S0-CFD-785

WEIRD LOUISIANA

POSTED
STRICTLY FORBIDDEN

Weird Louisiana

Your Travel Guide to Louisiana's Local Legends and Best Kept Secrets

By Roger Manley

Mark Sceurman and Mark Moran, Executive Editors

STERLING

New York / London

www.sterlingpublishing.com

WEIRD LOUISIANA

STERLING and the distinctive Sterling logo are registered trademarks of Sterling Publishing Co., Inc.

Published by Sterling Publishing Co., Inc.
387 Park Avenue South, New York, NY 10016

Distributed in Canada by Sterling Publishing
c/o Canadian Manda Group, 165 Dufferin Street
Toronto, Ontario, Canada M6K 3H6
Distributed in the United Kingdom by GMC Distribution Services, Castle Place, 166 High Street, Lewes, East Sussex, England BN7 1XU Distributed in Australia by Capricorn Link (Australia) Pty. Ltd. P. O. Box 704, Windsor, NSW 2756, Australia

10 9 8 7 6 5 4 3 2 1

Manufactured in China.

Photography and illustration credits are found on page 271 and constitute an extension of this copyright page.

Layout and production by bobsteimle.com

Sterling ISBN: 978-1-4027-4554-6

For information about custom editions, special sales, premium and corporate purchases, please contact Sterling Special Sales Department at 800-805-5489 or specialsales@sterlingpublishing.com.

Contents

Dedication

This book is for my parents, Richard and Zora, who knew from the outset that it takes a while to get where you're going, and for my brother Mark, my constant friend in all the many strange places we grew up. But most of all it's for my wife, Teddy: my dream, my companion, and my love. How I got lucky enough to wind up with any of you in my life remains the most inexplicable mystery of all. —Roger Manley

A Note from the Marks

O*ur weird journey began* a long, long time ago in a far-off land called New Jersey. Once a year or so we'd compile a homespun newsletter to hand out to our friends called *Weird N.J.* The pamphlet was a collection of odd news clippings, bizarre facts, little-known historical anecdotes and anomalous encounters from our home state. The newsletter also focused on the kind of very localized legends that were often whispered around a particular town but seldom heard outside the boundaries of the community where they first originated.

We had started the publication with the simple theory that every town in the state had at least one good tale to tell. *Weird N.J.* soon become a full-fledged magazine and we made the decision to actually do all of our own investigating and see if we couldn't track down just where all of these seemingly unbelievable stories were coming from. Was there, we wondered, any factual basis for these fantastic local legends that people were telling us? Armed with not much more than a camera and notepad we set off on a mystical journey of discovery. Much to our surprise and amazement, much of what we had initially presumed to be nothing more than urban legend actually turned out to be real, or at least contained a grain of truth that had originally sparked the lore.

After about a dozen years of documenting the bizarre, we were asked to write a book about our adventures, and so *Weird N.J.: Your Travel Guide to New Jersey's Local Legends and Best Kept Secrets* was published in 2003. Soon people from all over the country began writing to us, telling us strange tales from their home states. As it turned out, what we had first perceived to be a very local-interest genre was actually just a small part of a much larger and more universal phenomenon. People from all over the United States had strange tales to tell that they believed to be true, and they all wanted somebody to tell them to.

When our publisher asked us what we wanted to do next, for us the choice was simple: "We'd like to do a book called *Weird U.S.*, in which we could document the local legends and strangest stories from all over the entire country," we told them. So for the next twelve months we set out in search of weirdness wherever it could be found in these fifty states.

In 2004, after *Weird U.S.* was published, our publisher asked us once more where we wanted to go next. In the year that it had taken us to put together *Weird U.S.* we had come to the conclusion that this country had more great tales waiting to be told than could be contained in just one book. We had discovered—somewhat to our surprise—that every state we researched seemed to have more fascinating stories to offer than we actually had pages to accommodate. Everywhere we looked we found unwritten folklore, creepy cemeteries, cursed locations, and outlandish roadside oddities. With this in mind, we told our publisher that we wanted to document it *all*, and to do it in a series of books, each focusing on the peculiarities of a particular state.

When asked to think of a "weird" state, for most people some likely candidates will spring to mind first: New Jersey (of course), California (naturally), and another that is usually near the top of most people's list—Louisiana. Just saying the name of the state is enough to conjure up all sorts of strangeness in one's imagination. It is a land of voodoo, hoodoo, and backwater bayous; cultures like Creole and Cajun, which seem mysterious to, and are often misunderstood by, people who live elsewhere in the country. It is of the United States, but a state with roots deep in French, Spanish, and Caribbean culture. It is a land of haunted Old South plantations, French Quarter mansions, and cities of white marble and limestone towers to house the dead. It is also home to Mardi Gras, without a doubt *the* most surreal and extravagant celebration of collected weirdness in the entire country, if not the world.

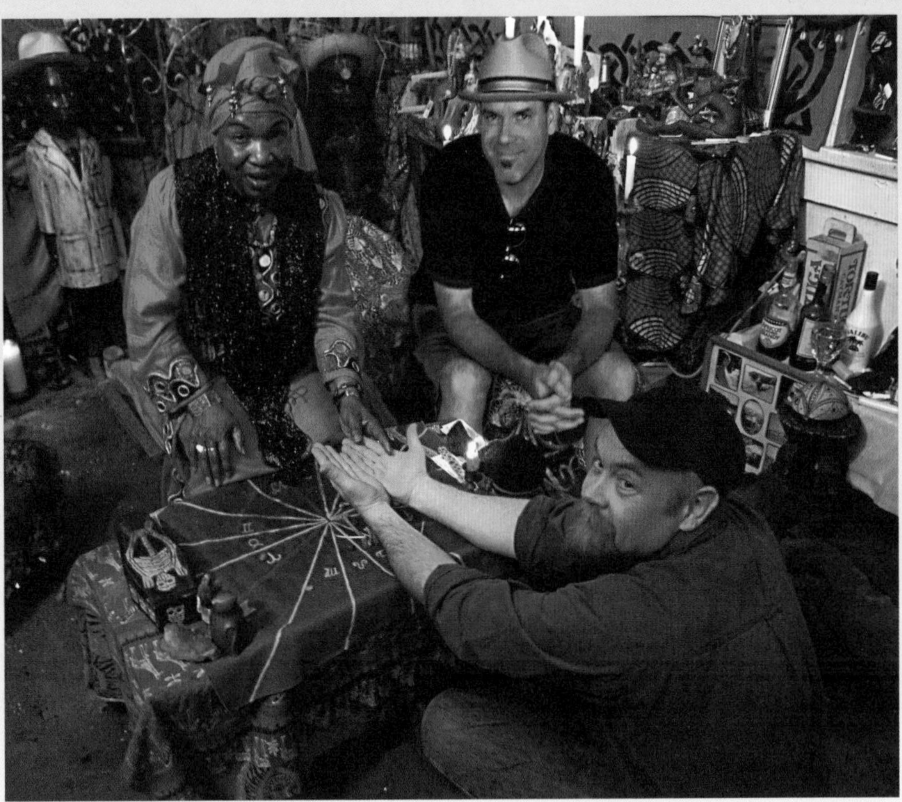

We had the distinct pleasure of visiting Louisiana ourselves on a number of occasions. We wandered the cemeteries of New Orleans, participated in the reenactment of the Bonnie and Clyde ambush in Gibsland, and witnessed the miraculous healing powers of a "traiteur" near Octave Fontenot. But we knew when it came to writing *Weird Louisiana* we'd need to find someone who truly spoke the local language. (Heck, we had enough trouble just trying to pronounce *Octave Fontenot*!)

Fortunately, when it came to selecting a local author to collaborate with on this book, there was really only one choice in our minds—Roger Manley. At the time, we had just finished work on *Weird Carolinas* with Roger and had been truly astounded by the almost incomprehensible volume of bizarre material he was able to dig up on the two states. Not only is he a dogged investigator of the weird, but he also possesses the photographic and storytelling expertise required to bring his unusual subjects to life in the pages of a book. When Roger told us that he had spent his formative years catching gar in the bayous and would relish the opportunity to revisit his old home on Weird forays, we jumped at the chance to work with him again on *Weird Louisiana*.

So come with us now and let Roger take you on a tour of the Pelican State, with all of its haunted history, colorful characters, and surreal sites. It's a uniquely fascinating state of mind we like to call *Weird Louisiana*.

—*Mark Moran* and *Mark Sceurman*

Introduction

D***riving down back roads*** in the Bayou State in search of the bizarre, if I saw some old-timer out in front of his house, I'd pull over and introduce myself.

"Hi there, sir. Hello. I'm writing a book about weird things, and I'm wondering if you could help me find some around here."

"What you mean, *weird*?"

"Well, you know, stuff like ghosts, sudden disappearances, bottomless ponds, secret organizations, Indian mounds, swamp beasts, snake farms, hubcap ranches, creepy graveyards, abandoned insane asylums . . ."

"Whoa there," he'd usually interrupt, cutting me off before I could finish my spiel. "You said 'weird.' What's so weird about all that? You're talking reg'lar life here in Loosiana!"

Weird is in the eye of the beholder—what's odd or eerie to one may be business-as-usual to another. I learned this lesson early on in life, having spent a significant part of my childhood in the Pelican State. Odd or off the wall, creepy or curious, I knew the stories were out there—the legends and lore of Louisiana—I just needed to find the right folks and ask the right questions. So I'd take a deep breath and keep on chatting up one soul after another, hoping to evoke a response.

"What about buried treasure, lover's leaps, lost towns, or swamp midgets? Or what about sand geysers, black hail, Siamese-twin otters, or snake-oil inventors? Or giant accordions, ghost trains, glowing crosses, abandoned convents, fish falling out of the sky? Know about any serial killers, freak vegetables, UFOs, or over-the-top taxidermy? Any mad scientists or devil sightings? Now surely that can't *all* be considered completely normal, can it?"

One roadside informant might ask, "Did anyone ever tell you about the Concrete Man near Hobart? That might be something for your book." Or another might say, "Have you heard the story of the cursed woods of Kurthwood? My dad used to tell me about camping out there and hearing the Indians drumming away in the middle of the night."

Yet another would tell me about the vampire of Verda; the monster of Fricke's Cave; or the Creole Cat of Dekattrois, a six-foot, two-legged beast so famous for stalking the town in the late nineteenth century that residents started an annual festival to celebrate its capture—until the whole town was blown away forever in a 1922 hurricane. Maybe then I'd hear about Morgan Hite's brick-and-mortar rocking chair in Mandeville, or the man-tree on Bennett

Bridge Road in west St. Tammany Parish, the German-socialist colony near Minden, the witches' church in Houma, or the poltergeists of Patterson.

In Shreveport, I heard about the armed robber who tried to hold up Blalock's Beauty College and was almost beaten to death by beauticians wielding curling irons. In Baton Rouge, they told me about the pet-cloning lab and the 1949 LSU–Tulane football game that was predicted by an unknown psychic graffiti vandal, who painted the exact score all over the stadium the night before the game. In Monroe, they told me about octogenarian radio DJ Pearly Tolliver, and about Verdiacee Hampton Goston, a.k.a. Verdiacee Turner, the founder and former mayor of the nearby town of Richwood. Evidently, the mayor's chair left her with a taste for power, for she went on to become Her Highness Verdiacee Tiari Washitaw-Turner Goston El-Bey, empress of the Washitaw de Dugdahmoundyah, claiming a separate nation within the United States and applying for an ambassador's seat in the UN. It only goes to prove my point yet again: In Louisiana, anything is possible.

Never for a second was I disappointed, for in Louisiana there's enough eerie, odd, and outrageous to fill an entire shelf of books. The only tricky part was digging up stories that Louisianans themselves would enjoy reading.

My hope is that each of you will discover your "weird eye," a term Mark Moran and Mark Sceurman use to describe the ability to see and appreciate the weird, wacky, and wonderful world we live in. So, open up that weird eye and take a good look around—I guarantee you'll like what you see. Trust me on this one, y'all. —*Roger Manley*

Legends of Louisiana

Hanging in the lobby of the New Orleans Athletic Club on Rampart Street is a plaster cast of the hard-hitting right arm of legendary boxer John L. Sullivan. On July 8, 1889, Sullivan became the last world champion heavyweight bare-knuckle boxer after an almost unbelievable seventy-five rounds in the ring with Jake Kilrain.

Almost unbelievable, we thought. Legendary, too, in the sense that people still talk about Sullivan and that bloody fight, while pointing to that big muscled arm as proof that it happened. This tells you something about the nature of legends. When historical facts seem borderline unbelievable they're often on the verge of becoming the stuff of legends. Ordinary facts become extraordinary when they don't agree with our understanding of reality—Who among living boxers could fight for two hours and sixteen minutes today?—or when coincidences start to seem astronomically unlikely. Take the grisly legend of Captain Michero, who fell overboard and drowned when his boat wrecked on the Mississippi many years ago. Days after the tragedy and fifty miles downstream, Michero's son was fishing at the family dock when he thought he'd hooked a big one. He reeled in the line and screamed . . . and you can guess how that one ended.

Legends often try to explain or make sense of the unbelievable in our already crazy world. And there's plenty about Louisiana that's pretty hard to believe. As you read through the pages that follow, keep one thing in mind: Local legends are often as important to the storytellers as they are to

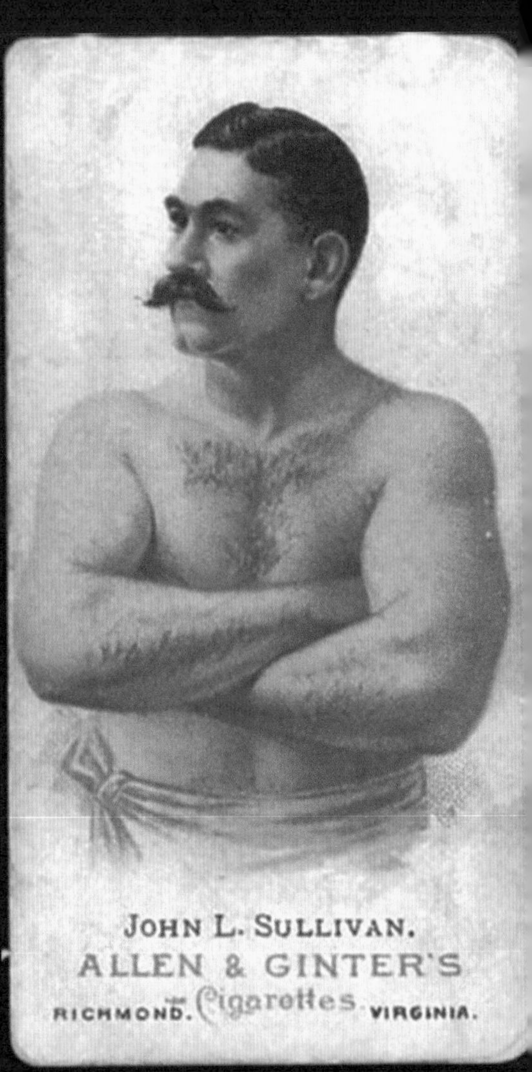

The Rougarou

Mention the rougarou to an elderly Cajun and he's likely to take a quick glance over his shoulder before responding with a tense whisper. The word *rougarou* is a variation of *loup-garou*, which in old French means a sorcerer who can change into a wolf. In Louisiana, the *rougarou*, often characterized as werewolves, can use magic ointments to morph into any number of creatures—snake, bat, or on rare occasions a household pet or bird—but most often they transform into wolves. Unlike the classic Hollywood werewolves of Lon Chaney and his ilk, a rougarou is not necessarily beholden to phases of the moon. Most Louisiana legends about the creatures characterize them as men who are outcasts from society; in France, *loup-garou* can also mean "lone wolf" or "loner."

If it howls when you sing "*hallelujah,*" it's a *rougarou.*

You have to whisper when you talk about the *rougarou* lest you be overheard. If they think you're wise to their disguise, they'll come after you seeking revenge. And you definitely don't want a rougarou coming after you, since they can be very difficult to kill. The only tried-and-true way, in fact, is to shoot them with a bullet that has been blessed by submersion in holy water before an image of Saint Hubert, the patron saint of hunters. And even then the bullet is only sure to find its mark if you also happen to have a four-leaf clover (a naturally occurring symbol of the cross) in your pocket. It requires a bit of premeditation, so don't just go hog wild and start shooting at them—it won't do a bit of good.

While its origins are older than Christianity, the *rougarou* is not a pagan belief that the Catholic clergy ever railed against with much conviction, probably because they seem to be on the same team, more or less. *Rougarou* primarily feed on sinners by scavenging corpses of the unblessed who haven't had last rites properly administered by a priest. They are particularly active during the season of Lent between Mardi Gras and Easter. Anyone bitten by a *rougarou* while breaking a classic Lenten restriction (such as the consuming of the flesh of ungulates during daylight hours on a Friday) may spend the next 101 days as a lost soul, which are all but indistinguishable from zombies in the legendary lore. If you pass away of some other cause during this period, your prospects for spending eternity on the sunny side of the street are not all that encouraging.

Fortunately, *rougarous* are easier to repel than the average Louisiana mosquito. Although they are said to be inordinately afraid of frogs, lugging a frog around all the time just in case you might need to throw it at a *rougarou* could become a hassle. Lucky for us, singing church music is apparently enough to convince them that you aren't the catch of the day. In fact, that's the best basic way to tell a *rougarou* from other kinds of swamp monsters, since people who've caught a glimpse of them often describe something that sounds a little Bigfooty: hairy, shaggy, smelling bad, and so on. So the rule of thumb is: If your hymns don't stop the big, scary, furry creature in its tracks, it's a Bigfoot. If it howls when you sing "hallelujah," it's a *rougarou*.

Legend of the Cabildo Gates

According to a legend often told to tourists in New Orleans, the intricate wrought iron gates of the Cabildo, the old government headquarters, were constructed using reforged iron that came from torture devices of the Spanish Inquisition. When the monk Antonio de Sedella arrived in the city in 1788, he announced that he had been sent on a secret mission: As an agent of the Inquisition, he was ordered to organize a tribunal for the express purpose of ferreting out heresy in the city and punishing it severely. The Spanish governor at the time, Don Estevan de Miró, likely reasoned that if all the heresy and sin in New Orleans were indeed to be punished, nobody would remain to do the punishing except Sedella himself. He had the monk summarily arrested and sent back to Spain.

The squealing and groaning sounds coming from the Cabildo's old iron hinges whenever they open or close are, according to the more imaginative tour guides, the tormented screams of former victims of harshly dogmatic Spanish Catholicism. But since Miró acted quickly to remove Sedella, we're not inclined to believe this. The real and far more lasting torture inflicted throughout the offices of the Cabildo more likely came in the form of all the elaborate regulations, legal documents, tax forms, and property deeds required by the original French founders of the colony.

Don't forget, we get the word *bureaucracy* from the French.

Frisbee's Fitting End

Louisiana legends are full of stories about men famous for their downright evil orneriness. Col. Norman Frisbee, a plantation owner in Tensas Parish, was notorious for his indiscriminate cruelty, his expensive tastes—and his deserved death.

Shortly before the Civil War, Frisbee ordered the construction of what would have been one of the grandest homes in the state, to be erected as a showplace in the middle of his twelve-thousand-acre plantation. He sent away for the finest, most ostentatious fittings—solid silver doorknobs, twenty-four-carat gold basins and chandeliers, gold flatware, and even a two-hundred-pound bell cast from melted-down silver dollars. When the war began, however, only eighteen rooms on the first floor of the house had been completed. As word reached him that Union soldiers were heading toward Tensas Parish, the colonel realized he would have to hide the treasure to keep it from falling into enemy hands. All of the fittings were loaded into two wagons, each driven by a single slave, while Frisbee rode a horse alongside them. They drove the wagons onto a part of the property that had not yet been cleared or planted. Without telling the drivers what he was doing, Frisbee picked a spot by lining up two pairs of unusual trees to establish sight lines, then pointed to the ground with the butt of his whip and told them to dig a hole to bury the precious metals there. After the hole was filled and smoothed over, Frisbee ordered the slaves back to the plantation and headed in the direction of his brother-in-law's plantation.

Orlando Flowers, who owned the next plantation over, was an affable young man and generally well liked—nothing like the terrible colonel. One of Flowers's mules had run loose in Frisbee's cotton fields. After the drivers left with the two wagons, Frisbee approached the mule, shot it, cut off its ears, and rode over to Flowers's house. When Flowers stepped out onto the veranda, Frisbee tossed the mule's ears at his feet. He loosed his whip and snapped it across Flowers's cheek. However, the sight of the mule ears had sent the young man into such a cold rage that he could feel no pain, and instead of flinching from the whip he grabbed it and gave it a yank so hard that Frisbee fell off his horse. A second later, Flowers was on top of him, and before anyone else could intervene, he'd stabbed his dastardly neighbor to death.

It's not at all surprising, given the colonel's reputation, that no one ever pressed charges on Flowers for the murder. They all agreed that Frisbee got what he deserved. Folks did, however, hunt for the treasure for years afterward, and still do. Most people think it must be somewhere in the northern tip of Tensas Parish, between Big Lake and Bayou Macon. So strong is the faith in this "legend" that locals say the Frisbee place changed hands a number of times based largely on the belief that the property held treasure. And who's to say it isn't true?

In Wet Pursuit

In early December 1924, a tanker ship based in New Orleans was returning to its home port via the Panama Canal after delivering a load of petroleum to the West Coast. Capt. Keith Tracy of the SS *Watertown*, a vessel owned by Cities Service Company, ordered seamen Michael Meehan and James Courtney to go down and clean the empty cargo tanks. The two men didn't return at the end of their watch. When their fellow sailors went looking for them, they found Meehan and Courtney unconscious in the cargo tank—they had been knocked out by the fumes and asphyxiated. Not long afterward, a brief ceremony was held and their bodies were commended to the sea.

The next day, December 5, 1924, Captain Tracy was informed that something truly strange was taking place onboard his ship. Two human faces were seen in the roiling water of the craft's wake. Although he dismissed the first reports as an optical illusion enhanced by the emotional state of the grieving crew, as more information reached the bridge he decided to go observe the phenomenon himself. What Captain Tracy saw rattled him to the core and planted a seed of fear in his soul: The clearly recognizable faces of Meehan and Courtney loomed in the frothy mist just above the churning wake no more than forty feet behind the ship.

Tracy ordered the engines cut. As the ship slowed, the faces disappeared. When the command was given to resume normal speed, they came back once again. In fact they stayed with the ship, hovering at roughly the same distance from the stern's fantail for the rest of the voyage. Every man on board the SS *Watertown* saw the faces of the two men who had lost their lives servicing the vessel.

No captain would risk his reputation by reporting something he did not believe to be true. So when Captain Tracy reported the strange sightings to his superiors at Cities Service Company, they struggled to overcome their own incredulity. In an effort to get an objective handle on the situation, one of the officials suggested that on the next voyage Tracy should try to obtain some photos of the faces, should they reappear. A sealed roll of Kodak 130 black-and-white film was handed to him for this purpose.

Sure enough, as soon as the *Watertown* left the New Orleans docks and revved up to its cruising speed, the faces reappeared. The assistant engineer shot all six frames on the roll and then put the camera away. Meehan and Courtney's phantom faces followed the tanker throughout its run to the Pacific coast and back. Looming in the distance to torment the captain's uneasy conscience, the faces seemed intent on reminding him, day after day, of the terrible mistake he'd made in ordering the two seamen into the fume-filled hold to clean it.

At the end of the voyage, the roll of film was returned to the company, to be developed as the supervisors had requested, so that there could be no tampering with it. When the negatives came back from the lab, one of the images on the roll proved that at least the captain and his crew weren't insane or delusional. It showed the floating faces of the two dead seamen, exactly as the captain had reported. But this was little consolation to Tracy—for if what he had witnessed could be photographed, the vengeful spirits that seemed to be pursuing him were real. The Burns Detective Agency had analyzed the film at the request of Cities Service and could find no evidence that the image had been faked.

Tracy soon put in for retirement, and as the saying goes, he "faded into history." After he left the *Watertown*, the faces no longer appeared, or at least were never reported again. His first mate, who had relayed the order to Meehan and Courtney without questioning it, soon died, as did the company supervisor who had commissioned the voyage in the first place.

The clearly recognizable faces of Meehan and Courtney loomed in the frothy mist just above the churning wake no more than forty feet behind the ship.

The Divided House

When Abraham Lincoln said, "A house divided against itself cannot stand," he was talking metaphorically about the young American nation, not an actual house. Speaking in 1858 as a Republican candidate for the U.S. Senate, he was hoping to fend off a Civil War that he could already see coming, knowing that it would pit brother against brother in an awful and bloody conflict.

When Andrew Sellers died, he bequeathed his house in Lafayette to his two sons. A dispute among surviving family members culminated in the two brothers dividing the house down the middle—literally. Unable to come to any compromise, they sawed the house into equal halves and each took his portion to a separate piece of property.

Each half of the house stood just fine, although many decades later one of the halves had to be knocked down to make way for a newer home.

The other half still stands, and the current owners have reconstructed its missing part so that it's a whole house once again. There should be some deeper metaphorical meaning there, too, if only Abe were still around to work it into a speech.

Railroad Station on Riverside Drive

According to a local legend, an unusually large hollow magnolia tree still growing alongside Riverside Drive in Monroe was once a way station on the Underground Railroad. Escaped slaves would hide inside the tree, waiting until a signal came from a smuggler's boat temporarily anchored in the Ouachita River. Responding to the signal was tricky. Both the boatmen and freedom seekers were supposed to hoot like owls in case anyone happened to overhear their communications. Many of the runaways found it hard to do, though, because in both African and Native American mythology, the sound of an owl was often considered an omen of death. —*Kathy Jordan*

Doomed Dome in New Orleans

Back when the New Orleans Saints weren't much of a force to be reckoned with on the football field, fans sought reasons for the team's seemingly endless streak of bad luck. And since the team was based in the Crescent City, most fans were also at least vaguely familiar with voodoo. According to one of the tenets of voodoo, there always has to be a reason for something. Poor performance on the gridiron doesn't just happen. Something (or *things)* has to be causing it.

To clear the way to build a civic center, the old Girod Street cemetery had been unearthed and moved in 1957. Today the Superdome sits on top of a portion of what had been hallowed ground for almost 150 years. The spirits had been uprooted and could no longer rest in peace. It didn't matter that the cemetery had already been officially deconsecrated, or that the remains of all the relatives of forty-four white families had been successfully gathered up and redeposited at the Hope Mausoleum on Canal Street, or that the rest of the human remains had been sifted out of the ground and heaped into a mass grave at Providence Memorial Park. According to folks who openly believed a breach of trust had occurred, this was why the Saints could rarely seem to complete passes, score touchdowns, or kick successful field goals.

Football boosters naturally played all such speculations down, pointing out that the dead of Girod Street had long

been disturbed already. Bums had moved into the crypts, they said, and prostitutes had been plying their trade between the tombs, and few of the graves were well maintained. With those arguments, they quickly pushed their agenda through, won the NFL franchise for New Orleans, and saw to it that what was then the world's largest dome was built. But the spirits may have had the last laugh. For years the Saints struggled against what seemed like supernatural opponents. Talk of a curse on the doomed dome became commonplace.

The curse seemed to end only when the Superdome was finally put to some use other than sports and entertainment. Although the damage inflicted by Hurricane Katrina and its aftermath required $193 million in repairs, the dome had sheltered some thirty thousand people through the worst of the disaster. After that, the curse seemed to lift. When the facility reopened in 2006, the Saints won their very first game and kept up a winning season that took them all the way to the NFC championship game.

Those who knew about the ghosts that populated the old cemetery under the dome complex also knew why the losing streak ended in 2006. The old man who told us about the legend laughed as he pointed toward the giant curving roof. "See?" he said. "They just wanted to frustrate those money people. Soon as the dome finally did some *good*, well, them ghosts must have reckoned they could leave it alone."

Slave Ghost of Hangman's Tree

Off of Robert E. Lee Boulevard in New Orleans there's a strange area where you'll find Hangman's Tree. Right where Robert E. Lee crosses over Bayou St. John there's a fort known historically as Old Spanish Fort. It's remained virtually untouched in the outskirts of the city for more than two hundred years and the famous voodoo queen Marie Laveau performed a few voodoo ceremonies here. There's an oak tree on the levy next to the fort. A disobedient slave was hung here and his ghost still haunts the tree to this day. Sometimes, if you go to the tree late at night, you can see the outline of the slave who was hung. On rare occasions, if you walk closer after you see the outline of his body, his head actually turns and he looks at you. It is a very eerie spot. Just approaching the tree gives me goose bumps. —*Matthew Muller*

Songs of Saint Louis

Whenever "eyewitness" TV news journalists want to instantly convey the message that they are on location in the Crescent City, there's always one place they go—the square in front of the St. Louis Cathedral. Although the present building dates back to the early 1790s, there have been churches on the site since 1727.

Some of the lore surrounding St. Louis Cathedral seems farfetched. Persistent stories that during the French Revolution the Place d'Armes (as Jackson Square was then called) resounded to the horrifying rattle and thunk of a falling guillotine blade are almost certainly untrue, since the colony was under Spanish rule at the time of the Reign of Terror. But other stories that sound untrue, such as that voodoo queen Marie Laveau got married in the cathedral, can be easily proved by old church records. Many natives of New Orleans say that you'll stand a far better chance of encountering her ghost in the church than at her heavily visited "grave" in St. Louis Cemetery No. 1.

Although no heads rolled during the Spanish era, the period of their rule wasn't without the occasional atrocity, and herein lies the source of another spirit that lingers at the cathedral. Much to the horror of the Creole settlers who had lived under French rule since the territory had been

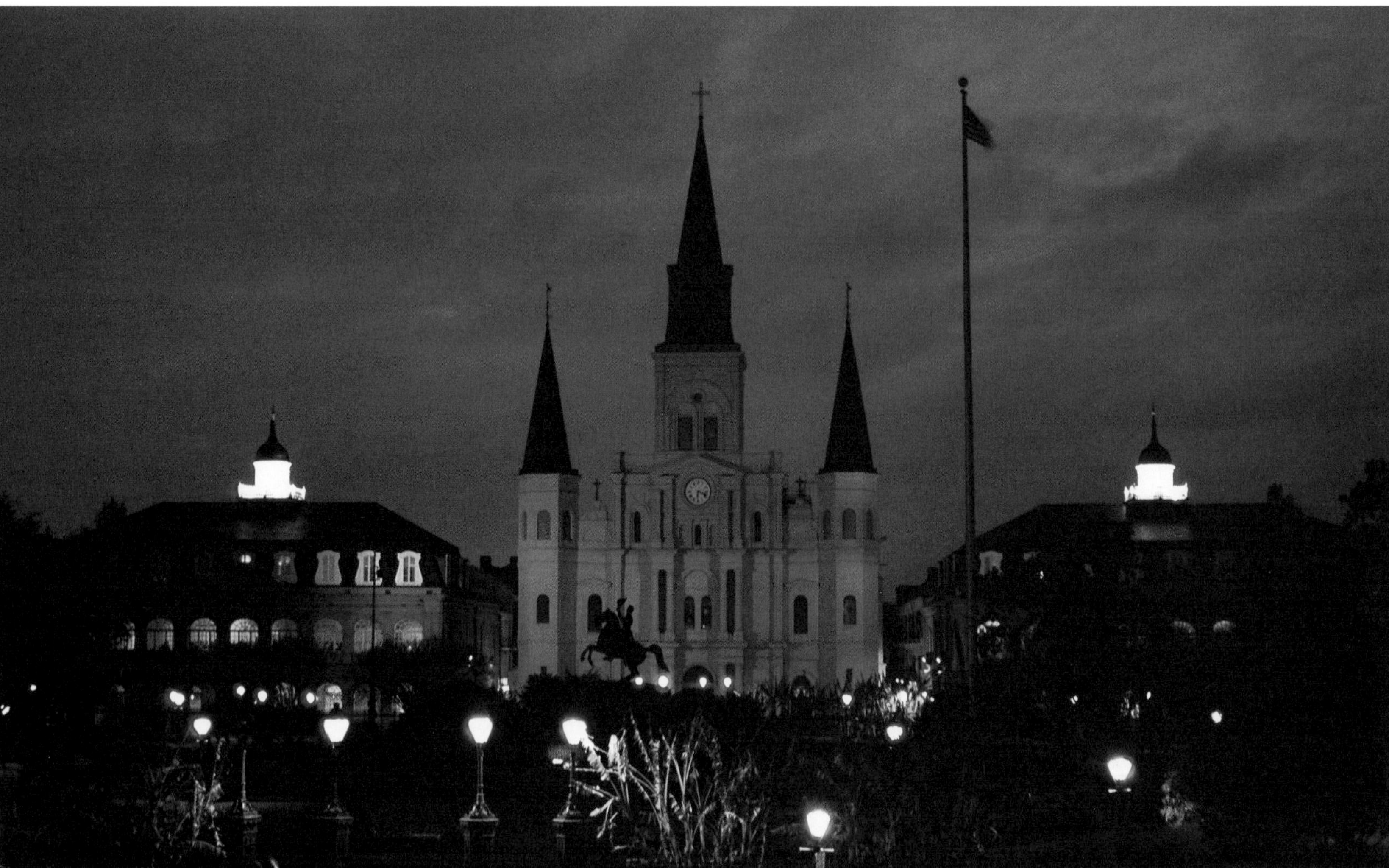

claimed for France in the 1680s, Spain acquired Louisiana from France in 1764 via a treaty signed at the end of the Seven Years' War (known in America as the French and Indian War). Locals almost immediately began plotting the overthrow of their new rulers, even before the first Spanish governor arrived. Antonio de Ulloa lasted barely two years before the Creoles chased him out of the colony. The Spanish crown then retaliated by sending a major fleet of ships loaded with soldiers to take back Nouvelle-Orléans and turn it into Nueva Orleans. A tough Irish-Spanish military commander, Field Marshal Alejandro O'Reilly, led the force. O'Reilly landed with two thousand troops from Cuba and made quick work of putting down the rebellious Creoles and arresting their leadership.

O'Reilly ruled by fear and made an example of anyone who resisted Spanish rule. He sent some of the rebels away to life imprisonment in Havana and had six others summarily executed. As a flourishing touch, he ordered that their bodies be left to rot where they fell. This was considered an incredibly harsh punishment in a time when failing to perform last rites or funeral masses was thought tantamount to putting the deceased persons' souls at risk in the afterlife.

One evening, as a mist was rolling in from the swamps, a Capuchin monk named Père Dagobert approached the soldiers standing guard over the bodies. He was personable and engaged the bored sentries by telling them humorous stories and inquiring about their lives in Cuba. Dagobert then asked if he could take a look at the six corpses and explained that he had been too busy to see them during the daytime. He reasoned with guards: Since the bodies had been left out on display in order to make an impression, he wanted to be shocked and awed just like everyone else. They waved him by.

The fog continued to thicken and soon obscured the monk from view, but they could hear him loudly singing "Kyrie eleison" through the mist, so they ignored him. Given Dagobert's jolly nature, the Spanish-speaking guards probably mistook the litany—Greek for "Lord have mercy"—for a French folksong. Unknown to them, however, the song masked the sounds of the priest's accomplices, who had snuck past the checkpoint while he was entertaining the guards, while they made off into the night with the bodies rolled up in blankets. Dagobert strolled back by the gate, slapped the guards on the shoulders, and wished them a good evening.

When the fog lifted at dawn, the soldiers were shocked to discover the six bodies had vanished.

When the fog lifted at dawn, the soldiers were shocked to discover the six bodies had vanished. There was little they could do, since no one had actually witnessed Dagobert spiriting the bodies away. It's also likely that O'Reilly was somewhat relieved by the disappearance, since by then there had been plenty of time for the pile of rotting cadavers to have served its purpose, but to have rescinded his order to leave them there might have made him seem weak and irresolute. A Catholic himself, this way he might not have to worry so much about his own mortal soul. In any case, he didn't pursue the popular priest and let the matter lie. That same night, after leaving the scene, Père Dagobert had managed to get the bodies to the cathedral, conduct a mass, and see to it that the men were safely deposited in a secret grave in St. Louis Cemetery No. 1 before sunrise.

Some say that the remarkable incident must have left a permanent presence at the church. On certain foggy nights, if you listen carefully and if there's not too much other activity going on around Jackson Square, you can hear the faint, medieval melody of "Kyrie eleison" drifting around the church and up Orleans Street toward the cemetery.

The Good Darky Tells the Way Home

It's one of the weirdest, most controversial, and most useless monuments in the Pelican State. The statue greets visitors to Louisiana State University's Rural Life Museum in Baton Rouge. It depicts an elderly black man doffing his hat and offering an indirect greeting. Although its official name was the *Service Memorial Statue*, from the day it was first erected in Natchitoches in 1927 until it was moved to Baton Rouge in 1972, it was called "the Good Darky."

The name came from the wording on its original plaque that said, "Erected by the city of Natchitoches in grateful recognition of the arduous and faithful services of the good darkies of Louisiana. Donated by J. L. Bryan, 1927." A legend that attached to the statue soon after it was unveiled was told in the white community of Natchitoches often enough to end up in a compilation released by the Works Progress Administration in the 1940s. The legend said, "Plantation Negroes, inebriated after a spree in town, go to the statue to ask the way home and the Good Darky never fails to tell them the right direction."

Historian James W. Loewen has pointed out that the purpose of the legend and the Good Darky statue was to further the aims of white supremacists, since the submissive grin on the former slave's face suggests that he doesn't really mind being downtrodden: He'd kept the home front going while his owners tried to perpetuate his enslavement.

The statue was rescued after civil rights demonstrators tossed it into the Cane River in 1968. The Natchitoches city council said it had been planning to move the statue to construct traffic islands that would improve vehicular movement, so the Good Darky stood in a field behind the city water filtering plant for several years. Then it was moved to Baton Rouge and acquired by the Rural Life Museum, minus its original plaque.

There are many who say that if exhibited at all, the statue should probably be mounted in another kind of setting, among more appropriate artifacts of the past like signage for segregated drinking fountains, burned crosses, armbands, and tickets for the rear seats of the bus. But for now it stands among flowers in a traffic circle at the entrance to the museum, setting a very outdated tone for a public institution, as an elderly, realistic, life-sized bronze lawn jockey.

From Interstate 10 in Baton Rouge, exit at Essen Lane and head south to the first traffic signal. Turn right (west) into the road leading back about a mile to the museum.

Horse Thief Hellhole

The old Caldwell Parish hanging tree in Columbia is no more, but in the days when justice was meted out on a quick, local basis, almost any tree would do, including one located conveniently within the bounds of a cemetery. Lee Erwin has passed on the lore surrounding a peculiar slab in the middle of Oakley Cemetery in nearby Franklin Parish: "Seven horse thieves were caught red-handed back in 1903 and each was hung by the neck until he quit kicking." Then the bodies, we've been told, were dumped into a large open pit and sealed over with a foot-thick slab of concrete. This slab is marked off on top at designated intervals with wide spaces—coffin-sized spaces—and separate dividing lines. "By my count," Erwin says, "there are five body-sized spaces, suggesting, to me anyway, that if there truly were seven horse thieves as folklore tells it, a couple of those marked-off graves are certainly double dippers."

Whether this uncomfortable-sounding burial is true or not, the slab and the surrounding cemetery are known for a number of strange phenomena. People have seen brilliant lights shining up out of the other slabs' cracks, fireballs shooting up above the trees, and—before it was torn down—the church across the road suddenly and inexplicably lighting up from inside, even though no one was there for services and electricity hadn't been extended to that part of the parish yet. The old cemetery marks one corner of what some locals jokingly (but nervously) refer to as the "Bermuda Rectangle," the other angles of which are formed by Peck, Extension, and Jigger Streets. In the middle is Metropolis, and the whole thing seems to focus on a point just across the Boeuf River at the Wade Landing Indian mounds. Within this zone, according to Erwin and others, there are an inordinate number of haunted places, including the infamous Moaning House on Old Columbia Road.

Diamonds in Her Soup

In late 1946, teenager Billie Earp of Shreveport was in the process of making lunch with a can of Campbell's condensed vegetable soup when she heard a "plink" as something hard hit the bowl. Fishing around in the thick broth, she discovered a diamond engagement ring. She contacted the company to ask if there had been any publicity gimmicks that included diamond giveaways and, if not, maybe someone wanted their ring back? Campbell's asked her to describe the ring, but young Miss Earp asked *them* if anyone among their employees could describe anything that might have gone missing. When they never responded, the ring was hers to keep.

That wasn't the strangest thing that ever happened to her. Many years later, after careers as a nurse's aide, dental assistant, and military mom, she was walking out of a mall in Houma when she saw a ball of light hovering over some nearby trees. A phone call to the radio station revealed that quite a few other people had seen it, too, and that the Air Force was investigating. No one knows what it was, but one eyewitness described the unidentified flying object as looking "bright as a diamond in the sky."

Speaking of which, the most popular point of origin for flying saucers and other UFOs is Alpha Centauri, which, at only 25.8 trillion miles from Baton Rouge, is in the closest star cluster to the Sun. In March 2008 the Harvard-Smithsonian Center for Astrophysics announced the discovery that a white dwarf star within the same constellation contains a diamond almost 1,870 miles in diameter, making it the largest precious jewel in the known universe. Twinkle, twinkle!

The Vampire Murders

One of the most interesting stories I've heard is about the vampire murders in New Orleans. I don't know if they actually happened, but the legend goes as this: For the past two hundred years or so, bodies have been turning up in alleys all over New Orleans. Some versions of the story say victims had no marks on them but that they were somehow drained of blood. Other versions say the bodies had the stereotypical vampire bite marks.

In the beginning of the twentieth century, two brothers were arrested in connection with the murders. They were tried and put to death, but the murders continued. Rumors started to spread that the boys were vampires, and because they were executed by hanging, they were still alive—or undead. Soon, the rumors were rampant, and the mayor ordered their crypt opened. The seal of the crypt was unbroken, but the brothers' bodies were gone.

Legend says that the murders are still being committed today. —*Clifton Knight*

A Gold-Fashioned Wedding

Bridezillas of today, craving to create a wedding no one will ever forget, could scarcely do much better than to emulate the legendary nuptials that Charles Durand of St. Martinville arranged for two of his daughters. Perhaps he was trying to rebuild his reputation in the eyes of his colleagues and neighbors, for he not only pulled out all the stops but also found some stops to pull that no one had ever previously known existed.

Durand had moved to St. Martinville from France not long after the War of 1812 and speedily established one of the most successful sugar plantations on Bayou Teche. To symbolize his having "arrived," he created one of the state's most impressive private allées leading up to his mansion. Almost three miles long and lined by hundreds of alternating pine and oak trees, the intended effect was to create a tunnel of foliage that would encourage guests to anticipate their arrival at the grand estate.

Durand lived happily in the house with his wife and twelve children until his wife's sudden death. A showman through and through, he advertised his grief, visiting her grave on a daily basis. He commissioned a sad-faced cast-iron statue of himself, cloaked in a raincoat and kneeling on the hard ground before her tomb in desolate misery. A plaque mounted at the base of the sculpture repeated his vow never to take the hand of another; he would remain true to his soul mate until death rejoined them.

Despite his pledge to remain chaste, Durand remarried in less than a year, leaving the statue alone to carry on the graveside vigil. Local gossip went into overdrive, culminating in an act that Durand could not ignore. Someone broke off the head of the grieving statue and under the plaque carved the words *Ne dites pas de tels mensonges*, meaning "Don't tell such lies!"

Whether this motivated how he responded when two of his children announced simultaneously that they had found their future husbands, no one can be sure, but Durand decided to plan a wedding event that the local citizenry would never forget. Although the practical

details aren't clear, he somehow acquired a tremendous number of large spiders and set them loose among the trees leading up to the house a few days before the big event. The spiders did just as he had expected, and created thousands of webs in the branches overhead.

At dawn on the morning of the double wedding, all the household servants were given gold and silver powder and instructed to dust the webs with the precious glitter. Oriental carpets were laid on the road, and tables set with food and drink were lined up along it. Bands spread out along the entire length of the alley, creating a tunnel of sound and spectacle. Thousands attended the daylong event that ended with fireworks and the departure of the four newlyweds on a steamboat heading down Bayou Teche toward New Orleans.

Durand succeeded in restoring his name—in fact, people in St. Martinville still talk about him almost a century and a half later—but it seems he may have blown his bank account. When he died a few years later, there was almost no inheritance remaining for his heirs. Locals, who couldn't believe that he would have gone to such lengths as to beggar his descendants, spent a lot of fruitless effort digging for buried treasures on the former Durand estate.

Unexplained and Unnatural Phenomena

W*hether folklore or fact* (or somewhere in between), we've found a bounty of bizarre in the Bayou State. In 1860, for starters, many people in Shreveport looked up at the sky and observed ". . . a strange light in the heavens . . . It appeared to the naked eye, about 300 yards in length, extending from north to west . . . just above the tallest trees." Many interpreted it as a heavenly sign, perhaps something to do with the general feeling of unease that accompanied talk of civil war, but whether the omen was good or bad, they couldn't say.

In 1988, John and Mary New of Sulphur (Calcasieu Parish) spotted the Virgin Mary in the base of a magnolia tree growing in their yard. Crosses have appeared in bathroom windows in Baton Rouge, Alexandria, and Violet (St. Bernard Parish); figurines have cried tears of blood in a Chalmette religious supply shop; and an image of Jesus showed up in a recently repaired space heater in Lutcher. Would you recognize a miracle if you were faced with one or try to convince yourself that it hadn't happened?

Folks from Louisiana know a thing or two about the eerie and unexplained. Rain of fish in Marksville, a weeping idol in Kenner, the flaming fountain in Colfax, a candle with an eternal flame in Cameron—that's just the tip of the iceberg.

OUR LADY
OF
TICKFAW

Supernatural Light Shows

A flash of light tears through the sky. Is it a shooting star? A piece of space debris falling back into Earth's atmosphere? The aurora borealis? Or is it some other kind of celestial spectacle that defies scientific explanation?

Consider the series of mysterious light shows that took place all across Louisiana in March 1989. On consecutive evenings, a fantastic display of red, green, and purple lights lit up skies in several rural communities. Witnesses who were alarmed by the events contacted their local fire departments to report possible brush fires and explosions. In Baton Rouge, police communications systems went haywire for hours as the pandemonium spread across the country and Canada—power grids from New Jersey to Texas were affected, and the Hydro-Quebec grid in Canada went out for more than nine hours. In this case, the origins of the events can be explained by science: The Sun released a tremendous amount of magnetic energy into the solar system, creating a brilliant display of color and light while also causing malfunctions in electrical grids and communications systems. Other events, like the celestial spectacles described later, walk the line between science and supernatural.

Early one morning in November 1967, Louisiana State Police spotted mysterious, color-changing lights in a rural area near the town of Crowley. A short time later, the bright beams were seen bouncing around within the city limits before dispersing into the neighboring communities. That same morning, the lights were observed in the towns of New Iberia, Kaplan, Jennings, and Abbeville, where witnesses described them as red and slow moving. Although credible sources in five towns described seeing the colorful light show, no UFO sightings were reported and nothing strange turned up on any military or air traffic control radars.

On an evening in March 2006, areas north of Lafayette were treated to another light show. From Baton Rouge to Jefferson Davis Parish, the sky lit up with a greenish flash of light that prompted dozens of eyewitnesses to phone their local radio stations and sheriff's offices. A witness in St. Landry Parish saw the lights pass directly overhead in the direction of a neighboring field, but when he searched the field the following morning, he found nothing. NASA officials were unable to identify the origins of the flashing lights; and because the agency tracks large incoming space debris, scientists felt it was unlikely that asteroids or man-made space junk had broken through Earth's atmosphere on this evening.

Fresh Meteorite in Baton Rouge

In early June 1969 Gillis Chaisson found a rock in his backyard in Baton Rouge sitting in a patch of smoldering grass. Roughly six inches long, four inches wide, and three inches thick, the rock nearly singed Chaisson's hands when he touched it. Was this an ordinary rock or a piece from a so-called "fresh" meteorite?

Scientists at the Louisiana State University physics department weren't convinced the object came from space, arguing that there would have been widespread sightings if a ball of fire did, in fact, fall through our atmosphere. Those who believed in the rock's galactic origins countered that meteorites can enter Earth's atmosphere at any time of day, including the daytime, when they are less visible to the naked eye and thus less likely to be witnessed en masse. And while there wasn't evidence of a crater at the site where the rock presumably landed, it's also true that most meteors that hit our atmosphere burn up long before hitting the ground. Considering twenty thousand to eighty thousand meteorites larger than ten grams (about a third of an ounce) fall to Earth each year, it's not much of a stretch for us to believe Chaisson's rock was, in fact, a meteorite.

Meteorite Hazard at Audubon Golf Course

At the northern end of the eighteenth hole fairway in New Orleans's Audubon Park Golf Club course is one weird hazard. An iron meteorite weighing in at more than fifteen tons juts out nearly six feet from the well-manicured grounds of the old course. The *Picayune* described the meteorite's arrival on March 31, 1891:

> *The terrific explosion and detonation which startled all of Carrollton just previous to daylight yesterday morning, shook houses and smashed panes of glass, proves to have been caused by the fall of an enormous meteorite. All people throughout the city who happened to be awake heard the noise and felt the shock. Indeed, the effects were felt as far away as Biloxi, and no doubt at more distant points.*
>
> *The few who were on the streets or rushed to the doors and windows saw an immense glare of fire in the sky and the hissing of flames, which ceased as suddenly as they appeared.*

Initial descriptions measured it at eight feet high and twenty-one feet in circumference at its widest point. But in the nearly 120 years since it slammed into the park, rust, ground subsidence under its enormous weight and souvenir collecting have diminished the spectacle somewhat. In fact, after it was determined that it probably posed little or no danger to the park or its visitors, city officials soon realized that the greater danger was to the meteorite itself from the swarms of souvenir hunters. Twelve lesser masses of space iron and thousands of smaller chunks and fragments scattered around the site were quickly carried away as mementos, many of which still grace mantels and curiosity cabinets throughout the region. By late afternoon on the day the interplanetary traveler arrived, a committee headed by the commissioner of public works, E. T. Leche, decided to post a guard of armed policemen around the site until an iron fence could be constructed to preserve it for future citizens to enjoy and admire.

It turns out the best way to preserve an intergalactic artifact is to tell a lie about it. A false rumor was started, claiming that the rock hadn't come from space at all. Instead it was touted to be a giant sample of iron ore from Alabama's famous Red Mountain quarries near Birmingham. It purportedly had been abandoned in New Orleans after the World's Industrial and Cotton Centennial Exposition of 1884–85.

This version of the origins of the meteorite gained momentum after readers realized that the original newspaper article had come out on April 1, although the event itself had happened the day before. It did not explain, however, how such a big chunk of "iron ore" had completely escaped notice until then, or why, if Alabamans had thought it was so impressive before the fair, they had decided it was so worthless afterward. What is more, in a region with almost no outcroppings of solid rock at all, surely over the course of six years of supposedly sitting in plain view in a park surrounded by hundreds of daily visitors, someone would have noticed it, if it had really been there all along.

After the fake meteorite story began circulating, the public quickly lost interest. The Public Works office quietly canceled plans for the elaborate fencing as the meteorite

Rain of Fish

There was something fishy about the morning of October 23, 1947, in the town of Marksville—and we don't mean figuratively. For nearly ten minutes, fresh fish fell from the sky over an area about eighty feet wide and almost a quarter of a mile in length. Hickory shad, largemouth bass, black bass, sunfish, perch, and minnows bounced off rooftops, pelting pedestrians and even knocking a newspaper delivery boy off his bike. There was no rain that day, and according to the Louisiana Weather Bureau, there had been no tornados or waterspouts that week that could account for the heavenly haul.

Once the rain of fish ended, curious Marksvillians scrambled to get a closer look at the fallen fish. They found that many were frozen, most were very cold, and all were absolutely fresh and fit for consumption. Local folks seized the opportunity, snatching up armfuls of fish to take home for supper that evening. Marksville's cat population feasted on the leftovers.

The Great Shreveport Peach Pelting

On the afternoon of July 12, 1961, carpenters working on the roof of a house at 2065 Lovers Lane in the town of Shreveport had to take cover from a heavy downpour—of peaches! Hundreds of green peaches, the size and consistency of golf balls, came pouring down from a small, dense cloud hovering directly overhead. According to reports, the peaches fell only in this very concentrated area and not on adjacent houses. The weather station at nearby Barksdale Air Force Base was unable to explain the event, as there hadn't been any winds strong enough to strip peaches from the trees nor any whirlwinds or other updrafts powerful enough to lift them into a cloud and deliver them onto the hapless house builders.

Tornado Chair

On November 14, 1947, tornados flattened a major part of downtown DeRidder. One of the strange discoveries in the aftermath of the twisters was a cane-bottomed chair and picture frame that cyclonic winds had firmly embedded in the vertical exterior wall of a weather-boarded house. A photo provided by Doris Ledoux shows officer Vallery Sanders examining the chair's point of impact.

Weather Cutters

Louisiana lore claims that fishermen of bayou brown shrimp have a special gift: They can deactivate tornados and waterspouts by "cutting the weather." Jules Nunez and Michael Bouisse of Barataria are among several in the coastal seafood industry known to possess the ability and have been observed on many different occasions severing threatening waterspouts.

How do they do it? Witnesses say that the so-called Weather Cutter goes head-to-head with Mother Nature, facing the oncoming funnel cloud and using a sharp knife to make a cross or X in the direction of the storm. The funnels then break at the indicated point and fizzle away to nothing. A 1981 article in the *Times-Picayune* quotes Nunez saying, "I picked it up from my mama who was afraid of them. When she would see a waterspout coming, she would tell me to run get the butcher knife."

Cop Car Combustions

A bizarre series of spontaneous combustions of New Orleans Police Department squad cars swept through the motorized force during the spring and early summer of 1980. Black-and-white cars suddenly burst into flames for no apparent reason on May 20 and June 3. After two more mysterious fires broke out on the morning and afternoon of June 8, injuring at least one patrolman, the department headquarters issued orders that arrested civilians and prisoners could no longer be transported in police vehicles, for fear that someone could be burned alive while in locked custody, trapped behind the grills in the squad cars' backseats that had no interior door handles.

The source of the fires remained an enigma. At first it was thought that overworked air-conditioning units might be the cause of the problem, but some of the fires occurred during early-morning hours when the AC was neither turned on nor under any strain. Frustrated with the situation, police spokesman Gus Krinke said that city cops might need to "play police and fireman at the same time," by fighting fires while fighting crime. After two more unexplained spontaneous combustions, Ford Motor Company inspectors examined the 1980 LTDs that seemed to be the focus of the unsettling phenomenon, but they were unable to determine the source of the blazes.

Death by Brain Freeze?

Sure, it hurts like hell, but can a brain freeze kill you? The answer may be yes, at least in the case of Placide Richard. According to a parish coroner, young Placide, depicted in this old, hand-tinted photograph from the Acadian Museum in the town of Erath, suffered a fatal brain hemorrhage after a friendly prank went horribly wrong. As Placide lay sleeping in the hot afternoon sun, his friends poured ice water on his head, which had the unintentional effect of killing him in a matter of minutes.

Flaming Fountain at Colfax

Flanking the steps leading up to the Grant Parish Courthouse in the town of Colfax is a circular planter filled with rangy shrubs. You wouldn't know by looking at it today, but this modest concrete container was one of Louisiana's great natural wonders for more than forty years. Once called the Colfax Miracle, and known locally as the Burning Well, it was a deep bore with a colorful history.

In 1899, the town of Colfax hired the Hart Well Company of Plaquemine to search for an alternative freshwater source to the nearby Red River. Drilling began in March of that year; and by June, they had sunk the second deepest well in the state and were piping water from a depth of 1,103 feet at enough pressure to shoot 60 feet in the air. Water surged upward at an estimated rate of fifty thousand gallons a day, but unfortunately it was too salty to use for farm irrigation and unsuitable for human consumption. It was also soon discovered that the water was impregnated with methane and other combustible hydrocarbons. Driller L. B. Hart learned this firsthand after volunteering to take a sip of the well water—his beard and eyebrows were singed off when his cigar accidentally ignited the flammable water.

Boosters of the expensive well project quickly attempted to spin the disappointing results, claiming that it was a blessing in disguise and that the pressurized water could be used to power water mills while the natural gas might be tapped to fuel a factory. Unfortunately, after the initial pent-up pressure subsided, the well's water flow wasn't continuous. Twice a month, the water and gas would roar out for a few days at a time before subsiding to barely a trickle. The great project's only real boon to the local economy turned out to be its role as a peculiar tourist attraction. As Grant Parish Planning Board Chairman G. C. Smith wrote in the late 1940s,

> *When the well comes in someone with a lighted match is never missen to set it on fire just to see it burn. . . . Especially during the late war maneuvers, did the well arouse a lot of wonderment and speculation from soldier boys who received their training in this section of the state. Many of these soldier boys told others about the burning well after they left for foreign service and a number of them have actually written back to have the tale verified by the local Post-Mistress, Mrs. Emma Straughan, thinking that they were being duped by such tales of a well whose waters burned as they flowed out into the basin that has been constructed to catch them.*

By the 1960s, the novelty of the Colfax Miracle had worn off, and a growth industry in liability lawsuits suggested that a flaming fountain on public property wasn't such a good idea anymore. As Christmas presents suitable for kids transitioned from jackknives and shotguns to LEGOs and rubber dinosaurs, the architects of a kinder, gentler America capped off the old firewater wall, filled its basin with potting soil, and disguised the tired old miracle with ornamental shrubbery.

Our Lady of Tickfaw

On the morning of March 12, 1989, more than ten thousand people from all over the country showed up for an open-air Mass on Alfredo Raimondo's property in rural Tangipahoa Parish after he spread the word that the Virgin Mary had given him a message requesting that they gather there to honor Saint Joseph. During the events of the day, some worshippers witnessed strange lights radiating from the sun while others had visions of Mary, Jesus, and Joseph; smelled the scent of roses wafting on the breeze (a sign of the Virgin's presence); or discovered that their silver rosaries had turned the color of gold.

Raimondo, a retired oil field pipe fitter, compares his former vegetable patch outside the town of Tickfaw to Lourdes—the famous pilgrimage and healing center in southwest France where the Virgin Mary has made regular appearances since 1858. He points out that the French grotto where the Virgin announced her immaculate conception to Bernadette Soubirous had long been used by local townspeople as a garbage dump, while his own garden lay atop a former Tickfaw landfill. And, as at Lourdes, the humble surroundings didn't deter the thousands of worshippers who flocked to Our Lady of Tickfaw, as the Raimondo field became known. The blessed site seemed well on its way to becoming a major pilgrimage destination and the town of Tickfaw, population 664, had never seen anything like it.

For several years following the 1989 Mass, believers came to Our Lady of Tickfaw by the busload. Some of them stayed long enough to help build a scattering of shrines and prayer sites on the land, including a small sanctuary and gift shop. Others volunteered to serve as guides, leading new arrivals to the many sacred areas of the property. An apparition of Jesus had appeared in one spot, where photos later revealed a divine presence that had been invisible at the time the pictures were taken. On one occasion, Padre Pio's image appeared in the bark of the holly tree—where most of the site's miracles were concentrated—and worshippers who were gathered around it were spattered with what appeared to be blood. For several years, Mary herself showed up during subsequent Assumption Day celebrations, held annually in mid-August. And during the very hottest days of the summer, visitors often saw apparitions in shadows on the trunks of trees or up in the clouds, witnessed strange light displays, or experienced the sun as a spinning, multicolored orb hovering in the heavens. At another point a white ball had appeared in limbs of the tree with the image of Mary floating inside it. Other miracles, such as the appearance of facial hair on a statue of the Christ Child in the sanctuary, defied explanation or interpretation, even though photos still exist to prove they happened.

Over time, however, enthusiasm for the Tickfaw miracles seems to have waned. Nowadays Our Lady of Tickfaw is a bit difficult to find, although the shrines are maintained, the religious shop is open for business, and the sanctuary is still there to be used by anyone who wants

a chance at a closer walk with the Virgin. Many locals seem unsure of its location and tend to direct curious out-of-towners to Our Lady of Pompeii, the mainstream Catholic Church in town. But persistence pays off. Across Interstate 55 on Antioch Road, near the Natalbany River, is a place where miracles still do happen.

Hail Mary, Full of Tears

In the last five hundred years, the Vatican has officially recognized only three miracles. Each of the divine events involved the appearance of the Virgin Mary—to an Indian peasant in Mexico (1531); to a fourteen-year-old girl in Lourdes, France (1858); and to three children in Fátima, Portugal (1917). Apart from these three, none of the widely reported appearances of Mary, Joseph, Jesus, the Holy Cross—on mildewed drywall, weathered adobe, potato chips, double-paned plate glass windows, grilled cheese sandwiches, or cloud formations—has received full ecclesiastical recognition. Nor have any of the paintings or statues that weep tears, oil, blood, myrrh, or resin been awarded official acknowledgment.

Even so, this hasn't stopped Louisiana's faithful from seeking out special signs from the heavens. In October 1996, an icon at Our Lady of Perpetual Help Church in Kenner, a suburb of New Orleans, began to weep. Moisture gathered around the eyes of the Blessed Virgin in enough quantity that a makeshift trough lined with cotton balls was placed beneath the icon to catch the drops as they fell. So many people came to see the phenomenon that lines stretched around the block and visitors were escorted into the sanctuary in small, supervised groups so they could observe the miracle. The icon's tears were never fully explained, but eventually the weeping abated enough that the catch-trough below the picture could be safely removed. A handful of parishioners still treasure the swabs of cotton that had absorbed the Virgin's tears.

This Little Light of Mine

Hurricane Audrey tore through southwest Louisiana in June 1957. At the time, the category four storm was the most destructive hurricane to hit the United States since 1938, and it was also the worst storm ever to form so early in the season. The town of Cameron in Cameron Parish was hit hard—more than 80 percent of its homes were damaged or completely destroyed. After the storm subsided, Rev. A. L. Gilbert entered the ruins of St. John's Catholic Church to survey the damage. Amid the dirt and debris he saw a light—a candle on the altar had survived the tempest with its flame burning brightly.

Meaty Miracle

In early March of 1999, a maintenance man at the Ascension of Our Lord Catholic Church in the town of LaPlace found a communion wafer on the floor of the sanctuary and turned it over to the pastor, Rev. Benjamin Piovan. Church rules stipulate that under such circumstances the priest must either eat the wafer himself or dissolve it in holy water—he naturally chose the latter.

When Father Benny retrieved the jar a few days later, he found that instead of dissolving, the wafer had transformed. It was swollen with a stringy reddish texture and looked very much like a piece of meat floating in the holy water. On March 14, Father Benny began taking the jar to his Masses, and parishioners lined up by the altar waiting to catch a glimpse of the meaty miracle.

“I thought I would have to strain to see it,” church member Denise Stein told reporter Martha Carr, “but I could see it from about three feet away. . . . There was no doubt in my mind that it was definitely Jesus’ flesh and blood.” The rest the congregation shared her feelings. Jona Christy, another member of the church, cried when she saw the jar. “I believe it is real,” she said. “It is a beautiful, blessed thing. Maybe the reasons it happened are yet to come.”

Strange Occurrence at Lake Peigneur

For more than a century, Lake Peigneur had been little more than a scenic backdrop for an Iberia Parish mansion built by the well-known nineteenth-century character actor Joseph Jefferson. Many years later Jefferson's estate was developed into a resort called Rip Van Winkle Gardens by John L. Bayless, Jr., who named the place after Jefferson's most famous stage role. Bayless eventually built his own home, a visitor center, and a camellia conservatory on the shores of the 1,300-acre lake. In early 1980 he had finally settled into the house to enjoy his retirement. But he would spend less than nine months there before disaster struck.

Perhaps it could have been foreseen. Near the resort was the entrance to a huge underground salt mine owned by the Diamond Crystal company, which had dug vast caverns beneath the lake in the process of extracting salt from subterranean dome deposits. Meanwhile, Texaco had secured a lease to prospect for oil in the general area. By November 1980 it had maneuvered a floating drill rig into the middle of the shallow lake and begun drilling. Somehow, no one considered that these two activities might conflict with each other.

In the predawn hours of Thursday, November 20, 1980, the drilling machinery came to a grinding halt somewhere around 1,200 feet below the lake floor. After a few hours, during which the drillers struggled to free their equipment, they discovered that the rig had begun to shift and tilt. Concerned that the platform might give, they headed to shore to work out a plan to realign it. But to their amazement—and soon, their horror—instead of tipping on its side (the water in the middle of the lake was only six feet deep), the entire rig disappeared below the surface of the water.

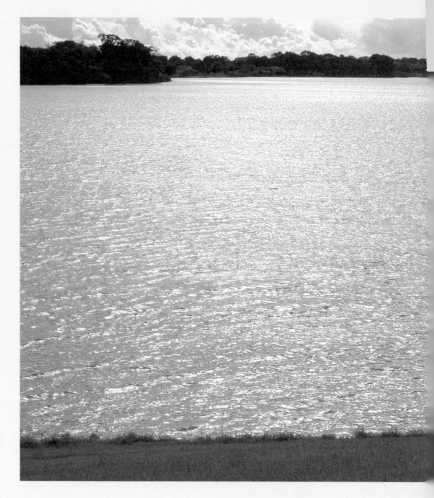

Meanwhile another drama was underway in the salt mine below the lake. Water had begun surging into the mine from a ceiling crack and was rapidly filling the shafts and tunnels. Alarms sounded and, luckily, all fifty-five miners were able to evacuate using their emergency escape cages.

It soon became clear what had happened. Due to a simple miscalculation, the oil prospectors had accidentally drilled into the salt mine. As the lake water drained into the mine, it dissolved the columns of salt that had been left

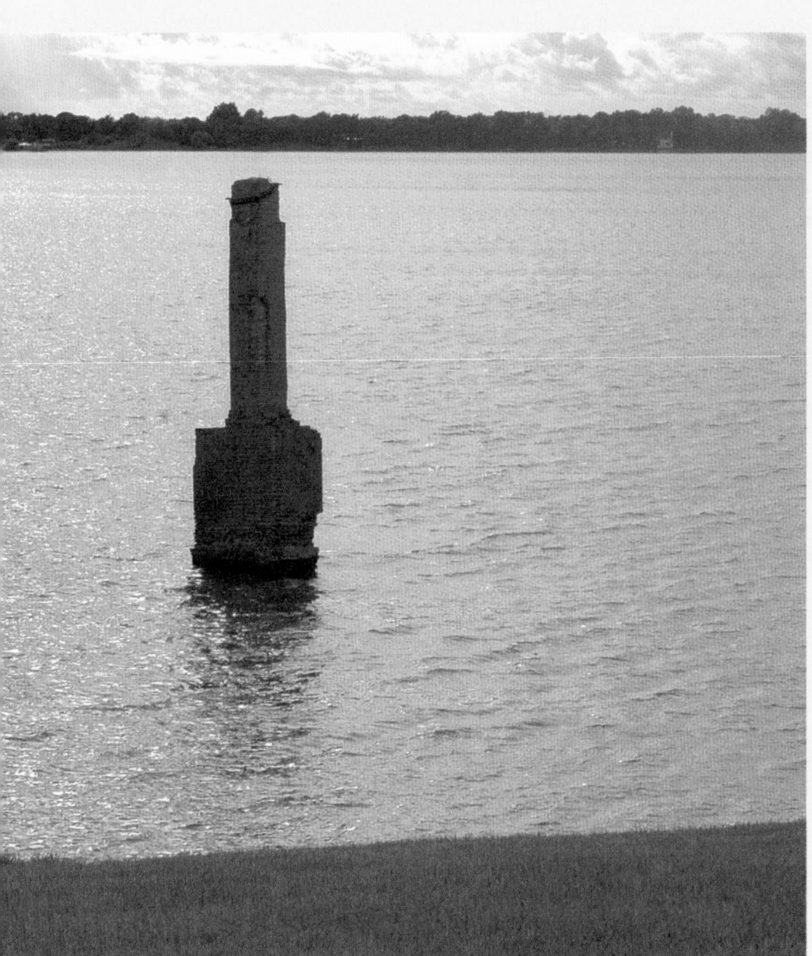

to support the tunnels. When these began to collapse, the entire mine became a mammoth sinkhole, sucking water in at such a rate that all the air remaining in the mine began roaring out of its entrance shaft to form a four-hundred-foot geyser that blasted water, equipment, and debris over a wide area.

The widening hole in the bottom of the lake then turned into a giant whirlpool so powerful that it eventually sucked down eleven full-sized barges and a second drill rig. Finally, as the lake drained, the Delcambre Canal, which had always flowed away from the lake, reversed its direction and cascaded back into the lake to create a huge, roaring waterfall. Over the course of the next two days, nine boats, a mobile home, five lakefront houses, and Lyle Bayless's retirement dream home, his camellia conservatory, and sixty-five acres of Rip Van Winkle Gardens were washed into the lake by 3.5 billion gallons of salt water pouring in from the Gulf of Mexico.

Eventually it all stabilized once water from the lake completely filled the mine and the Gulf waters had refilled the lake. But Lake Peigneur was forever changed. Before the day of the "mistake," it had been a freshwater lake only six feet deep. Now it's more than 1,300 feet deep and full of salt water. Amazingly enough, no lives were lost during the spectacular goof-up. Texaco acknowledged the error and, along with the company that managed the rig, paid $32 million to the Diamond Crystal mining company and another $13 million to local residents whose property had been swept into the lake.

This may not be the end of the story, however. A few years ago, residents around Lake Peigneur began noticing a plume of foamy bubbles gathering in one spot on the lake's surface. Fourteen years after the drilling disaster, an Atlanta-based energy company obtained a license to create two huge artificial caverns farther below the abandoned salt mine and now uses them to store up to 9.4 billion cubic feet of natural gas at pressures up to 2,700 pounds per square inch. The escaping bubbles suggest there may be a crack forming in one of these giant underground containers. If that's the case, then someday a spectacular light and sound show may prove far more astonishing than even the simultaneous waterfall, geyser, and whirlpool were.

Heavenly Bathroom Experiences

On the evening of Monday, October 11, 1976, while standing in his bathtub, James Barrow saw a brilliant crucifix made of light through his bathroom window. News of the heavenly apparition spread quickly, and by five thirty the following evening, hundreds of people had flocked to the Barrows' home in Scotlandville, a community on the northern outskirts of Baton Rouge. By Thursday night, the crowds had grown unruly, and law enforcement officers were called to the scene. It was then that the Barrows decided to make their bathtub-miracle viewing opportunities available to the public by appointment only.

By the end of that week the media had been alerted to the nightly event and an article in the *Advocate* (Baton Rouge) featured Mrs. Barrow describing the cross as "reaching from the sky to the ground" and explaining that it remained visible all night but would begin "disappearing and reappearing during the morning hours." By ten thirty each morning it had vanished entirely, only to return once again after sunset.

Amazingly, this wasn't the only cross-in-a-bathroom sighting in Louisiana at the time. There had been reports of similar experiences in Independence and Slidell, and there were signs that the blessed phenomenon was spreading across the state. After viewing the Barrows' bathroom miracle, witnesses often went home to discover that the mysterious cross was visible in their own bathrooms as well. Officials were stumped. They couldn't explain the crucifix apparitions, nor could they say how or why the phenomenon had spread across the state.

Sgt. Royal McCastle helped solve the mystery. He and his cousin Henry McCastle discovered that the Scenic Highway Glass Service had recently been stocking and installing a kind of frosted glass with fine-grained striations that caused any light that shone through it to form a cross. This would explain, Sergeant McCastle pointed out, why people would often report seeing a "bloody cross" through their bathroom windows whenever he drove up to help with crowd control at cross sightings throughout the area. What witnesses saw was the red light atop his car, while the other crosses were just streetlights. He attributed the whole thing to a kind of mass hysteria. "People would go see one, and they had it on their mind," he explained, and "then they would get home and see a cross in their [own] bathroom window. . . . They had never noticed it before, [and] now they saw it [and] thought it had followed them home."

Despite the fact that the McCastle cousins cracked the case of the bathroom miracles more than thirty years ago, devout Louisianans still flock to see divine manifestations as soon as they are announced. As recently as 2004, huge crowds formed outside the Shirley Cross home at 1804 Dublin Road in Alexandria to spend a few moments standing in her tub and gazing up in awe at the symbol of sacrifice looming mysteriously through her bathroom window.

Green Balls of Fire!

The twenty-two-room mansion on the shores of Lake Peigneur at Rip Van Winkle Gardens is believed to be haunted by the ghost of Joseph Jefferson, who built the property in 1870. Green balls of lightning-like electrical discharges sometimes hover over the house even when skies are calm. Heavy chairs, especially those with upholstery supported by hidden steel springs, have been observed sliding along waxed floors. So what's going on here? Could it be the acclaimed actor's spirit still lingers in his beloved home?

Where paranormal researchers have described the sound of ghostly footsteps, scientists with a stronger bent toward physics have attributed the mansion's eerie green illuminations to the interaction between the lake's water and the collapsed salt mine that surrounds the property. And the mysteriously mobile furniture? Scientists offer up static-cling attraction—the same force at work when you rub a piece of cellophane on a wooly sweater—as an explanation. Whatever the cause, witnesses of the Jefferson mansion's green balls of fire find it eerie and literally hair raising!

Unidentifed Hovering Object

In the spring of 1969, a saucer-shaped object more than 150 feet in diameter was documented hovering over the Mississippi River Bridge in Baton Rouge by *Advocate* photographer Charles Gerald. According to one onlooker, "the tremendous wind force given off by the craft seemed to cause the bridge to tilt slightly as if sinking into the river." The unidentified hovering object was observed for only a few minutes before it vanished.

Saucer Gumbo

South-central Louisiana is one of the world's hot spots for UFO activity. There have been hundreds of credible sightings within about eighty miles to the north and south of Highway 190, some dating back as far as the end of World War II. In fact, many experts believe that atomic weapons used at the end of the war signaled extra-terrestrials and encouraged them to visit Earth. Here are a few notable saucer-related encounters:

Bright Lights, Big Screams

A pilot heading toward Dallas, Texas, vanished on July 27, 1967, after his plane crashed somewhere between Leesville and Alexandria. In his calls for help, which were picked up by CB radio operators as far away as Seneca, South Carolina, and Saskatchewan, Canada, he reported being chased by a red glowing object. He said the object approached the side of his plane and then hovered around the tail section as it forced the craft down. The pilot then radioed in that he would attempt to land the plane on either Highway 28 or 121 in Vernon Parish. After the crash landing, he survived long enough to scream that something with a bright glowing light was hovering over the wreckage where he was pinned. Then the radio went dead. Neither the wreckage nor a body was ever recovered.

Saucer Sightings in '73

During mid-October, 1973, a wave of UFO sightings that many witnesses likened to a saucer attack occurred in a concentrated band stretching from Zachary to Gonzales. Several days in a row, witnesses saw a slew of unidentified objects in the sky. According to the *Advocate* in Baton Rouge, one man encountered a UFO at around six in the morning on October 19 at the intersection of Airline Highway and Florida Boulevard. The object followed his vehicle into Gonzales, where he was able to go into a café and convince more than a dozen customers to come out to the parking lot, where they saw it, too. Onlookers described the object as very bright and with four inverted V shapes behind it.

Meanwhile a woman in Zachary reported that six-foot strands of a "white, silky substance" fell out of the sky onto her seven-year-old boy on October 18, shortly after he saw a cigar-shaped object passing overhead. This description of the peculiar material agrees with reports by other witnesses who said "angel hair" had been found drifting in the air. According to expert UFO-ologists, this material is often associated with UFO encounters and may have something to do with their propulsion, communication, or perhaps even with saucer waste evacuation. As in the other cases where it had been reported, the strands that fell on the young boy disintegrated or dissolved harmlessly soon after landing on him.

The following week, all the flying saucer activity finally seemed to die down, only to be revived almost exactly a year later. In the fall of 1974 a number of well-documented sightings in Holden, Gonzales, and Livingston led up to a famous alien abduction in Pascagoula, Mississippi, which many serious UFO-ologists still consider among the top ten most significant encounters in UFO history.

Time-Stopping Trinity

On the night of October 25, 1996, two men standing in a Calcasieu Parish field between the town of Iowa and Lake Charles observed three glowing objects, each emanating a bright white light. The objects, which made humming noises as they hovered about fifty feet above the ground, appeared one at a time. The first changed from a saucer shape to a ball shape, then the white light turned red before it vanished. A few minutes later a second object showed up directly overhead and seemed to paralyze the men somehow. This one, which had a triangular shape, was also white to start with but turned a silvery blue color. It remained overhead for several minutes before slowly lifting up and taking off at high speed.

One of the men looked at his watch and noticed that it had stopped running, even though it was a self-winding watch with no battery. As he made this observation, a third object—triangular in shape with dim lights—appeared, hovering about five hundred yards away. It rose to join the other two objects and took off. The stopped wristwatch had paused at 2:04 A.M., but as soon as the UFOs left the area, it began ticking once more.

Mr. T's Polaroids

On the chilly overcast day of January 12, 1967, a middle-aged fisherman known only as Mr. T took several Polaroid photos of a saucer-shaped object flying above Old River in Livingston Parish, according to journalist Ron Albritton, whose report appeared in the March 12 issue of the Baton Rouge *Sunday Advocate*. Mr. T was out in his boat checking the trotlines when he first spotted the craft. He happened to have a Polaroid camera on hand and was able to snap a blurry shot of the weird object before it flew off into the distance. While still on the river later that evening, Mr. T heard a vacuum-cleaner type noise overhead, but it was too dark to see anything.

"...sounded like a million crows, chattering like crazy in a clump of trees across the river."

The next morning, Mr. T noticed an unusual number of dead fish floating in the river. He grabbed his rifle and camera and headed to the shore. While walking along the riverbank, he heard a flock of birds that "sounded like a million crows, chattering like crazy in a clump of trees across the river." Then suddenly he saw it again: The saucer-shaped craft from the day before flew out from behind the trees and approached him. Again, Mr. T managed to snap a few shots of the saucer. Moments after the craft disappeared, he peeled back the developer strips and saw that the pictures were sharper than those he had taken from his boat a day earlier.

Experts later examined the images and declared them to be authentic, pointing out that it would have been extremely difficult to fake Polaroid images (as opposed to prints made from film negatives) and that the sequence of the shots agreed with his account. Dr. Edward Condon, professor of physics at the University of Colorado, was among the experts who acknowledged Mr. T's version of the incident. According to the *Advocate* article, Condon was the recipient of a $131,000 government grant to investigate strange aerial phenomena, and in late 1966 and early 1967 these were being reported at the rate of "two to three thousand U-F-O sightings a month." But rare indeed were sightings like Mr. T's on Old River, where an apparently responsible witness with nothing to gain was able to back up his story with such solid documentary evidence.

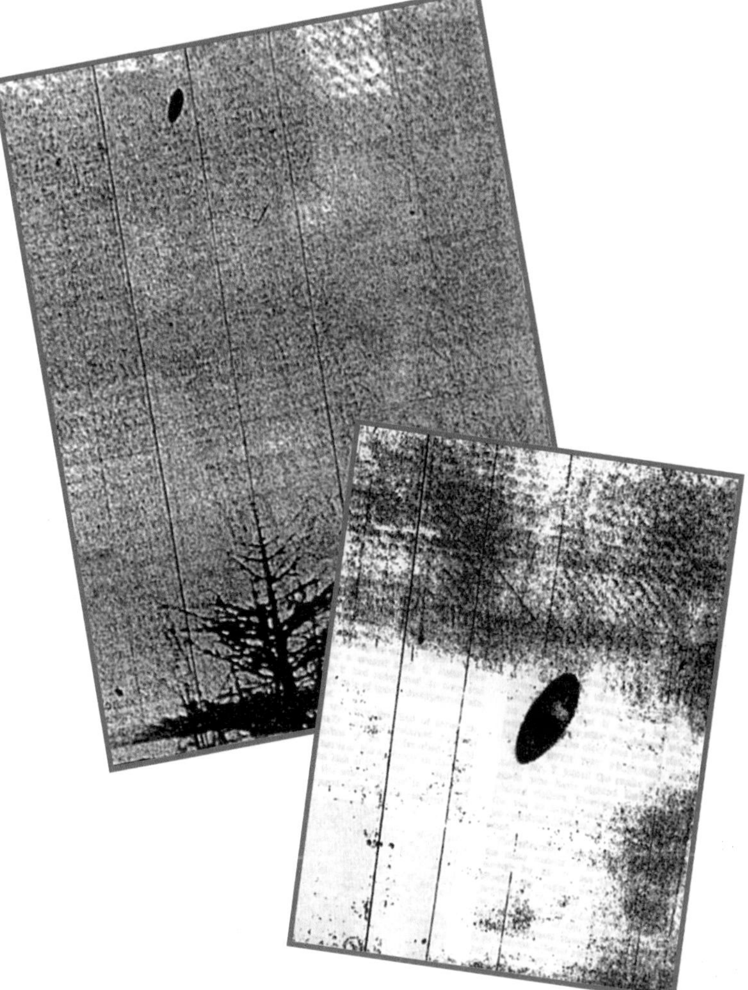

Fabled People and Places

There often comes a point in each of our lives when we discover that some of our most cherished beliefs may not actually be true. So why do we accept fables in the first place? The most obvious answer is that they help explain things.

As long as fables keep helping us make sense of the world, we hang onto them. As soon as a better explanation comes along, we can let them go. But what if you live in one of those places where it's not so easy to tell fact from fiction? Louisiana can often be like that. So much of what is true can seem outlandishly unbelievable and bizarre, while so many falsehoods can masquerade as the gospel truth. Louisiana is the very heartland of masking and masquerading, after all, and sometimes the healthiest approach to trying to make sense of this lifelong carnival may just be to kick back and enjoy watching it all roll by.

The Casket Girls

In 1717, when New Orleans was established, there were only twenty-seven women living there. We kid you not. At the time, the young Louisiana colony was a settlement with an uncertain future, and for the city to take hold and thrive, the imbalance between the sexes needed to be rectified. The city needed women, and lots of them. The government had a few ideas—some brighter than others.

A Few Good Women

In 1719, Philippe II, the Duke of Orleans, proposed rounding up women from hospitals and prisons in France and shipping them to New Orleans. The majority of these women were prostitutes or petty criminals from urban areas, and many didn't survive the long voyage across the Atlantic. Those who made it to New Orleans found the lifestyle change difficult to deal with and never settled into their intended roles as farmer's wives.

The city's second effort to improve the male-to-female ratio involved bringing over boatloads of Ursuline nuns starting in 1727. The nuns did a great deal of good in the city, building a convent, a hospital, and the Ursuline Academy—the oldest continually operating Catholic school for women in the United States today—but their hearts were dedicated to the Lord, so they didn't do much to help grow the city's population.

In 1728 the government tried a third scheme. Teenage girls and women from French or Canadian orphanages were offered free transportation to New Orleans, a guarantee of marriage, and a small casket or chest containing two dresses, two petticoats, six hats and scarves, and an assortment of ribbons, buttons, bows, and toiletry items. Once in New Orleans, the Ursuline nuns looked after these so-called *casket girls* until they were married off.

The program was a wild success compared to the previous two efforts, since it made the colony more attractive to men. Soldiers who agreed to marry casket girls were excused from duty and given a cow, rifle, and plot of free land. Under the new plan, the town of Nouvelle-Orléans leaped from a 1721 census count of 470 to 7,500 by 1731. Although the steady flow of young women into the city certainly helped the population boom, relations between the casket girls and the Ursuline nuns weren't always idyllic. Behind the convent's closed doors there was tension. And over the thirty years that the casket girl initiative lasted, the tension escalated, giving rise to some of the legends that surround Ursuline Convent.

Supernatural Stakeout at Ursuline Convent

According to one of the more gruesome legends, the earliest boatloads of casket girls were forced into the roles established by the dubious behavior of the "corrections girls" who had preceded them. When word reached the French government that many of the young women were put to work as prostitutes and slaves, ships were dispatched to take them back to France. When they arrived back in the old country, French peasants who hadn't heard about the casket program noticed that each of the girls carried a small chest that she refused to open for anyone. Before long, rumors grew that the little caskets held the remains of dead babies that had

been conceived when the girls had been raped or held in prostitution. The little caskets eventually spawned such unrest they were confiscated and returned to the Ursuline sisters in Louisiana. The nuns permanently sealed the caskets and hid them on the third floor of the convent, where they remained for the next two centuries.

Then, in the late 1970s, there was renewed interest in the caskets. A group of paranormal researchers who tried to investigate the convent were denied access, so they decided to stage a stakeout. They set up video equipment on the sidewalk in front of the building and took turns monitoring the site throughout the night. When the third shift of investigators arrived at dawn they were horrified to discover their colleagues from the previous shift lying dead beside the convent wall. Both men's throats were ravaged and looked as if they had been bitten. Autopsies later revealed that their bodily fluids had been drained.

The video equipment remained undisturbed. When the team members played back the half-inch reel-to-reel tapes for the police, they saw a stationary view of the convent in grainy black and white and heard the two investigators chatting. Long minutes passed with nothing but small talk. Then one of the researchers said, "Something's moving! Hey Matt, can you see something up there? Is something moving?" The picture on the screen jiggled as they hurried to zoom in. When it refocused, one of the dormer windows was open and something dark without a clear shape became visible. A scream was heard. The camera got knocked over. Then there was silence.

The police and investigators who returned to the scene were puzzled. The dormer windows were not only closed, they were nailed shut. And although the paranormal investigators insisted the tapes were new, the police speculated that the movements caught on tape were the result of a technological glitch, as if the tapes had already been used. Nothing else made sense.

It wasn't long before rumors of demons and vampires began circulating around the French Quarter, many of them fed by the sudden focus of attention on the Ursuline Convent. Whatever the cause, the double murder of the two paranormal investigators was never solved.

Archbishops Rest in Pieces

According to Joy Dickinson, legend has it that the preserved hearts of all the archbishops of New Orleans are buried under the altar of a chapel in the Ursuline Convent. The Church has refused to refute or contradict this legend, and the custom would certainly be in keeping with many shrines and cathedrals in Europe, especially in France.

Priestly Possession

The Ursuline order gained notoriety a century before the nuns arrived in New Orleans in 1727. Father Urbain Grandier, a French Catholic priest, was accused of bewitching a convent of Ursulines in Loudun, France. Mother Superior Sister Jeanne of the Angels claimed that Grandier had used black magic to seduce her. As hysteria swept through the convent, dozens of other nuns said that Grandier had put them under demonic possession. The priest was arrested, tortured, and found guilty after prosecutors managed to produce documents purporting to be written agreements between Grandier and the dark forces of hell—bearing not only Grandier's signature but that of none other than Lucifer Beelzebub Satanas himself, signed backward! Grandier was sentenced to death and burned at the stake.

Saint Expedite

Our Lady of Guadalupe Church, on the corner of North Rampart and Conti Streets, was originally called the Mortuary Chapel and had been built exclusively for holding funerals. By the time it was erected in 1826, New Orleans had already suffered through thirty years of annual summer outbreaks of yellow fever, malaria, and other deadly epidemics. At the time, no one knew that these diseases were carried by mosquitoes. They thought instead that they were generated by poisonous air. (*Malaria* comes from *mala aria*, Italian for “bad air.”) Such poisonous air could come, they believed, from a variety of sources, like swamp gas or nighttime breezes, but especially from the last breaths and foul smells seeping out of the mouths and nostrils of dead people.

“ST. EXPEDITE”
PRAY FOR US

Therefore, they thought, one way to minimize the spread of disease would be to build a chapel alongside the cemeteries on the edge of town and hold all the funerals there instead of in the main St. Louis Cathedral downtown. That way, only the immediate family would risk infection from the dead. Following the funeral, relatives of the departed could go next door for a quick and convenient internment ceremony.

Over the years, the Mortuary Chapel assumed a number of roles, becoming a church for Confederate veterans in the late 1860s, then renamed St. Anthony’s Chapel in the 1870s. In 1918 it was renamed Our Lady of Guadalupe, when it was earmarked for use by Spanish-speaking locals. In 1921, a collection of plaster statues of saints was shipped to the church and arranged around the main sanctuary. In addition to transporting well-known saints like Joseph, Martha, Michael, Peter, and Anthony of Padua, the shipment included statues of some lesser-known martyrs: Saint Raymond, patron saint of midwives and nicknamed Nonnatus or “the unborn” because he was delivered by C-section after his mother died in labor; Saint Florian, patron saint of fire brigades; and Saint Dymphna, patron saint of the insane.

Finally there was Saint Expedite, who many religious scholars suspect probably never existed. According to a local legend, one of the boxes in the shipment of statues and relics had been received with the word *Expedite* stamped on it. The nuns, finding no other identifying labels with the box, mistakenly thought it must be the name of the saint and set it up as a shrine to Saint-Expédité—and the name stuck. The statue of Saint Expedite, just inside the door to Our Lady of Guadalupe, brandishes a cross with the word *hodie* on it (Latin for “today”). Because of this, Saint Expedite is thought to be the saint to invoke when avoiding procrastination, making quick decisions, and providing speedy answers. Therefore he is considered the patron saint of computer hackers, programmers, and book authors facing imminent deadlines.

Red Rum

In Chalmette, some ten miles east of New Orleans, is a historic park preserving the spot where the Battle of New Orleans was fought during the War of 1812, culminating with a great American victory on January 8, 1815, and marking one of the final episodes of the war. In fact, as every schoolkid in Louisiana learns, the war officially ended on Christmas Eve, 1814, with the Treaty of Ghent. But because news of the treaty was slow to reach the British or American forces in Louisiana, the battle continued into the new year.

On January 8, although outnumbered almost two to one, American forces under the command of Gen. Andrew Jackson suffered only thirteen deaths and fifty-eight wounded while the British incurred more than two thousand casualties. News of the miraculous victory quickly spread through the entire region; but when it reached the Ursuline Convent, the nuns were hardly surprised. They had prayed to the Virgin (actually to the statue of Our Lady of Prompt Succor) to protect the troops. The previous evening the nuns had prayed before the venerated idol; and during the next day's continuation of the battle, there was

a front-line miracle: A thick fog settled on the battlefield. British troops began to advance in standard formation when suddenly the wind shifted, blowing the fog away, and leaving them standing in their red coats, in full view of the Americans, who picked them off like targets in a shooting gallery.

But that wasn't the first time the nuns had asked for the Virgin's help. In 1812 a terrible fire tore through the French Quarter and threatened to burn down the Ursuline Convent. Thanks to the nuns' prayers, it is believed, the wind suddenly changed direction, blowing the fire away and sparing the convent.

Despite her blessed nature, however, the Virgin may also have a wicked sense of humor, if one story told about the aftermath of the War of 1812 is true. British Gen. Edward Pakenham had been killed during the battle, but rather than bury him in foreign soil, his redcoat compatriots decided to return his body to England, where it could be interred with honors. Without access to refrigeration or embalming fluid, they did the only thing that could be done back then to preserve a corpse—pickle it in rum. Every British sailing vessel was well stocked with the stuff, since it helped alleviate the boredom of the lengthy voyages, kept the sailing men reasonably happy, and warmed the extremities of anyone standing watch during long winter nights. A full keg was appropriated for the purpose and General Pakenham was summarily submerged in liquor for the voyage.

On the way back to the general's homeland, however, the ship was captured by American privateers—government-licensed pirates who had been given permission to attack non-U.S. ships that wandered too close to the coast. These enterprising fellows hijacked the entire cargo and took it with them to Charleston, South Carolina, to be sold. As soon as the privateers unloaded on the Charleston docks, a man bought one of several barrels of the rum that had been seized from the British vessel and took it home to Fairfield County. When he got there, he invited all his neighbors over for a frolic. The rum was especially good that evening, they said, and the party it led to was especially wild. When it came time to break up the barrel for firewood, it was still too heavy for one man to lift alone, so they smashed it where it stood.

Much to the partygoers' surprise, out fell the perfectly pickled cadaver of General Pakenham, still dressed in his uniform with all his decorations. The man who reported the event afterward joked, "At least they could say they finally knew what a good, full-bodied rum was supposed to taste like."

Funky Bunkie

How the Avoyelles Parish town of Bunkie got its name is a weird story. The town was originally established as a "railhead" town, used to ship local products to market. When the Louisiana Pacific Railroad representatives asked what the name of the town was going to be, the founders were at a loss.

However, one of the founders had a young daughter who was born with a speech impediment. The little girl had accompanied her father to the meeting along with her pet, a small spider monkey. The monkey jumped out of her arms and she ran after it, calling, "Come back, bunkey!" The founders, not having arrived at any kind of agreement, heard her and decided on the spot that the name of the town would thenceforth be Bunkie.

Strangely enough, there is a small lake in Avoyelles Parish called "Reynolds Lake" that surrounds an island that is (or at least was thirty years ago) populated by a troop of monkeys said to be descended from the little girl's pets. I know this much is a fact: There were monkeys on "Monkey Island" when I was a kid, because when my father and I duck hunted on Reynolds Lake, he always pointed out the monkeys. *—Frank*

The town of Bunkie was originally named Irion, after a Major Irion who fought in the War of 1812 and settled in Avoyelles Parish ten years later. But when they put the railroad through, the Haas family donated part of their land for the train station. As a gesture of thanks, the railroad company gave Col. A. M. Haas the honor of naming the station and he named it Maccie, after his daughter. Maccie had a toy monkey her dad had brought back from a trip to New Orleans and she called the toy monkey Bunkie. So, really, the town is named for a child's mispronounced name for a toy. *—Nancy*

Turkish Delight

A few blocks behind St. Louis Cathedral on the corner of Orleans and Dauphine Streets in New Orleans is a tall house with lacy iron verandas that jut higher above the pavement than those of its neighbors. For many decades it was often referred to as "the Sultan's House," although the legend behind that moniker has faded with time. Today a plaque identifies it only as LE PRETE HOUSE.

Jean-Baptiste Le Prete moved into the house in 1839 and lived there until 1878 when, unable to repay a major debt, he lost it to Citizens Bank. After that the house changed hands many times and gradually deteriorated over the years. By 1922, it had been subdivided into small dingy tenements and was in such bad shape that an article in the *Times-Picayune* said that ". . . time has left its scars on those high-flung walls and . . . the interior has lost much of its plaster and every vestige of paint [so that it] gives only the slightest hint of its former glory."

According to rumors that gradually grew into divergent legends, Le Prete had lost much of his fortune after a remarkable new arrival showed up in New Orleans one day. Sometime during or shortly after the Civil War, so one version of the story goes, a stranger stepped off a boat that had just landed at the city docks, dressed in baggy silk pants gathered in at the ankles, a red silk cummerbund tied around his middle, and wearing a turban atop his head. He spoke with a thick accent, muffled by a drooping mustache. Among his belongings was a heavy, padlocked wooden casket that nobody was allowed to touch. After making inquiries about possible places to find lodging, the newcomer was directed to Monsieur Le Prete's house, saying that the owner was generous to a fault, was known to welcome any and all into his home for frequent parties and salons, and was sure to be a delightful host. Not only had many of the most prominent people in Louisiana been wined and dined there, including many foreign dignitaries, for Le Prete, they said, took special pride in both the quality and variety of his guests. The stranger smiled when he heard all this and immediately made his way up rue d'Orleans to find the door.

As soon as Le Prete invited him in, the turbaned man introduced himself and told his story, while carefully observing his eager host to see which way the plot should unfurl and how far he could elaborate on the details. To his delight, Le Prete seemed ready to listen to anything he told him, so he had some fun with the narrative. The foreigner was, he claimed, a wealthy Turkish merchant who had come to the city on behalf of his brother, a sultan back in Istanbul. His brother had sent him to consider making certain major investments in Louisiana; and to be more specific, he hoped they would be able to purchase several sugar plantations. The two brothers had made their fortunes in the spice trade back in Turkey, so importing high-quality Louisiana sugar would be the natural next step.

However, his immediate needs were, he said, more mundane, for unfortunately he had arrived with neither French nor American currency but only certain "valuables" that might take a few weeks to convert into cash. As he said this, he looked meaningfully down at the locked casket in his lap. If Monsieur Le Prete would only allow him to stay a while, it would not only be an act of supreme kindness, but perhaps they might even discuss becoming partners, for he didn't intend to remain in the Americas forever. He and his wealthy brother would need a local liaison to handle their plantations and sugar shipments, and La Prete might be just the fellow.

Le Prete fell for it. Not only could the Turk stay there, he said, but he could have run of the place. Le Prete had a plantation out in Plaquemines Parish and could stay in the country to free up the town house for the exclusive use of the guest. He would even advance the Turk a significant loan of cash for the time being, to tide him over until he could cash his valuables.

As he prepared to leave for the country the following day, Monsieur Le Prete made sure his friends and acquaintances were aware that a demi-sultan was a guest-in-residence at chez Le Prete. Of course the friends fell for the story as well and were soon fawning over the exotic visitor to impress him.

The stranger, meanwhile, began living high on the hog. Before long, the sound of raucous laughter and shrieks of female ecstasy reverberating out of the Le Prete house became a regular nuisance, but even if wary neighbors were suspicious of the imbalance between the few men who entered the house and the many women who were seen coming and going at all hours, they tried for a time to excuse it by reminding one another that back in his own country, the Turk had probably grown accustomed to keeping a harem and was merely trying to make himself feel more comfortable in a foreign land.

But even the folks of New Orleans know that good times don't last forever. Just as Lent arrived to put an end to Carnival, the high life at the Le Prete place eventually came to a screeching halt, although there's some confusion about how it all unraveled. According to the "public" legend, which assumes that the stranger really was who he said he was, the older sultan back in Turkey finally realized that his younger brother was squandering the family fortune and sent a team of assassins to straighten things out. During one of the young Turk's wild parties, this gang of henchmen suddenly swarmed into the room, attacked him and a few of his guests with their daggers and scimitars, and then packed up the remnants of the casket of jewels and headed back to the Golden Horn.

Another version of the tale has it that things came to an end when neighbors, eager to profit from the cachet of the intriguing foreigner, invited him over for dinner. They

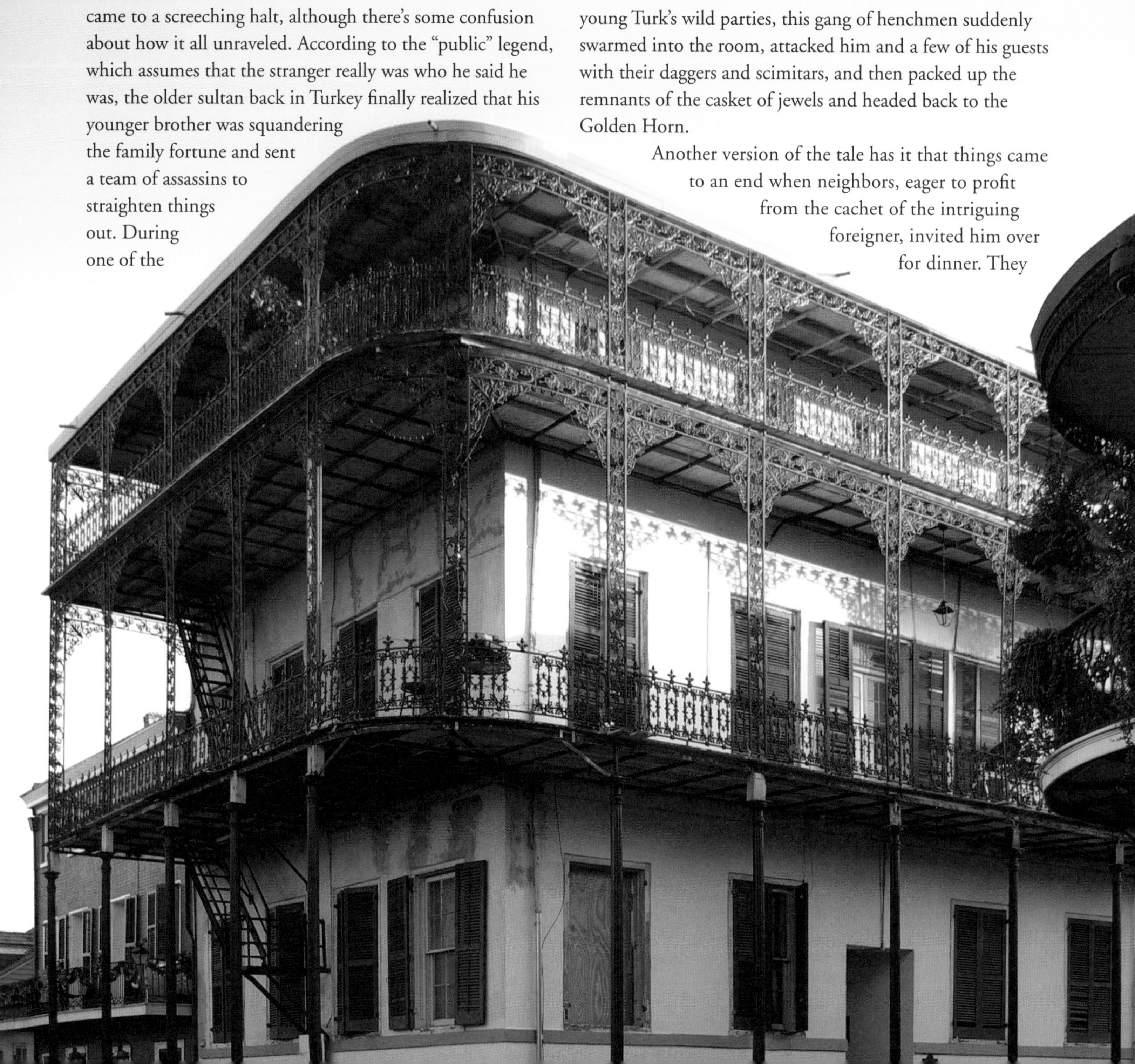

prepared a variety of foods and were gratified to see him enjoying plentiful servings of every dish set before him. Afterward, however, it dawned on them that not only had his accent become less Turkish and more Cockney as the evening wore on, but he also had been especially fond of the ham—and no dyed-in-the-wool Ottoman Turk would have touched any pork. The neighbors alerted Le Prete that he might be harboring an imposter and the well-meaning and generous host promptly kicked him out, but not before the scoundrel had spent the entire loan and destroyed the place.

This version seems a little more plausible, but for one small problem. Over the years, numerous occupants of the property have seen a shadowy mustachioed man in baggy attire, who began appearing in various rooms and seemed to take no notice of locks or doors. In a 1979 *Times-Picayune* article by Lorena Dureau, former tenant Virgie Posten admitted that back in the 1950s she had moved out within two months of signing a rental contract because she had seen an apparition in her bedroom.

> *My two-room apartment had only one door. . . . I always kept it locked, and even if whoever it was had had a key, I think I would have at least heard it turning in the lock. Yet there was nothing. Only silence. One minute he was there . . . the next he was gone. . . .*
>
> *After [a] second time, when I woke up in the middle of the night and saw him standing at the foot of the bed staring at me, I made up my mind to get out of there. . . .*
>
> *My third and last experience, however, was the most frightening of all. We were standing in the dimly lit hallway in the empty house, as I locked the door, when we suddenly heard a blood-curdling scream . . . somewhere at the top of the staircase just a few feet from us. It was petrifying – a long shrill scream that ended in a horrible gurgle! We ran as if the devil himself were after us to the street door. For a moment we even got wedged in the doorway, as both of us tried to get out at the same time. We laugh about it today, but it was pretty frightening at that moment. The very next day I got my things out of there.*

It is tempting to dismiss either version of the story of the sultan—or rather, of the sultan's younger brother—as merely another colorful New Orleans legend. But was he merely evicted, as the mild version of the story has it, or was he killed by a posse of assassins? Neither quite makes sense, especially if you lend any credence at all to the possibility that the witnesses really did see some kind of apparition. Perhaps this is one of those cases where the truth may lie somewhere in that nebulous zone between seeming fact and obvious fiction.

Big Myth Understanding: Louisiana's Many Made-Up Markers of History

One of the proudest sites in the historic little town of St. Martinville is a grand old live oak standing on the banks of Bayou Teche that marks the place where the Acadian heroine Evangeline Bellefontaine anxiously searched for her lost lover, Gabriel Lajeunesse, who had vacated the premises only shortly before she arrived. Utterly frustrated at the narrow miss, she stood on this very spot and cried, "O Gabriel! O my beloved! Art thou so near unto me, and yet I cannot behold thee? Art thou so near unto me, and yet thy voice does not reach me? Ah! How often thy feet have trod this path to the prairie! Ah! How often thine eyes have looked on the woodlands around me! Ah! How often beneath this oak, returning from labor, thou hast lain down to rest and to dream of me in thy slumbers! When shall these eyes behold, these arms be folded about thee?"

After she missed running into him under the hallowed oak, she set off to find him. For years he barely managed to keep out of her clutches while she chased after him over most of the North American continent east of the Mississippi. Finally, decades later, she tracked him down to a poorhouse in Philadelphia, of all places. Too old to run from her anymore, he still managed to have the last laugh, for moments after she finally laid eyes on him, he died. But Evangeline decided to look on the bright side of things and adopted a "better late than never" attitude. She stole a quick, necrophilic kiss and then thanked the Lord for getting them back together. And then she died, too, and they were buried in an unmarked grave.

Why anyone would ever believe such a nutty series of events is a real mystery, but luckily we don't have to, since it turns out that it's all just a long poem by Longfellow (as in Henry Wadsworth), written in 1847.

The real story—documented in *The True Story of Evangeline* by Judge Felix Voorhies—ends somewhat differently. Like Longfellow's couple, lovers Emmeline and Louis were separated when the British ordered the French Acadians to vacate Nova Scotia, and after many years they wound up in Bayou Teche. But unlike the poetical pair, Emmeline and Louis actually did stand face-to-face under the aforementioned mighty oak, not in a Philadelphia slum. And in contrast to the more decisive way that Gabriel handled the reunion, Louis didn't die right then and there, though it might have been better if he had.

Instead, he told Emmeline that he had "pledged his faith" to someone else since they'd last kissed a number of years earlier, so she should forget about the past. And with that heartless send-off he just walked away, leaving her dumfounded—so dumfounded, in fact, that she went insane. Wandering around the banks of the bayou picking flowers and muttering to herself, she eventually managed to die in her own mother's

arms. She was buried next to the church of St. Martin de Tours in St. Martinville, where her monument stands today, offering mute testimony to the power love has to make victims of those who partake of it carelessly.

It's a sad story. If only any of it were true. But despite the title of Voorhies's piece, it's just as fictional as Longfellow's. The "grave of Emmeline Labiche" is empty, since she never existed. The "portrait of Evangeline" atop Emmeline's tomb (are you keeping up with this?) is really that of Mexican actress Dolores del Rio, who played Evangeline in a 1929 Hollywood movie and decided to donate a statue of herself to the town. Local boosters seized its arrival as an opportunity to make the Voorhies short story seem more believable, so they created a "tomb" and mounted the statue atop it to make it real. Their success at this was so complete that it caused a lot of local embarrassment when French Canadians petitioned to have Emmeline exhumed so she could be reburied in the land of her birth.

But if there was no Evangeline—or Emmeline—then what's all the to-do about that oak? Surrounded as her tomb is by elaborate fencing, set aside in a little park by itself, and accompanied by several historical markers—surely she must be real, right?

Unfortunately, no. In fact, this is Original Evangeline Oak Number Three. The first two died of lightning and disease. Each time an Original Evangeline Oak keels over, the town simply chooses another stately tree, moves the signs and benches to the new location, and goes right back to business as usual.

St. Martinville isn't the only place in the state to try to profit from blurring the line between fiction and history. Out-of-staters looking for Tara, Scarlett O'Hara's fictional plantation in *Gone with the Wind*, may find themselves directed to Chretien Point (the estate whose staircase supposedly did provide the model for the one in the movie where Rhett Butler turns and says, "Frankly, my dear, I don't give a damn," before he heads on out into oblivion). In New Orleans, tourists hunt eagerly for the home of Stanley Kowalski on the Desire Street streetcar line, and though the latter no longer exists and the former never did, locals are only too happy to point off into the distance and tell them to "Head down thataway and take the third left. You can't miss it."

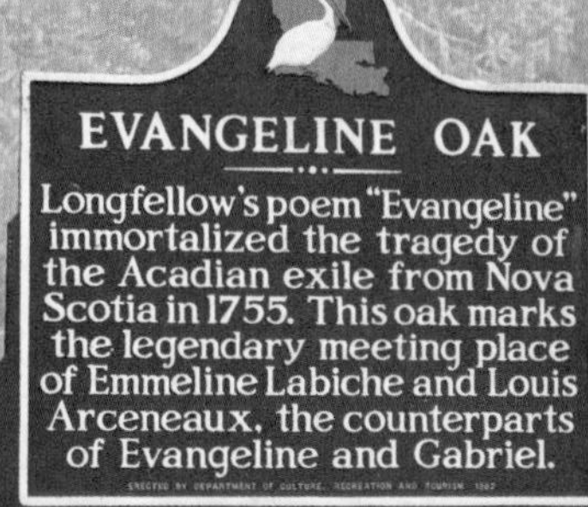

EVANGELINE OAK
Longfellow's poem "Evangeline" immortalized the tragedy of the Acadian exile from Nova Scotia in 1755. This oak marks the legendary meeting place of Emmeline Labiche and Louis Arceneaux, the counterparts of Evangeline and Gabriel.

Uncle Tom's Cabin

One of the greatest Lost Imaginary Historical Sites of Louisiana has to be Uncle Tom's cabin. Until not so long ago, tourists driving between Alexandria and Shreveport would stop off at Little Eva Plantation near Chopin to take pictures of an old shack identified as the very cabin where the kindly old slave had lived out the last years of his wretched life. After reverently soaking in the historical impact of the decrepit hut, visitors could walk up a hill to frown at the grave of the infamous Simon Legree. A few steps farther brought them to a fenced-in area where they could gaze solemnly at the actual grave of Uncle Tom, the slave that Legree had mistreated. In fact, Legree was so cruel that when Harriet Beecher Stowe described the racial situation in her 1852 novel *Uncle Tom's Cabin, or, Life Among the Lowly*, the book's release became one of the pivotal events leading up to the Civil War.

The only problem is that Stowe, like Longfellow, never visited Louisiana. In 1853 she wrote a follow-up to her novel, called *A Key to Uncle Tom's Cabin*, in which she made it clear that the plantation described in the book was based on one she'd visited in Kentucky, and Uncle Tom was a character based on a composite of many stories she'd heard about slavery since her childhood. But never mind; the tourists needed to see the cabin so they could take pictures of it, and there one stood in Chopin.

But it was even more artificial than they realized. Built in 1959, the cabin was made to *look* old, but a few steamy Louisiana summers also weathered it nicely.

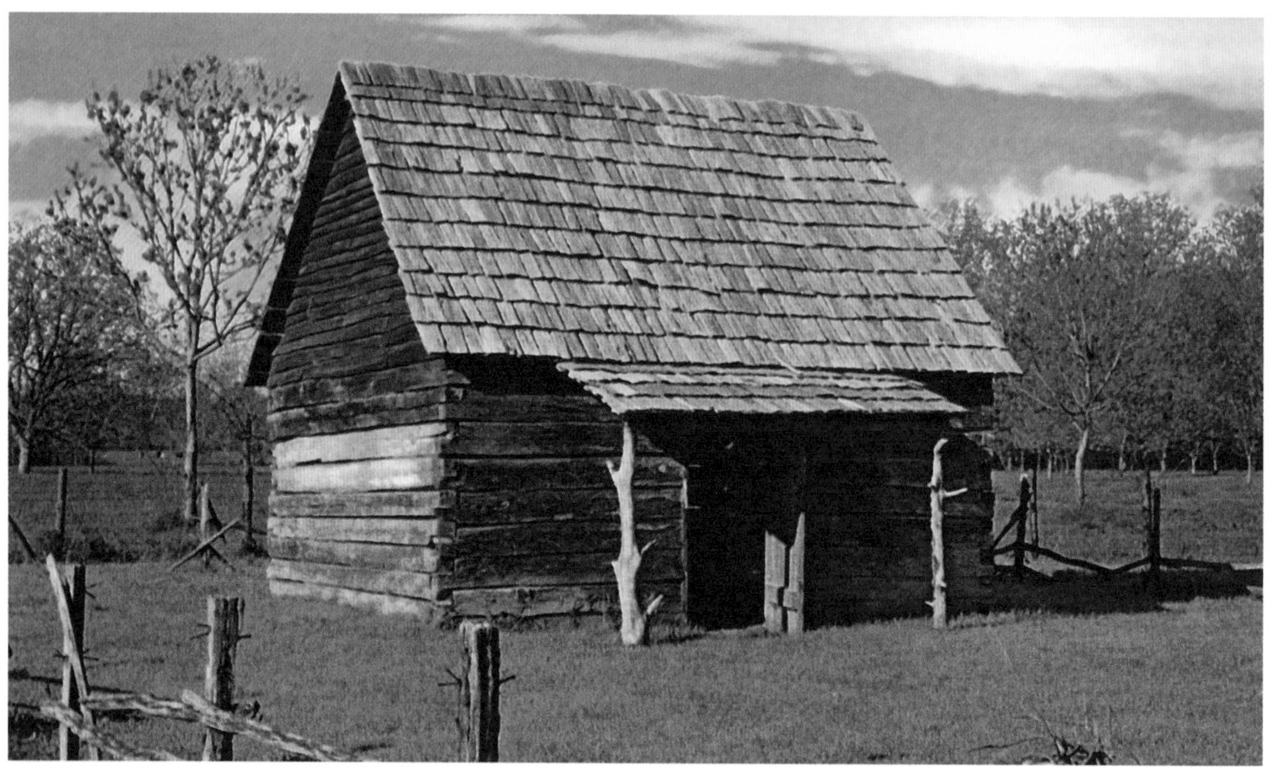

Ratted Out

The old sailors' proverb about rats abandoning a sinking ship seems to have some basis in fact, but is it possible that rats can tell not only when a ship is already sinking but also when it is likely not to survive its next voyage? In other words, could rats have the gift of prophesy? If a tale about the wreck of the steamer *Paris C. Brown* is true, they just might. When the steamboat docked at Plaquemine in early January 1889, crew members noticed two rats scurrying frantically off the vessel to get to shore. Three of the crew, believing wholeheartedly in the old proverb, promptly followed suit and abandoned the ship as well. No amount of threatening or cajoling could convince them to reboard, and the boat set off upriver for Cincinnati without them. The next day, when barrels, boxes, and other items that had been among the nine hundred tons of freight loaded onboard came floating down the Mississippi past Baton Rouge, the three men who had jumped ship knew that the rats had steered them right. The next day news reached the city that the *Paris C. Brown* had hit a snag and sunk eight miles below St. Francisville. Nine members of the crew and a passenger who had locked himself in his room were lost in the disaster. It was the ninth Mississippi River sinking in three weeks.

The Long "Arm" of the Law

When the new Police Administration Building opened in New Orleans in 1968, the public quickly discovered a bit of decor that many felt sent the wrong message. Inside the lobby was a very large copper statue of a man who was said to represent "the defensive and protective hands of the police." But his hands weren't the focus for most folks, who noticed right off the bat that he was altogether rather nude. Police Superintendent Joseph Giarrusso said he would "get right on it," meaning he'd talk to the architect about talking to the artist—Chicago modernist Eldon Danhausen—about the possibility of downplaying the "heroic-sized billy club" by way of some kind of cover or alteration. "I'm a proud member of the NOPD," Giarrusso said, "but I realize that not everyone is as turned on by art as we are."

Curse of Valcour Aime

An unprepossessing clump of trees and thick undergrowth next to the parking lot of the Sixth Ward Elementary School a few miles west of Vacherie, in St. James Parish, hides one of the most bizarre archaeological sites in the entire United States. Here, behind a rusting fence, is what remains of one of the grandest houses of the antebellum era and of the elaborate fantasyland that once surrounded it. The ruins are now covered with vines and crawling with snakes and spiders, but those aren't the only deterrents to trespassers. The place, according to local people, is haunted by a curse uttered by a fallen but still prideful man.

During its heyday, the home was known across the region as Le Petit Versailles, and its owner, François Gabriel "Valcour" Aime, was referred to as the Louis XIV of Louisiana, a nod to the French king who is Louisiana's namesake. But Aime himself called his plantation by a more workaday name: the Refinery. He had been the first planter in the state to successfully refine sugar, and the sweet, white crystals produced at his St. James Refinery had made him the richest man in the South.

Born in 1797, Aime came into his inheritance at the age of twenty-one and married his childhood sweetheart, Josephine Roman, who quickly bore him four daughters. But Aime longed for a son to carry on the family name; and in 1826, a male heir was born with his father's name, Gabriel.

The fame of Aime's home was most firmly established when Aime announced in 1843 that he would begin construction of an English garden on the estate grounds. Not merely borrowing English landscaping design, the Refinery would be the ultimate private playground. Four years later, enough of it had been completed that Eliza Ripley, a writer who visited the property, described it as having *a miniature river, meandering in and out among the "parterres," the tiny banks of which were an unbroken mass of blooming violets. . . . [I]t was spanned at intervals by bridges of various parapets. There were summerhouses draped with strange, foreign-looking vines. A pagoda [stood] on a mound . . . the entrance of which was scaled by a flight of steps. It was an octagonal building, with stained glass windows, and it struck my inexperienced eyes as a very wonderful and surprising bit of architecture.*

The entertainment was no less lavish than the setting. On one memorable visit by Prince Louis-Philippe, later the French king, a solid gold service was used for the evening meal. After dinner, Aime ordered the plates and utensils tossed into the river, saying grandly that it would be a disgrace to ever use them for a lesser purpose. Many a treasure hunter has gone seeking after the Refinery's table service, but since the river has changed course, it now lies perpetually preserved in the silt for some future civilization to rediscover.

Aime not only funded the construction of St. James Catholic Church but also commissioned an artist in Rome to create paintings to adorn it. With his fellow planters, he openly shared his agricultural discoveries and the practical expertise he'd gained from experimenting with steam power for his sugar refinery, so that many other Louisiana family fortunes were made with his help. Within his community, which extended up and down most of the Mississippi, Valcour Aime was regarded as a living breathing hero.

But scholars of classical mythology talk of something called the "heroic flaw." The ancient Greeks understood that not only is perfection is impossible, but if it *were* possible, it would quickly become boring and insufferable. Like Achilles with his vulnerable heel, they believed every hero had a tragic defect. And sure enough, Valcour Aime had at least one major imperfection all his own, which proved to be his ultimate undoing. It was his belief—unfortunately shared by many other male heads of household in his day—that sons were more valuable than daughters.

As his son, Gabi, grew up into a handsome youth, Aime saw to it that he received the finest education he could afford. The boy was trained in all the business skills and civilities that would eventually enable him to take over the family empire, and by his midtwenties he was being sent on trips abroad, where he was encouraged to live in a style that would reflect well on the elevated status of his parents back in Louisiana. The Aime daughters, meanwhile, were allowed to pursue their interests only as hobbies and were tutored in the home and expected to serve only as dutiful helpmeets to their husbands once they married.

By mid-September 1854, advance word had reached the Refinery that twenty-eight-year-old Gabi had just returned to New Orleans from his latest voyage and would be arriving home at any moment. A feast to welcome the prodigal son was prepared and the house was decorated with bouquets of

flowers grown in the plantation's many conservatories. However, when Gabriel stepped off the boat and rode the estate's private railroad up to the mansion, he said he felt too ill to celebrate and asked if he could rest in bed. The next morning when a servant went to rouse him for breakfast, the young man was found dead, a victim of the dreaded yellow fever.

Valcour Aime was devastated. In his diary he wrote, "Continue qui voudra. Mon temps est fini. Il est mort le 18 Septembre. Je l'ai embrasse a 5 heures et encore le lendemain" (Whoever wants to can continue. My time is finished. He died on September 18. I embraced him at 5 o'clock and again the following day). Then he folded and sealed the page to keep it hidden.

From then on he was a broken man. Days passed when he would eat nothing and only stare into space, ignoring his wife, family, and friends. Weeds began taking over the gardens while mildew, mold, and vermin invaded the house.

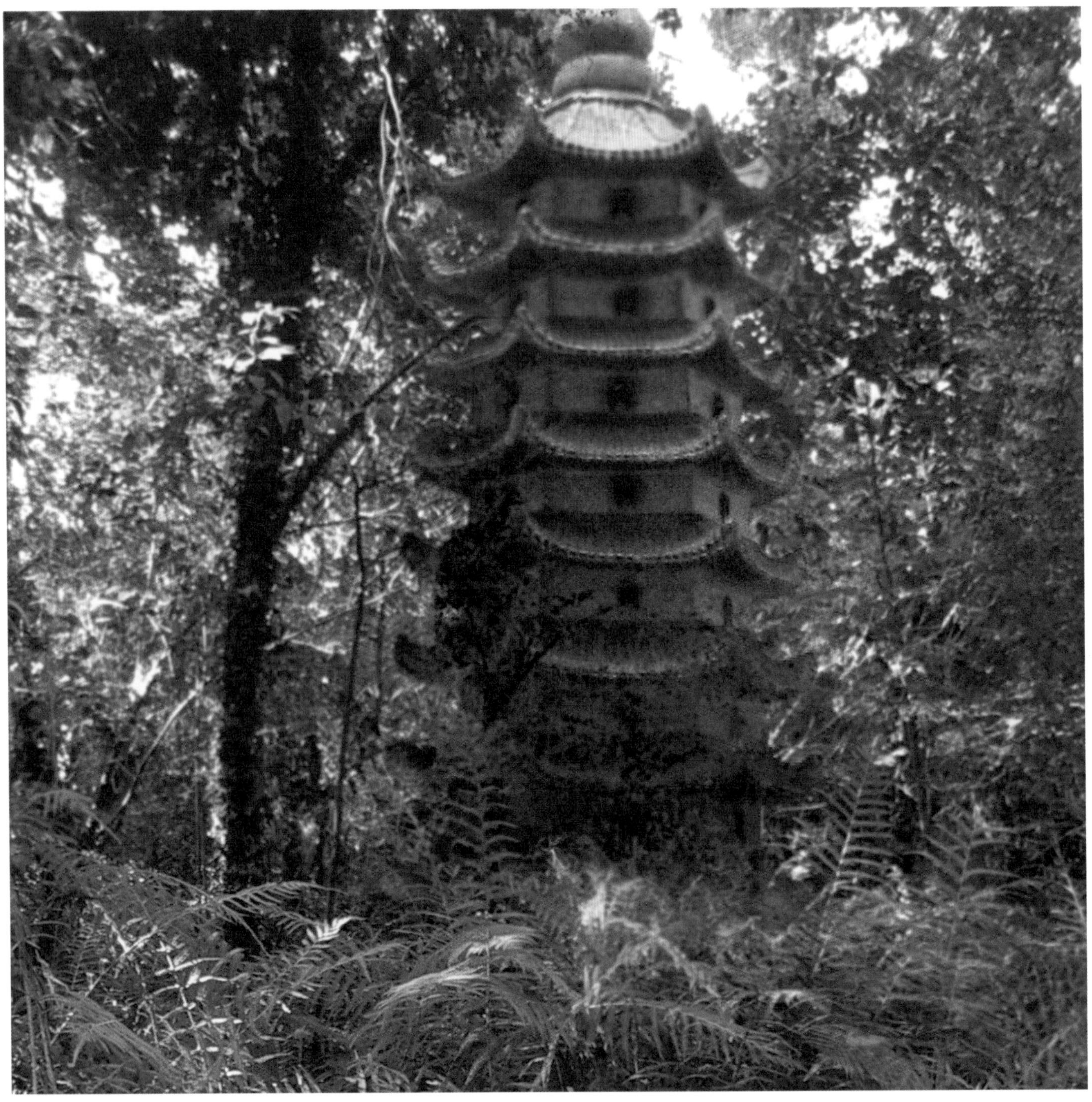

His wife, Josephine, grieved for the loss of both her son and her vital husband, and died only a short time later. It wasn't long before the bodies of two of their four daughters shared her tomb as well.

Valcour Aime retreated into solitary hermitage, moving out of the vast mansion into the overgrown garden. He spent his days kneeling and praying on the hard marble floor of the grotto hidden in the hollowed-out hill beneath the pagoda, and at night he slept on a hard bench in a tiny gardener's hut, decorated only with a crucifix and a portrait of his dead son. While out in the real world the Civil War raged and brought an end to the plantation slavery system, the fallen sugar king drifted aimlessly between the Stations of the Cross as an unkempt recluse teetering on the edge of madness.

On Christmas Eve 1866, Aime asked the priest of St. James Church if a special midnight Mass could be held only for him, so he could worship alone in the empty sanctuary. The kindly priest complied, but conspired with one of the two surviving daughters to prepare what they both thought would be a wonderful gift. At a prearranged point in the one-parishioner Mass, the priest gave a silent signal and a hymn sung in a clear, beautiful voice drifted down from an unseen singer. For years, Aime's daughter had begged him to let her develop her talents, for she had been born with an ability to sing and had longed to audition for the opera. Her tutors had said she was gifted enough to sing in Paris or Milan, but Aime had forbidden her to sing in public—not even a church and certainly not in a theater or opera house.

Recognizing the voice of his daughter, Aime jumped up in a screaming rage and turned toward the balcony where she stood in the shadows. Though no one else but he and the priest had heard her sing that night, and though she had only managed a few lines before he interrupted her, Aime cursed her for disobeying him and ran coatless and screaming out into the cold rain.

A fever settled into his body the following morning, and pneumonia confined him to his hut. By New Year's Day 1867, the great sovereign of sugar was dead.

Due to a peculiar clause in Aime's will, the mansion sat empty and rotting for the next four years, by which time the wind and rain had done so much damage that the surviving family members could no longer afford to restore it. Treasure hunters vandalized the gardens, digging around the pagoda and the mock medieval structures in search of the family gold, while the real treasures—the exotic tropical plants and birds that Aime had imported from the ends of the earth—either succumbed to the climate or thrived and found a permanent toehold in it. Among his many imports, Aime is credited (or blamed) for introducing both English ivy and Korean camphor to the South. In 1920 the abandoned house finally burned to the ground. Nine years later, the Mississippi River washed away the old St. James Church, but not before the Aime family bones were rescued from its cemetery and relocated to a relative's tomb in St. Louis Cemetery No. 2 in New Orleans. What fire and water didn't erase of Aime's legacy, rank vegetation now seemed capable of achieving.

Rumors of a curse began to circulate when some of the early treasure hunters succumbed to mysterious illnesses. After the fire, locals say, the first two men to enter the ruins died in horrible accidents. Kids from the adjacent school regard the dense twelve-acre patch that hides the ruins as haunted, and no amount of daring will convince them to enter and spend a night in the grotto where Valcour Aime raved. Though attempts have been made from time to time to restore the place, it seems doomed to remain the way it is, a ruined monument to its builder's family pride.

Weird Place Names

Beauregard Parish is probably no more blessed with peculiar place names than any other parish in the state, but between places like Turps and Tulla, or Oretta and Juanita (not to mention Junction, located at the convergence of 190 and 111), there are two burgs that stand out. Hen Scratch is west of Dry Creek. Meanwhile, east of Dry Creek is a place that was named in the early 1900s. A local rode up on horseback to ask the carpenters what they were up to, and when they explained that they were building a schoolhouse, he said, "Who'd a thought it?" Several generations of children subsequently earned diplomas at the Who'd a Thought It school, and old-timers still call the community by that name.

Suicide Oak

World War 1 poet Alfred Joyce Kilmer penned these deathless lines of poesy shortly before his own death in the valley of the Marne:

I think that I shall never see
A poem lovely as a tree.

A tree whose hungry mouth is prest
Against the sweet earth's flowing breast;

A tree that looks at God all day,
And lifts her leafy arms to pray . . .

He certainly wasn't picturing the Suicide Oak in New Orleans, which has what looks like a hungry mouth, all right. But this four-hundred-year-old arboreal monster has its yawning maw wide open for crunchy fare, like despondent lovers, businessmen whose investments have tanked, and folks who'll do anything to get a little attention.

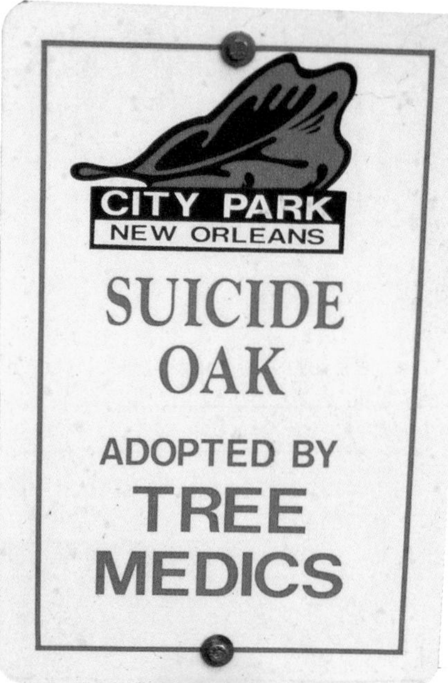

Postcards depicting the ancient oak were popular back in the early part of the twentieth century, when it became a landscape feature of City Park. Back in the 1920s, the body count was less than two dozen folks who dangled from its limbs or were propped up against its trunk after self-inflicting razor or gunshot wounds or taking poison. But as the tree continued to pull in despondent victims through the Great Depression, World War II, and Vietnam, it was no longer touted as such a popular tourist draw. Nowadays, runners on the jogging path nearby pick up their pace in the vicinity of its creaking limbs, while singles seeking dating advice from Internet forums post queries to their online buddies like, "Can anyone recommend any really pretty spots in the park? (Not Suicide Oak!)" In New Orleans, the dark gloom overshadowed by the 125-foot spread of the tree is known as an accursed zone, and only the foolhardy or most uninformed tourist would dare picnic there. It's one place in the city where *les bon temps* just won't *roulez*. Our best advice? Don't go by yourself, and don't take anything along that can be used as a lethal weapon. There's something there that may try to turn you into your own worst enemy.

Angola Farm, Home of "Gruesome Gertie"

If gruesome is your kind of thing, may we suggest a visit to one of America's most peculiar small museums? It's at the end of a dead-end road—the dead end for many a criminal in Louisiana, too, because just beyond the end of the road is the main entrance to the Louisiana State Penitentiary, known to its inmates as the Farm and to the rest of the state as Angola, after one of the four plantations that were incorporated into its eighteen-thousand-acre spread. In geographical size, that makes it the largest single correctional institution in the United States. Until not so long ago, it was also one of the most feared prisons in the nation. By the midtwentieth century, Angola had become so brutal and degrading that in 1952 thirty-one inmates intentionally crippled themselves by cutting their own Achilles' tendons. As a result, they became physically unable to stand up and work in the fields. The few outsiders who got glimpses of the labor gangs said that the conditions behind Angola's walls and fences back then were far worse than antebellum slavery, since most slaves had at least been able to interact with members of the opposite sex and didn't fear for their lives during every moment of the day.

In the 1970s things finally began to improve as a series of reforms were instituted. Today Angola is considered one of the success stories among U.S. prisons. Inmates publish a magazine called the *Angolite*, run a radio station, attend churches and mosques, and participate in the Angola Prison Rodeos, one of the most popular public events of the year, held every Sunday in October. Prisoners compete in standard rodeo events like riding broncos and roping heifers, but they also participate in challenges like "Convict Poker," which consists of four seated prisoners at a card table in the middle of the ring who are visited by a rampaging bull released from a chute. The last guy to remain seated is the nominal winner. Loads o' fun!

"Guts and Glory" is another crowd-pleaser. For this game, a raging bull enters the ring with a few dozen prisoners, who are torn between running for their lives and trying to snatch a poker chip tied to the bull's forehead.

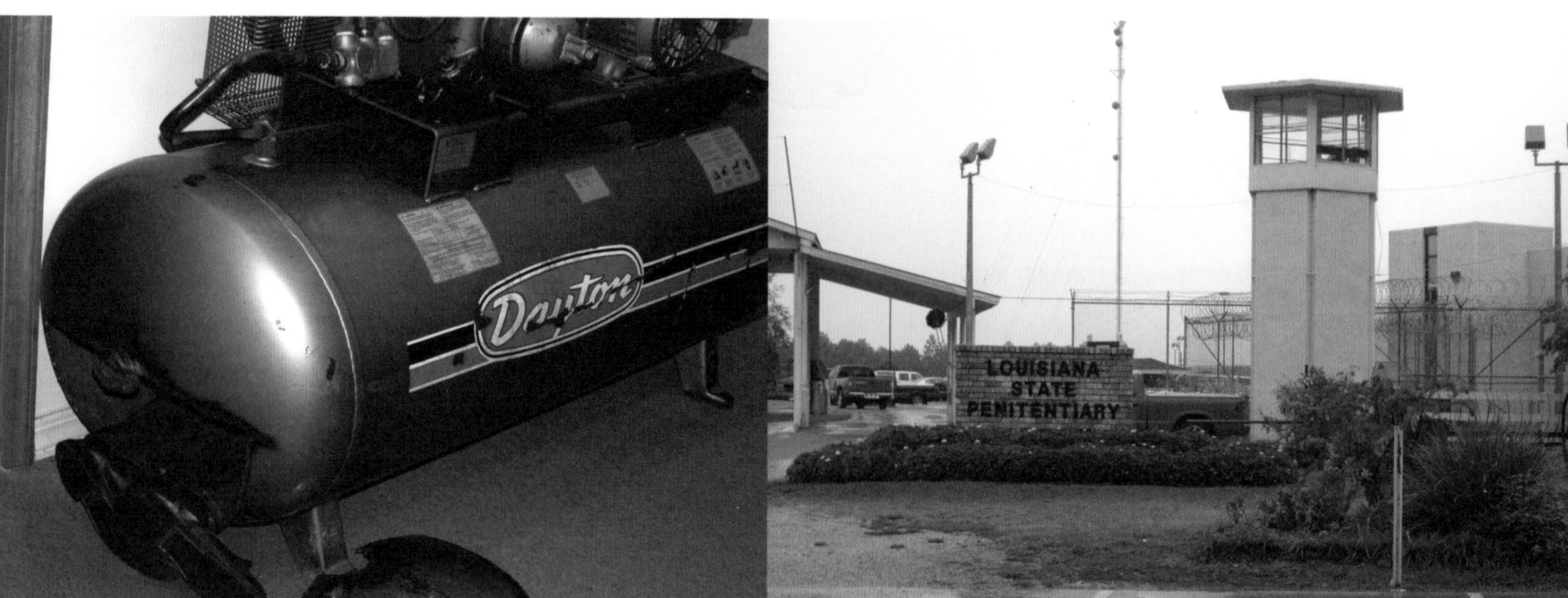

The "game" continues until someone grabs the red chip. It's apparently no big matter if someone gets trampled—that's half the thrill, they say, and besides, the prison has its own hospital. If necessary, it also has its own cemetery. Most inmates will wind up there sooner or later anyway, since the vast majority of Angola's convicts never taste freedom again. The average sentence is nearly ninety years, and few men are paroled before spending at least fifty years on the Farm.

A few prisoners serve as trustees, who work at the free public museum at the prison's entrance. For some, the gruesome photos on the walls of the museum (it's not a good museum for little kids) act as a deterrent to criminal behavior, but for others, the exhibits provide just about all the info they'd ever want to know about how to make deadly weapons from hundreds of innocent-looking items like three-ring binders, pencil sharpeners, floppy disks, toothbrushes, bottle caps, dental floss, and eyeglasses. After a visit to the museum, your home or office might suddenly feel like an arsenal just waiting to be developed into a lethal lair. If you've ever wondered how to make a homemade blunderbuss from a toilet, Louisiana State Penitentiary Museum is the place to find out. And if you want to brush up on some break-out-of-jail basics and learn about great near escapes, some exhibits feature clever ways to hide inside air compressors or rolled-up rugs or how to make rope ladders from unraveled socks.

The museum also houses the inmate-built, horse-drawn hearse that for many is their sole exposure to luxury or elegance, as they travel in style on their final trip to eternity. Although few Angola inmates can ever look forward to an ordinary life as those on the "outside" know it, they can count on their deaths—or at least their funerals—being handled with dignity. Early death imposed by the state hasn't always been so dignified. The most popular item in the museum is the former Louisiana State electric chair, known as Gruesome Gertie (some online guides call it Old Sparky, but that's a generic name for electric chairs everywhere). Originally Gruesome Gertie was not a permanently installed fixture at Angola but was trucked to whatever parish prison had need of her. During Gertie's fifty years of service (from 1941 to 1991), eighty-seven prisoners sat down in her embrace for the last time. Among them were Robert Lee Willie and Elmo Patrick Sonnier, whose crimes and biographical details were combined and adapted to create the murderer Sean Penn played in the movie *Dead Man Walking*. In 1991, lethal injection replaced electrocution as capital punishment and Gruesome Gertie was retired to a museum relic. Since electrocution has caused massive bleeding and has set convicts' heads on fire, nearly all thirty-six states that still have capital punishment now use lethal injection. Still, a few states allow the prisoner to choose between lethal injection or electrocution, while several others keep electrocution in their statutes as a back-up plan in case lethal injection is ever declared unconstitutional. Guess that's not so shocking after all.

Napoleon House

Legend has it that during a late-night party in 1821 several Louisianans came up with an idea to send Jewish pirate Jean Lafitte to remote St. Helena Island in the middle of the South Atlantic Ocean. Their plan was to kidnap Napoléon and bring him back to live in Mayor Girod's house on Chartres Street in New Orleans. But before they could follow through on such a plan, the deposed emperor of France died—and Jean Lafitte was exiled to a small island off the Yucatán peninsula, too. Nevermind; locals have been calling the building that Napoléon *might* have lived in the Napoleon House ever since. Not a bad trick; anyone can do it. In fact, we've started calling our own place the Mick Jagger Estate after offering to let him retire in our spare bedroom. He never wrote us back, but then . . . neither did Napoléon.

Dueling Duos

According to a comment printed in the New Orleans *Daily Picayune* on July 29, 1837, duels had become "as common these days as watermelons." On one typical Sunday that year, ten duels took place, three of them ending fatally for the losers. Easily insulted Creole gents could take offense at the drop of a hat, and then at the drop of a glove or handkerchief—the traditional signal for a duel to begin—they'd come out fighting.

THE OLD DUELING GROUNDS IN CITY PARK, SHOWING THE DE LISSUE-LE BOUISQUE DUEL IN 1841, NEW ORLEANS, LA.

There were a number of locations associated with dueling, including the square immediately behind St. Louis Cathedral, where the statue of Jesus with upraised arms stands today. The legendary spot for repairing even remote rifts to one's honor was "under the oaks," namely, under large trees that stood at the edge of town at the end of Canal Street—now located a few hundred feet south of the New Orleans Museum of Art. Or one of them still is, anyway. The others died or were blown down by storms years ago.

The traditional image of a duel—two guys in their shirtsleeves, taking ten steps in opposite directions and then turning to fire—was not as common in Louisiana as fighting with long, flexible rapiers and colichemardes (small swords from the late seventeenth and early eighteenth centuries). Dueling with such blades allowed for finesse. A slight cut or a deep gouge could be inflicted, depending on the nature of the grievance. And, in theory at least, dueling was regulated by a complex set of rituals and rules that made it sound like a game, which in many ways it was. Rule sixteen stipulated that "the challenged has the right to choose his own weapon, unless the challenger gives his honor he is no swordsman." Since most educated men in Louisiana were trained in sword fighting, this meant that whoever picked the fuss would occasionally find himself faced with alternative weapons, like double-barreled shotguns, squirrel rifles, bowie knives (a Louisiana invention), axes, champagne bottles, and cypress beams. At this point, they could either go ahead with the fight or bow out.

Buddy Stall, a local historian, has described two duels that were aborted in midstream when the weapon of choice just wasn't viable. In one case, following a scuffle, Creole aristocrat Albert Farve challenged S. M. Harvey (for whom the town of Harvey is named) to a duel. Since Farve was the challenger, Harvey, the former captain of a whaling ship, became "the challenged" and got to pick the weapons. His weapon of choice? A harpoon. After some consideration, Monsieur Farve decided to withdraw the challenge.

A fuss that began in Catahoula Parish also ended amiably when a blacksmith named Humble was challenged to a duel. Being nearly seven feet tall, he realized that he provided too big a target to fight with either swords or pistols and thus chose to fight the offended party, Bernard de Marigny de Mandeville, with ten-pound sledgehammers while standing in six feet of water. Marigny, who was not quite six feet tall, wisely opted to withdraw his challenge.

Robert Ripley, of *Ripley's Believe It or Not!* fame, once told the story of Alexander Grailhe, who suffered a debilitating injury during a duel with swords. Although he survived, an abscess in his punctured lung subsequently left him unable to walk upright. A few years later he, too, somehow managed to irk Marigny, who challenged Grailhe, crippled or not, to a duel with pistols. Marigny's bullet struck Grailhe in the chest and miraculously drained the abscess. Not only did he survive this second duel, but his posture was returned to normal and he remained hale and hearty for the rest of his life.

Voodoo Cures

Voodoo is a complex religion practiced in Haiti, Brazil, Trinidad, Cuba, and parts of the southern United States, especially on the islands near Beaufort, South Carolina, and around New Orleans. Taking a portion of its belief system from Roman Catholicism, voodoo worshippers believe in a principal God. They also honor ancestors, the dead, twins, and spirits called *Lwa*, which stem from African tribal spirits but are often identified with Catholic saints. Voodoo rituals invoke the spirits or saints by singing, drumming, and dancing, during which the *Lwa* may enter or take possession of the participants, allowing them to interact with the living and provide advice or perform cures.

At some touristic voodoo shops you might see lists of "recipes" for achieving certain outcomes. But following these without a skilled practitioner to guide you or tailor the rituals to your individual needs, personality, or situation would be as silly as prescribing your own conventional medicines. It may be harmless if your problems aren't really all that serious, but it's potentially harmful to address serious problems on your own if you haven't acquired the adequate knowledge to do so.

For example, there's probably no harm in removing spells from your house by taking a blessed candle from room to room and almost, but not quite, blowing it out in each space so that a bit of holy smoke will spread throughout the house. Throwing a little salt in every corner of every room may help, too, and at least won't cause ants or bugs to infest your house like sprinkling flour or sugar might.

But an old cure for snakebite involves taking a live chicken, cutting it in half, and then binding it against the bite with the meat touching the skin. The patient is supposed to leave it there for a few days, and only after the meat turns green is he supposed to remove it and burn it. The green color is considered a signal that the snake venom has been transferred to the chicken.

This is an example of a "cure" that relies heavily on the power of suggestion, since *any* raw meat left unrefrigerated

for a few days will begin to turn greenish whether it has absorbed any venom or not (which is extremely unlikely from simple contact). This cure "worked" because, by the time the believer had waited a few days for the meat to change color, he would have been well past the danger point for dying from the snakebite (though rapidly approaching the danger point for losing all his friends, since he must have smelled awful). This is an example of "Kids, don't try this at home!" If a snake or a dog bites you, seek a doctor right away. Voodoo may help put you in a prayerful state that encourages healing and luck, but antivenom and antibiotics are probably still a little better against bites or infections.

Here are some old-time Louisiana wart cures that we can't guarantee (but seem harmless enough): Cross two pins over the wart and then hide them where they can't be found; take a bone a dog has been chewing on and rub the wart with that, then put it back in the exact same position where you found it and never look at it again; collect "stump water" from a cypress knee at midnight during a full moon and rub that on the wart. Wart be gone!

If you get "the chills," put a little red chile powder in your socks for nine days, or drink tea made from willow roots. For measles, tea made from holly leaves or corn shucks may help. For a cold, try tea made from hogs' hoofs (but don't ask us where to get them), or tea made from pine needles and honey, or from nine prickly sweet-gum balls.

Aching joints may be soothed by carrying a raw Irish potato in your left front pocket or rubbing the joints with buzzard grease (you're on your own here, too). A silver dime (i.e., dated 1964 or earlier) with a hole punched through it (don't ask us how) and threaded on a string can be worn around the neck or left ankle to help prevent rheumatism.

Sometimes old folk remedies may be worse than the problems they are supposed to cure. For example, red bug bites can be cured by taking a red-hot branding iron or heated knife and applying it to the bite. Or else cut the swollen part off with a red-hot pocket knife and then bury it in the middle of a dirt road at midnight. That'll fix the bite, for sure, but now you'll have to see someone about that burned place where you're missing a patch of skin.

Surreal Celebrations

The motto for Louisiana should probably be something like *E Pluribus, Plures Festi*—roughly translating to "from many people, lots of parties"!

More than 135 annual officially named events celebrate just about every aspect of life in the state. In addition to dozens of festivals for every kind of music and ethnic group, there are festivals for agriculture (cotton, rice, pecans, peppers, watermelons, peaches, strawberries, sugarcane), transportation (wooden boats, buggies, cars, planes), terrestrial animals (bears, ducks, cattle, chickens, swine), aquatic animals (catfish, shrimp, crawfish, frogs, crabs, alligators), cooking (hot sauce, barbecue, seafood, French food, étouffée, jambalaya, gumbo, *cochon de lait*, smoked meat, cracklins, pies), and even a few crossover events like the Shrimp and Petroleum Festival in Morgan City; the Gas, Food, and Lodging Festival in Baton Rouge; or the Fest for All, a Baton Rouge tradition since 1973.

Festivals, saints' feast days, block parties, balls, parades, fraternal events, historical reenactments, church fetes, secret club gatherings—you name it, Louisiana's got a way to celebrate it. So sit back, turn the page, and *laissez les bon temps rouler*!

Mardi Gras

Mardi Gras is big and weird—and at the heart of what makes Louisiana the marvelously peculiar place it is. More than eighty publicly scheduled parades take place in greater New Orleans and the Lake Pontchartrain north shore between Epiphany (January 6) and Ash Wednesday, which can fall anywhere between February 4 and March 10. In addition, there are innumerable parties, balls, coronations, ceremonies, private soirees, secret rituals, and other events that take place throughout Louisiana during the carnival season and its climax on Mardi Gras. Honestly, the sheer number of options can be a little intimidating, even for locals.

Long-established social connections and vetted ancestries grant access to the secret society balls of the oldest and most elite carnival krewes but at the same time prevent association with groups like the Mardi Gras Indians, ethnic clubs, or voodoo celebrants—and the same is true in reverse. Although segregation is no longer official policy, separation continues to exist between whites and blacks; between French-descended Creoles and French-descended Cajuns; between Spanish descendants from the Iberian peninsula, Mexico, and the Canary Islands; between new immigrants and natives; and between dozens of other ethnic groups, social strata, religions, neighborhoods, parishes, schools, and churches. The differences between these distinctive subcultures contribute to the richness and diversity of life in Louisiana that few other states can match—and in one way or another, they all contribute to carnival and Mardi Gras.

The essence of Mardi Gras is masking. Donning a mask or a costume enables you to change your relationship to other people, either by emphasizing special connections within a group (as the carnival royalty or Mardi Gras Indians do among themselves) or by obscuring your normal identity so that divisions between groups are blurred. In either case, behind a mask you're free to behave in any way you want for the duration of the holiday. Music, food, and drink help enhance the role-playing experience while the parades encourage spectators to become part of the spectacle. A unique relationship forms between onlookers and the folks on the floats.

Mardi Gras Gifts

Fantastic floats. Decadent costumes. Over-the-top parades. New Orleans puts on quite a show for Mardi Gras, right? Well yes, technically, but we think it's time to let you in on a little secret: The show is just as much for the performers as it is for the audience. The folks who decorate and ride the floats and buy and toss the beads do it because it feels good to be the center of attention—riding along in public, constantly being beseeched for favors that can be answered merely by tossing out some plastic beads. Wearing a mask to preserve anonymity makes it easier to accept all the attention, but it also allows participants to stop playing that role at the end of the day when there aren't any trinkets left to

throw. The role of public gift giver is so highly coveted that people are often willing to pay hundreds or even thousands of dollars to ride on a float, a privilege normally reserved for members of the executive or legislative branches of government.

Not all Mardi Gras "gifting" is limited to beads, throws, or painted coconuts. The utter extravagance and awesome size of some of the floats and the grandeur or inventiveness of the costumes are *themselves* a kind of gift too—a visual feast to stir the imaginations of onlookers.

It has been said that a Scotchman has not seen the world until he has seen Edinburgh; and I think that I may say that an American has not seen the United States until he has seen Mardi Gras in New Orleans. —Mark Twain, 1859

First Floats in '57

Although the first Louisiana Mardi Gras was celebrated on March 3, 1699 (about fifty miles downstream from the future site of New Orleans), and although by the 1740s carnival balls were already a well-established annual custom, the first official celebrations weren't held until 1833 and the first parade in 1857, when the Mistick Krewe of Comus first rolled a few floats through the city mounted on wagons. The floats gradually increased in size and complexity until they were finally banned from rolling through the French Quarter in 1972. Nowadays the largest floats, like Captain Eddie's SS Endymion, the Krewe of Bacchus's Bacchasaurus, or the Krewe of Orpheus's Smoking Mary, may stretch nearly two hundred feet, weigh a quarter of a million pounds, and carry hundreds of riders, a band, stadium-quality sound system, fiber-optic light displays, smoke generators, and searchlights. Inside there are toilets, storage areas, and fridges packed with food and drinks.

Mardi Gras Indians

Have you ever seen the Mardi Gras Indians? If you have, you'll never forget them. The masking tradition followed by this loose confederation is one of the most unusual, over-the-top, and breathtakingly beautiful displays you're liable to come across during Mardi Gras in New Orleans. Ostrich plumes and other brilliantly dyed exotic feathers are set off with panels of beads or sequins. The vivid colors of the costumes are decorated with hand-embroidered scenes symbolizing power, mystery, or revenge. Some of the costumes weigh as much as a suit of armor, may cost up to $5,000, and require a year's effort to make. These are worn with incredible pomp during intricate ceremonies between members of roughly forty independent tribes belonging to either the Uptown Indians or Downtown Indians that, together, make up the Mardi Gras Indian Nation.

The origins of the elaborate tradition of Mardi Gras masking aren't clear. Some historians suggest that runaway slaves who sought refuge among Native Americans tried to pass as Indians and replicated their rituals as part of the act. Then, when an influx of Caribbean immigrants settled in Louisiana, these imitation Indians adopted folkways from them, too. Others think that when traveling spectacles like Buffalo Bill's Wild West passed through New Orleans in the 1890s, some locals were so impressed by the costumes of the Indian stunt riders and reenactors that they began making ever more highly wrought versions for themselves.

But whether or not the fabulous costuming became highly developed before the traveling road shows visited, the history of the Mardi Gras Indians as distinct groups dates back to pre-Civil War. With increasing urbanization, New Orleans's poorer streets and neighborhoods became aligned with various "gangs," groups, societies, or tribes—a few of which later gave rise to parading krewes like Zulu, or Mardi Gras maskers like the Northside Skull and Bones Gang—and borrowed traditions from Native Americans they found meaningful. These New Orleans tribes (also called gangs) would often clash violently after chanting derogatory comments "playing the dozens" (exchanging put-downs), and strutting and posturing threateningly. As time wore on, though, physical fights gradually gave way to trying to outdo one another in singing, dancing, and creating ever more showy "Indian suits." Nowadays, insulting remarks, threatening postures, stare-downs,

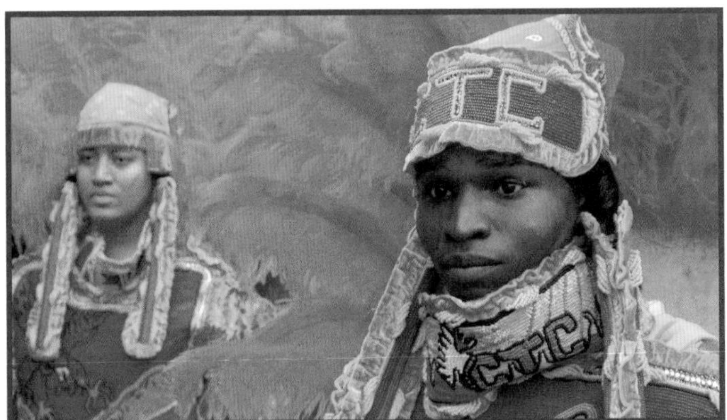

and put-downs between groups still happen, but actual fighting has become rare.

Members of Mardi Gras Indian tribes expend a lot of effort and expense on their participation, because their Indian suits need to be replaced (or at least greatly overhauled) every year. Thousands of hours are spent working on the costumes in secret, sometimes years ahead of the day they'll finally be brought out of hiding. Materials are important. Although both groups use blindingly bright feathers, the Downtown Indians decorate with sequins, while Uptown Indians decorate with beads and rhinestones. Emblems are often handed down within tribes; many of them have themes of vengeance while others tap into non-Indian themes like voodoo or African symbolism.

Although the leader of the tribe, the "Big Chief," can decide to have a procession almost any time of year (some of them now take part in folk festivals and civic celebrations), the best times for outsiders to observe Mardi Gras Indians include early afternoon on Mardi Gras, when a number of tribes converge on North Claiborne Avenue between Esplanade and Columbus, and around noon on the Sunday closest to March 19, St. Joseph's Day, when a parade assembles near where Bayou St. John and Orleans Avenue intersect. There may also be movements on St. Joseph's Day itself, although none of these get-togethers follows an exact predetermined route.

If you do see a moving band of Mardi Gras Indians, be sure to give them right-of-way, because pride and personal dignity may prevent them from stopping for anything. If need be, they may walk directly through traffic (and directly over any stopped cars that happen to be in the direction they are moving). The transformative power of their mighty costumes is such that when someone who has the right to wear one dons a Big Chief's suit, he literally becomes a "commander-in-chief"—and woe to anyone who gets in the way!

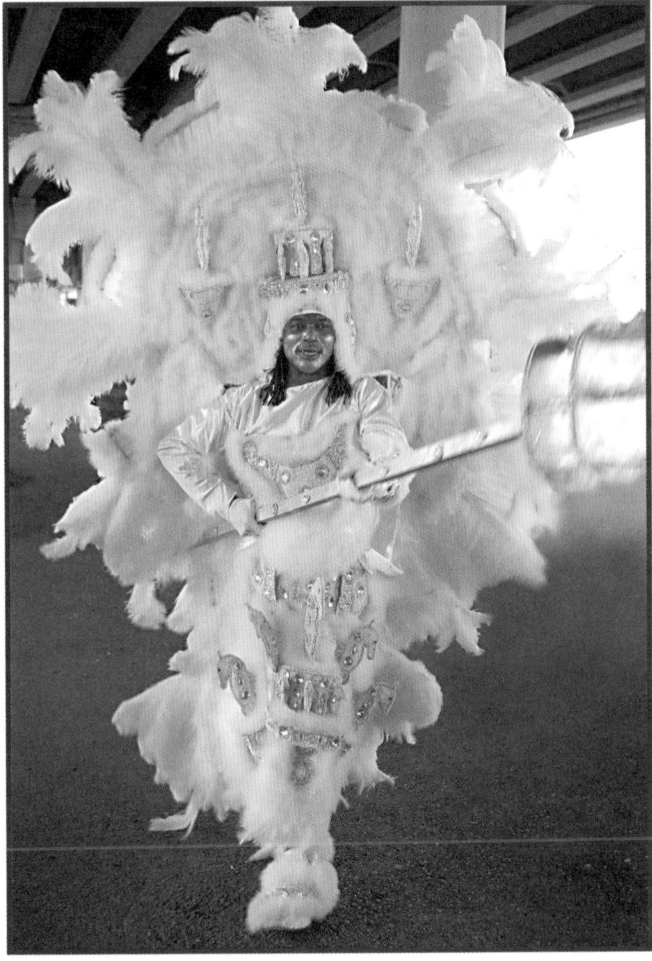

Zulu Social Aid and Pleasure Society

If you wake up early on Mardi Gras morning with a strong desire to conk someone with a blunt object, the only legally sanctioned way to do it is to get yourself into minstrel-show blackface, ride on a float in the Zulu parade, and do it with a coconut. Thanks to state law SB188, passed by the legislature and signed on July 8, 1988, by then governor Edwin Edwards, you can't be prosecuted. According to the "Coconut Bill," you're excluded from liability for injuries arising from coconuts thrown from Mardi Gras floats.

As one of the most venerated of all carnival krewes, the Zulu Social Aid and Pleasure Society has enjoyed a long history of doing things the weird way. In fact, the krewe's earliest parades were a spoof on the pomposity of many of the exclusive high-society krewes from early Mardi Gras celebrations. Participating in Mardi Gras for the first time in 1901 as a laborer's social club called "the Tramps," the group now known as Zulu was first organized as a club similar to a "benevolent society." In the days before mutual insurance companies, such societies pooled membership dues for emergencies ranging from providing meals during

illness to covering funeral costs for unexpected deaths.

In 1909, members of the group attended a musical comedy at the Pythian Theater, where they saw a skit about the Zulu tribe called "There Never Was and Never Will Be a King Like Me." After the show, they got together and decided to rename their group the Zulus. That same year, they marched at Mardi Gras in the bitingly ironic blackface-on-black, grass skirts, spears, and rags that became their emblem. The tribe's king wore a crown fashioned from a lard can and held a banana stalk scepter—a stark contrast to the ornate raiment worn by carnival royalty in the white krewes.

When the Tramps had marched in Mardi Gras parades, they threw gold-painted walnuts they called "golden nuggets," but in 1910, as Zulus, they began handing out gold-painted coconuts as a symbol of their expanding role in the community. By 1916, the group had officially incorporated as a society with more than 1,300 members and was able to mount a parade with a number of floats.

For more than fifty years, the Zulu parade followed a route that took it through the back streets of New Orleans. Not only was it banned from major thoroughfares because of racist legal restrictions, but since individual floats were sponsored by various cafés, bars, and clubs, the parade was obligated to make stops at each of them. As the day wore on, the parades invariably became less cohesive as floats took off in different directions to meet their individual sponsorship obligations.

The most difficult period in the history of the krewe came during the early 1960s, when the satirical wit that had formed the group's parading style came under attack from Black Awareness groups that didn't understand Zulu's brand of self-parody. Membership dwindled to only sixteen men, who kept their relationship to the organization a secret. By 1968, however, the group was back in full force, and for the first time it was allowed to roll down St. Charles Avenue and Canal Street like the other major parades. Since then, it's been one of the most eagerly anticipated parades because, as the first major parade on Fat Tuesday morning, it's the signal that Mardi Gras has begun.

Northside Skull and Bones Gang

Good luck trying to sleep in on Mardi Gras, especially in the Tremé district northeast of Louis Armstrong Park. Before dawn on Fat Tuesday, drumming and noisemaking from members of the Northside Skull and Bones Gang can be heard throughout the district. Sporting oversized skull masks and skeleton costumes, they remind revelers that life is short and death is inevitable. So, on Mardi Gras, get up and party—while you still can.

Distantly associated with the Mardi Gras Indians, some folklorists believe the custom of skeleton masking began after sailors returning from Mexico started emulating the fanfare they witnessed at Day of the Dead celebrations. But others see stronger connections with African customs brought over with the oral history and performance traditions of slaves who were permitted to dance and drum in Congo Square in the early nineteenth century.

If you miss their early-morning antics in the streets of the Tremé around St. Augustine Catholic Church (site of the Tomb of the Unknown Slave), catch sight of them and another Mardi Gras offshoot called the Baby Dolls (dressed in bonnets and bloomers with broad skirts like dolls from the 1930s) along with the Mardi Gras Indians under the I-10 expressway viaduct. They'll be in the vicinity of Ernie K-Doe's Mother-in-Law Lounge (1500 N. Claiborne) starting around noon on Fat Tuesday. Be careful, though—the skeletons can be unpredictable. After all, as one knowledgeable bystander pointed out to us, since they are already dead, they have nothing to lose.

Box of Wine, DIY Parade

Mardi Gras is a uniquely participatory holiday, especially when compared to mega-events like the Macy's Thanksgiving Day Parade in New York or the Tournament of Roses in Pasadena where onlookers stand back in awe of the event. In Louisiana, regardless of the size of the parade, a Mardi Gras celebration invites spectators to become part of the spectacle.

When Ann Marie Coviello wanted to do something to honor Bacchus as the god of wine, she and her friends founded Box of Wine (BOW) in the mid-1990s and created a mini parade with homemade floats and musical instruments to herald the coming of the Krewe of Bacchus parade. Box of Wine sets up on a side street in midafternoon on what has come to be called Bacchus Sunday—the Sunday before Fat Tuesday—and parades down St. Charles between Washington and Calliope, ahead of the main Bacchus parade, which usually reaches that stretch around twilight. Like many of the smaller parades, anyone with a costume, an instrument, an unusual pet, or an unmotorized vehicle can join in the fun.

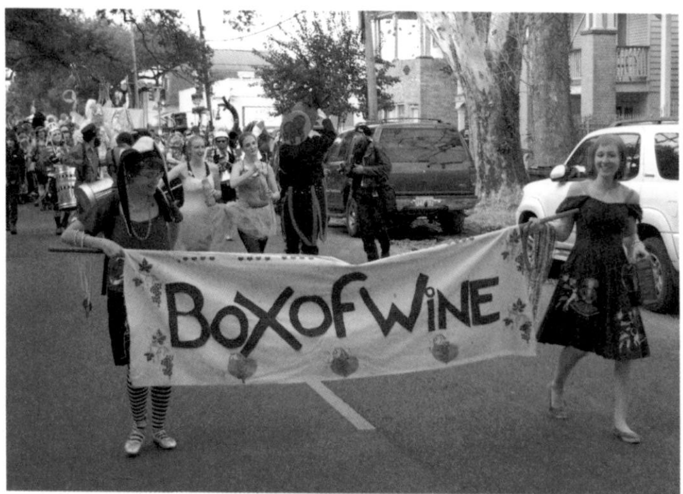

Small-Town Mardi Gras

Push Mow, a town parade founded by Ann O'Brien and held in Abita Springs, on the north shore of Lake Pontchartrain, is a small-scale celebration with big spirit. The parade features only one or two bands, one of which is a bagpipe ensemble called Kilts of Many Colours, and the floats are towed by riding lawn mowers or small ATVs—but the community-building spirit of exchange and recognition is the same as in the Big Easy.

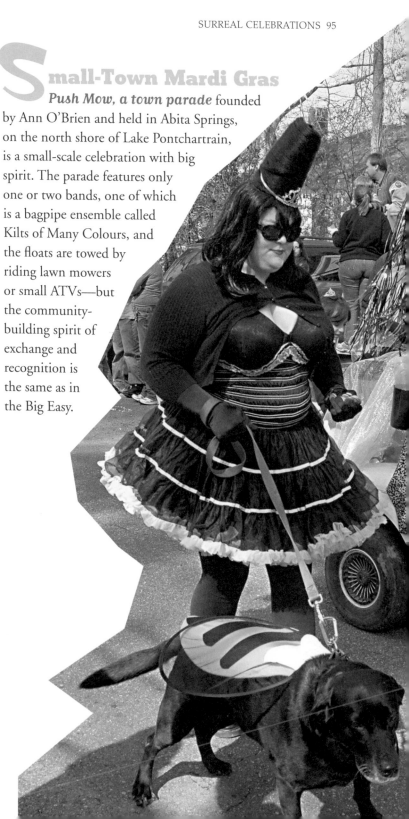

Mardi Gras World

You may not know who Blaine Kern is, but you're probably familiar with his work if you've been to a Mardi Gras celebration or seen pictures of the fanciful oversized floats parading down the streets. Since 1947, Blaine and the rest of the Kern family have been building floats for Mardi Gras and carnival celebrations throughout the world.

Kern began his artistic career as an apprentice sign painter in his dad's commercial art workshop during the Depression. When he was nineteen, he painted a mural in a local hospital to help cover his mother's medical bills. A doctor who saw the mural was impressed enough to hire Kern to design and oversee the building of a carnival parade for the Krewe of Alla, an all-male society that, by the way, celebrated its seventy-fifth anniversary in 2007. When that parade turned out to be a rousing success, Kern decided to make a career of it. He went on to study in cities rich with carnival tradition, including Cologne and Frankfurt, Germany; Nice, France; and Valencia, Spain, before returning to New Orleans where he began honing his skills. The result of Kern's extensive travel and training is a unique style that combines his knowledge of old-world tradition, innovative techniques, and modern materials.

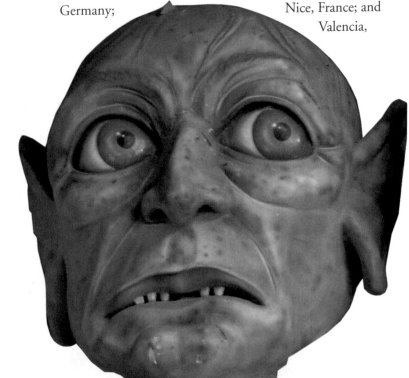

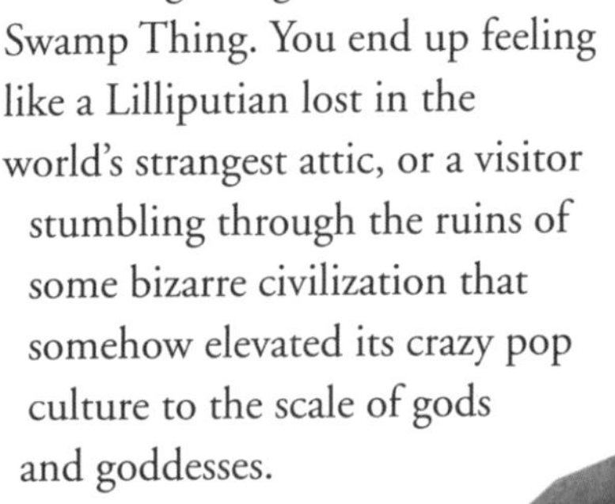

After founding Blaine Kern Artists in 1947, the family business grew to become the world's largest builders of parade floats. Since 1983, the company has branched out under the leadership of Kern's son Barry into the making of huge sculptural elements for many overseas parades and events, as well as for casinos, theme parks, hotels, airports, bowl games, and film sets. At the same time, it's continued to produce nearly fifty Louisiana Mardi Gras parades every year.

A lot of the props and sets begin or wind up back at Mardi Gras World, a cluster of huge hangarlike dens on the west bank Mississippi riverside in Algiers. In addition to guided tours through the working studios, construction shops, and warehouses, visitors may wander through to see the floats underway, leftover props, and giant caricature-like portraits of figures from the collective cultural consciousness, from King Kong and Salvador Dalí to Einstein and the Swamp Thing. You end up feeling like a Lilliputian lost in the world's strangest attic, or a visitor stumbling through the ruins of some bizarre civilization that somehow elevated its crazy pop culture to the scale of gods and goddesses.

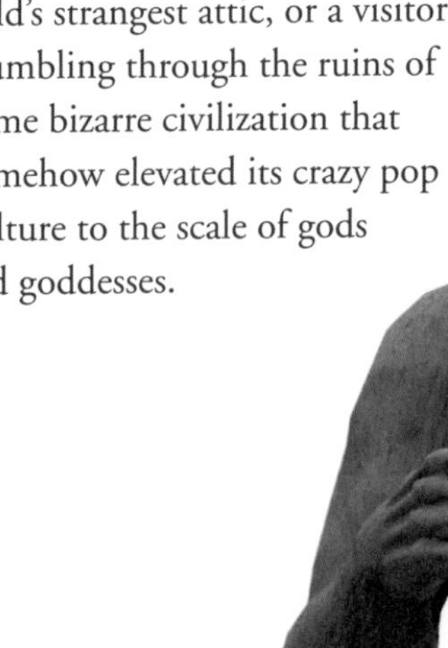

NMB

Courir de Mardi Gras

Drive about 150 miles west of New Orleans during the weeks leading up to Mardi Gras and you'll discover an entirely different breed of carnival celebrations in areas surrounding the city of Opelousas. Cajun and Creole folks in towns including Basile, Church Point, Elton, Eunice, Hathaway, LeJeune Cove, Mamou, Soileau, and Tee-Mamou-Iota don homemade costumes to participate in their local Courir de Mardi Gras (Mardi Gras Run). Costumed masqueraders, collectively called the Mardi Gras, travel across the countryside on foot, horseback, sulkies, or in the back of flatbed trailers begging for food from their neighbors. Following traditional routes, they stop at hospitable homesteads where the cape-clad leaders of the Mardi Gras, the Capitaines, approach the house and beg for ingredients to make a communal gumbo.

If the homeowners are amenable, the Mardi Gras storm the property, cavorting about in drunken revelry—singing, climbing trees, dancing atop their horses, and performing pranks on one another. On hands and knees they cry out for sausage, rice, small change, or a little something else for the gumbo pot. Using a braided whip to keep the rambunctious brood in line, the Capitaines are there to prevent injury and major property damage, and, perhaps more important, to reinforce tradition—those who party too much are as likely to get flogged as those with sour spirits.

During some celebrations, homeowners toss a live chicken up in the air as an offering to the visitors and the Mardi Gras gang scramble to catch it. The chicken-catching game continues until the Mardi Gras decide it's time to saddle up and head to the next hospitable homestead on the route. After a long day of drinking and cavorting in the countryside, the *courir* winds down in the late afternoon and the gathered ingredients are prepared into a gumbo. The festivities continue well into the evening with feasting, dancing, and more drinking.

The Courir de Mardi Gras is in part a centuries-old adaptation of a Roman Catholic celebration called the Courir la Chandeleur (the Candlemas Run), which was held just before February 2 each year. In seventeenth- and eighteenth-century Acadia (now Nova Scotia, where the majority of Cajuns' ancestors came from), a group of people would follow a leader bearing a decorated cane from house to house, to beg food for the Candlemas feast, and in turn would dance the *Escaouette* to thank them. Today Mardi Gras celebrations in predominantly French south-central Louisiana, also known as Acadiana or Cajun Country, combine the trick-or-treat aspects of Candlemas with the Native American tradition of fringed buckskin clothing (now colorful fringed cloth) and the masking of Black Creole ceremonies. The costumes worn in Acadian Mardi Gras celebrations are distinct from those worn in New Orleans and other urban areas. Common headgear is the *capuchon* (cone-shaped hat), although *mortieres* (mortarboards) or hats shaped like bishop's miters are also occasionally worn. Members of the Mardi Gras typically wear masks made of painted or ornamented wire screening, though the Capitaines go maskless.

Not every Courir de Mardi Gras is open to the public without an invitation, and there are significant differences between the various places where the runs take place throughout Acadiana. To find out which events are open for visitors to observe or participate in and when they take place, check the *Baton Rouge Advocate* or *Opelousas Daily World* Web sites a few weeks before Fat Tuesday.

M.O.M.s Ball

Now one of the premier parties of carnival season, M.O.M.s Ball began on a small scale one Christmas Eve in the late 1960s when two locals showed up at Jimmy Anselmo's bar with a turkey and offered to share it with anyone who was hungry. The folks at the bar that night surmised that only social outcasts, delinquents, and people without families would spend the holiday hanging out at a saloon and dubbed the turkey feast the Orphans and Misfits Annual Christmas Dinner.

The following year the Christmas dinner didn't happen, so a substitute event was planned—a public king cake party at the Veterans of Foreign Wars memorial hall for Mardi Gras. The event turned into a costume ball and the Krewe of Mystic Orphans and Misfits (M.O.M.s) was founded. The party was open to anyone who wanted to celebrate, provided participants wore costumes, and a small group of regulars banded together and agreed to cover the cost, in case any real orphans or misfits decided to attend.

To make it more like a regular Mardi Gras krewe, M.O.M.s had to have royalty. But in keeping with its tongue-in-cheek origins, only those who had been unemployed for at least six months and owed a sizeable bar tab were eligible to rule over the ball as Quasimodo, King of Fools. Several hundred people showed up to the first ball, making it an instant hit and firmly sealing its place in the annual Mardi Gras calendar.

The annual M.O.M.s Ball takes place on the Saturday evening before Fat Tuesday and has been held in the warehouses of Mardi Gras World for the past several years. Thousands of fully costumed revelers party late into the night to the music of the Ball's traditional band, the Radiators. Ironically, the party has evolved from a festive free-for-all to an exclusive invitation-only affair, and tickets are as difficult to come by as they are for the high-society balls it once spoofed.

Hop on Over to Rayne

Known as the frog capital of the world, the town of Rayne is located in the heart of Arcadia, about 150 miles west of New Orleans. Also designated the official Louisiana city of murals, renderings of the town's claim to fame can be seen in more than two dozen murals, many of which were commissioned from renowned muralist Robert Dafford. In early September every year, often on the weekend after Labor Day, thousands flock to the small town for the biggest frog party in the world, the Rayne Frog Festival. Events include a bullfrog costume contest, frog racing and jumping, and a Frog Derby Queen contest featuring girls dressed up as jockeys and urging their bullfrog buddies to hop like the wind!

Now a frog-friendly destination, in the 1800s frog legs were among the town's hottest exports after a local chef named Donat Pucheu began selling them to restaurants in New Orleans. Before long, a French duo known as the Weill Brothers stepped in and began exporting them by the ton to restaurants in New York and Paris. For much of the twentieth century, Rayne was the frog leg capital of the world, exporting a few thousand tons of appetizing amphibious appendages a year mostly to France, the world's leading consumer. Those glory days lasted until other sources in places like India, Bangladesh, Indonesia, Vietnam, and China replaced Rayne—much to the delight of Louisiana's abundant frog population, we're sure.

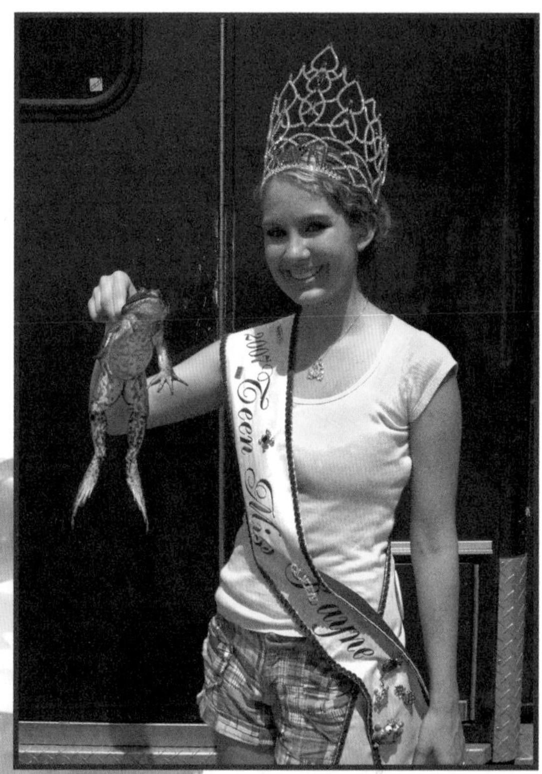

Society of St. Anne Parade

The Society of St. Anne parade has been a favorite among locals since 1969 and it's the only major parade that still passes through the French Quarter. There's no code, no competitive vibe (as well as no big, tractor-drawn floats), and anyone in costume can join in on the celebration as it assembles and sets off on Mardi Gras morning. Participants are encouraged to embrace the masquerading experience—beauty, color, artistic inventiveness, and flamboyance are key to the costumes. And we guarantee that you'll enjoy the Society of St. Anne parade more as a spectator if you make yourself part of the spectacle! Start with a mask, add a colorful wig, maybe a funny hat, and keep going from there—sequins, rhinestones, feathers, bottlecaps, aluminum foil . . . anything goes.

The starting point and the route vary slightly from year to year, but if you don your most outlandish garb and head to the Bywater district (roughly around Royal and Clouet Streets) before midmorning on Mardi Gras day, you're likely to find it. From there it forms behind the Storyville Stompers Brass Band and then typically proceeds along Royal to Canal to watch the Rex parade, with intermittent stops at bars and cafés along the way.

L'Omelette Géante

Abbeville's five-thousand-egg Giant Omelet Celebration has it all—a legend, a parade, international flair, and an *egg*cellent finale with free food for all.

Legend has it that Napoléon and his army were traveling through southern France and decided to rest for the night in the tiny village of Bessières, about 15 miles northeast of Toulouse. For dinner that evening locals recommended he sample a new dish invented by the village innkeeper—an *amelette* (derived from the Latin word *lamella*, which means "little flat thing"). Thankfully, Napoléon wasn't disappointed. In fact, he so enjoyed the meal he ordered the townspeople to prepare a giant *amelette* using all the eggs in the village for his army to feast on the following day. News of the new dish spread across France, and people started calling it an *omelette* to avoid confusion with *amulette*, an item used to ward off evil spirits.

The legend of *l'omelette géante* lived on in Bessières for more than a hundred years, and in the 1970s townspeople decided to reenact the cooking of the giant omelet. At first only the local poor attended the supersized supper each Easter, but before long, giant-omelet festivals spread to a handful of other small French-speaking cities around the world. Today the Giant Omelet Celebration is a tradition among seven cities that are members of the Confrérie Mondiale des Chevaliers de l'Omelette Géante (World Fraternity of Knights of the Giant Omelet). In addition to Bessières, the sisterhood includes Frejus on the coast of France; Dumbéa in the islands of New Caledonia in the South Pacific; Granby, Quebec; Malmedy, Belgium; and Pigüé, Argentina—and of course, Abbeville, Louisiana. Each of the cities has an annual Giant Omelet Celebration during which a giant omelet is made using ingredients from the region to give it a homegrown taste.

Abbeville's annual celebration takes place in early November, and the over-the-top omelet is made using ingredients like crawfish tails and Tabasco Pepper Sauce to give it a Louisiana zing. Two days of music, eating, and dancing build up to a special Mass at St. Mary Magdalen Church that includes the procession of the cooks and the cracking of the eggs. The giant omelet grows a little bit more giant every year—an additional egg has been added every year since the first official celebration in 1985; and in 2008, 5,024 eggs were used. Other ingredients include 52 pounds of butter, 50 pounds of onions, more than 6 dozen bell peppers, 3 boxes of salt, and 2 boxes of pepper. The cooking is done in a skillet with a twelve-foot diameter over a wood fire, and a forklift is poised to remove the omelet from the heat at just the right moment. We'd like to say that this is the world's largest omelet, but the crowds need to swell considerably to even hold a candle to the current record holder. In "Yolkohama," Japan, in 1994, a Japanese-style omelet was made using 160,000 eggs!

If you're interested in learning the *egg*sact recipe used for the giant omelet, visit www.giantomelette.org. The site also includes dates for future Abbeville *egg*stravaganzas through 2015.

Saint Rosalie, Heroic Hermit

Once a year in September in the town of Harvey, parishioners of St. Rosalie Catholic Church take the statue of their namesake saint out of the sanctuary and attach it to a carrying platform for a tour of the neighborhood. It's the highlight of the St. Rosalie Fair, which takes place beside the church. On the shoulders of stouthearted members of the congregation, St. Rosalie totters by booths offering games of chance or food, beer, and cotton candy, the idol's fair complexion counterbalanced by the Bible and human skull she clutches in her hands.

Rosalie, or Rosalia, is venerated in the town of Harvey and also in the neighboring town of Kenner, two communities that were settled largely by Sicilians. She is one of the patron saints of Palermo, Sicily, although very little is known about her life. According to most accounts, she was a distant descendant of Charlemagne who spent most of her adulthood as a hermit living in an artificial cave in an embankment near her hometown. In her mid-thirties in 1166 she died of unknown causes and was buried in the makeshift cave where her remains were discovered.

In 1624, a ship arriving from North Africa brought a plague to Palermo that spread quickly through much of the population. During the epidemic, Saint Rosalia appeared in visions to both a sick woman and a hunter with instructions on how to find her grave. The hunter did as instructed by the apparition. He unearthed the remains on Mount Pellegrino and carried the bones in a procession through the city—the plague miraculously ended. Grateful survivors built a sanctuary at the cave where her remains had been found and made her yet another local patron saint.

Saint Rosalie, as the Creoles call her, got her toehold on both banks of the Mississippi near the end of the nineteenth century, when an outbreak of anthrax spread among cattle belonging to Sicilian immigrants who had settled upriver from New Orleans. Remembering that she had been successful in handling similar epidemics before, the farmers prayed for her help. Once again she came to the rescue, this time saving most of the livestock. The descendants of these farmers have shown their appreciation by staging annual processions at Our Lady of Perpetual Help in Kenner and at the St. Rosalie Church in Harvey. Truly devout Sicilians participate barefooted; but the paved roads of southern Louisiana can still be pretty hot in September, so most people there wear shoes. Following the procession, the fair continues for the rest of the afternoon.

Halloween in New Orleans

While some consider it a second Mardi Gras, Halloween is really just another occasion during the year for Louisianans to exercise their creative muscle through costuming and dressing up, or masking, as most natives call it. Celebrated throughout the state, the current epicenter is lower Frenchmen Street in New Orleans's Marigny district, just a few blocks downriver from the French Quarter. The corner of Bourbon and St. Anne in the Quarter is another Halloween hot spot.

Elsewhere in the city you'll find the Coven Ball by Anne Rice's Vampire Lestat Fan Club, parades organized by the Krewe of Boo and the Jim Monaghan's, plus a plethora of private parties. There is, however, an undercurrent of unease beneath all the frivolity of Halloween mayhem relating to a rarely voiced truth: The city is a whole lot more frightening when it isn't trying to be scary. Whenever ordinary people dress up like ghosts or demons, any authentic ghosts and demons probably feel they can take the holiday off. But as soon as their stand-ins put away their costumes the real fiends return, rested and ready to go back to work.

Bizarre Beasts

Louisiana's mysterious melting pot serves up one seriously bizarre brew! Cypress swamps and slow-water bayous, prairies, thickets, and piney woods are set to a slow simmer, thanks to the summertime heat and the mild winters. Add refineries, sugar mills, and lumber and paper companies. Stir it all together and . . . well, something strange is bound to come crawling out of the mix.

There's the two-tailed heifer in Chalmette; Daisy, the four-eared feline in Jackson Parish; and the mystery sea monster off the coast of Grand Isle. Of course, there's also Louisiana's famous bad boy of swamp and screen and if that's not enough, we've thrown in a few amorous *arglefargin* and that "hairy fella," you know, the one with the big feet. There are plenty of bizarre beasts that go bump in the bayou. Turn the page to find out more—if you dare.

The Snake Whose Goose Got Cooked

In late July 1923, the *Lake Charles American Press* announced the discovery of a giant rattlesnake skeleton in a cave outside Junction City near the Arkansas state line. An elderly man who grew up in the Junction City area believed the snake had died nearly sixty years earlier. During his youth, he said, the giant reptile had terrorized Junction City until a party of field-workers decided to fight back and set fire to the woods the giant reptile called home. The snake was never seen again.

Evidence suggests that despite the protection of the cave, the snake was unable to survive the intense heat of the forest fire. Scientists who later examined the bones determined that the snake had been at least 107 years old when it died. Even after shriveling in the flames, the skeleton was more than ten feet long, and scientists estimate the snake measured twelve to fifteen feet while alive.

The Junction City rattler certainly was a sizeable snake, but compared to some of Louisiana's other legendary reptiles, it's pretty petite. According to herpetologists at the Louisiana State University Natural History Museum, water snakes more than forty-five feet long once inhabited the swamps and bayous of the state!

Beast Becomes Bayou

Over the millennia, the Mississippi River has changed course a number of times. The mouth of the river has shifted from near the location of present-day Morgan City (about 4,500 years ago), to near Chalmette (about 3,000 years ago), to near Golden Meadow in Lafourche Parish (about 700 years ago), and finally to its current location, near Pilot Town in Plaquemines Parish (about 400 years ago).

According to geologists, each time the Big Muddy changed course, it left its former waterways more or less intact, and these then became the principal bayous of today. In other words, Bayou Lafourche and Bayou Teche were once the Mississippi River.

The Chitimacha, a small tribe of Native Americans who have lived on the southern Louisiana coast for about 2,500 years, have another explanation, at least for Bayou Teche. According to a legend that survives in their oral history, a gigantic snake (*tenche* in their language) had wreaked havoc in their daily lives for ages, wrecking cornfields and ripping up fishing weirs. One day, a presiding chief decided to fight back against the super-sized snake. He gathered together the tribe's strongest men and organized a snake-hunting party. They made their way to the head of the snake near Morgan City and attacked it using only arrows tipped with garfish scales. How many primitive projectiles does it take to kill a 125-mile-long beast? Your guess is as good as ours—this is a legend after all.

As the days wore into weeks, their arms grew mighty tired, but they kept shooting as fast and as often as the women of the tribe could make new arrows and hand them over. Eventually the snake showed signs of weakening. Writhing, the snake coiled and wallowed, gouging out the channel that became Bayou Teche—after the body rotted away and left the bayou clear enough for navigation.

Hapless Hospital Hares

On January 5, 1955, Mr. J. B. Heroman of Our Lady of the Lake Hospital phoned the East Baton Rouge Parish sheriff's office with a report that something terrible had happened to eight of the nine rabbits that he kept in wire cages on hospital grounds. "Mysterious midnight monster marauders," he said, ripped wide holes through the heavy-duty mesh enclosures and massacred the captive hares.

When Lt. Tom Henderson and Deputy Jack Cullen arrived to investigate, they interviewed lab employee Frank Clack Jr., who had managed to catch a glimpse of two of the attackers as they ran from the scene toward nearby Capitol Lake. He described the assailants as covered "with black fur and [having] long tails." The officers soon discovered two pairs of mysterious footprints, each with four distinct toes or claws on their front paws or hands. According to an article in the *Baton Rouge Morning Advocate*, the "Deputies said they would patrol the lake shore in an attempt to find the 'monsters' and establish their identity," but it is not known if they ever successfully apprehended the beasts.

Some people think that there could be some connection between the Our Lady of the Lake Bunny Killers and a creature that Troy Stence and two friends observed one night in October 2003 while walking along Brown's Bend Road in Alexandria. The trio described seeing a ratlike humanoid that somewhat resembled "a gnome," according to Stence. "It was about four feet tall and had red eyes," he said, "but it wasn't a rat or a possum or anything like that. It looked like it had human arms and legs. It just ran off."

After they encountered it, Stence and his friends also ran—but in the other direction. To this day, nobody really knows what it was they thought they saw.

Those Amorous Arglefargin

In the *Old Natchitoches Parish Magazine*, reporter Bob Norman described a bizarre series of disappearances near Johnson's Chute, along the Cane River Bottoms. Those nineteenth-century mysteries were generally attributed to a monster known as the *arglefargin.*

Beginning in the 1860s, young men in the area would occasionally go missing. When their whereabouts were traced from the sites where they had last been seen, searchers would often come upon signs of a violent struggle. Along with scuffed earth and broken branches, they'd find huge monsterlike footprints mingled with the tracks of the missing youths. Occasionally they'd also come upon a mysterious word—*arglefargin* or *argilfirkin*—scrawled on a note pinned to a tree or scratched into the dried mud with a sharp stick. For a long time no one knew what this meant.

The hunt for the *arglefargin* was on. Farmers set traps baited with full-sized farm animals but caught only ordinary predators like bears or panthers. Then a local savant named Mrs. Jane came up with a novel explanation for the missing men, claiming "the people were being abducted by creatures from the moon to be used as slave labor." This was a little hard to believe, so one young man of spirit offered himself as bait for the traps. After days in the backcountry, he emerged exhausted, with the details of the truth. The *arglefargin*, he said, were not from the moon, but were humanoids who stood roughly between nine and eleven feet tall and looked ". . . something like a cross between the ugliest person who ever lived, a mutant gorilla, and a hackberry with Dutch elm disease." They also smelled like dead skunks and had a strong desire to mate. Yup, you read that right, the *arglefargin* were looking for love. According to the local lore that emerged following Mrs. Jane's human-baited trap, *arglefargin* were a long-lost branch from the human family tree. Their own species had gone into decline due to their size and low birth rate, and so they were attempting to reinvigorate the species bloodline with new genetic material from human male Louisianans.

Strangely, disappearances of young men in the greater Natchitoches area *increased* after this news spread, though few of them returned to tell the same tale as the first young fellow.

The last reliable sighting, according to Bob Norman, was by his own great-uncle Obie, who maintained all his life that he'd seen one in 1903. The fact that no pure-blooded *arglefargins* have been seen since does not prove conclusively that they died out completely. It is possible they simply moved deeper into the thick woods and emerge only on rare occasions in places like Arkansas or East Texas. Meanwhile a number of prominent midstate families still count ancient *arglefargins* among their hallowed ancestry, although most would rather face exile than ever admit it publicly.

Oh, You Lucky Dog!

In early July 1957, crewmen of the tugboat *White Castle* found a large brown dog more than fifteen miles off the coast of southwest Louisiana in the Gulf of Mexico. The dog was still swimming valiantly, although nearly unconscious after apparently being washed to sea when Hurricane Audrey had hit the coast almost a week earlier. The dog had a cut above his jaw, a gash on one side, and a crushed paw. The tug crew quickly dubbed the dog "Lucky Lou" because, according to the wife of a longshoreman, he "was found off Louisiana."

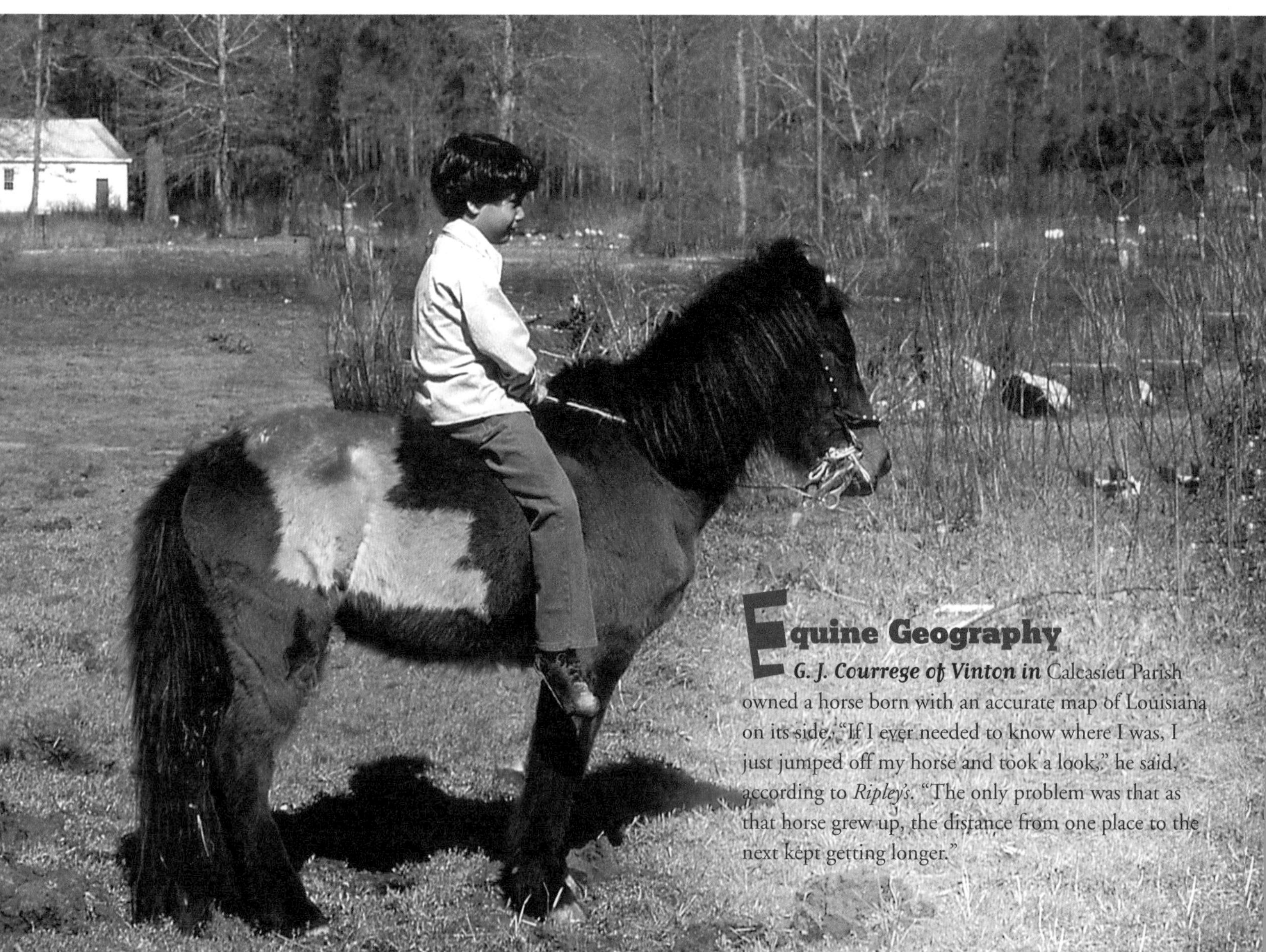

Equine Geography

G. J. Courrege of Vinton in Calcasieu Parish owned a horse born with an accurate map of Louisiana on its side. "If I ever needed to know where I was, I just jumped off my horse and took a look," he said, according to *Ripley's*. "The only problem was that as that horse grew up, the distance from one place to the next kept getting longer."

Bayou Bad Boy of Swamp and Screen

Shortly before the time his death was officially announced, Dr. Alec Holland had been operating a secret biology lab deep in a Louisiana swamp, where he was working on a biorestorative formula. According to reliable sources (who refused to be identified), the formula might have solved many of the problems caused by deforestation, carbon dioxide buildup, global warming, and human overpopulation, since it was said to be potentially capable of making "forests out of deserts." Unfortunately, just as the esteemed scientist was perfecting his discoveries, a bomb destroyed his lab. Covered in corrosive chemicals, Holland ran out into the swamp and desperately tried to put the flames out by rolling around in the mud.

Several months later, a frightening creature was spotted shambling through the undergrowth, covered in mud and leaves. Although Holland had already been declared dead, this thing had the memory and personality of the missing scientist. Hard-core comic book aficionados may recognize this as the backstory to *Swamp Thing*, a DC Comics series that began in the early 1970s and continued in one form or another for more than two hundred issues. In fact, even though it's in its fourth decade, it, or one of its spin-offs, sporadically shows up even today wherever comics are sold.

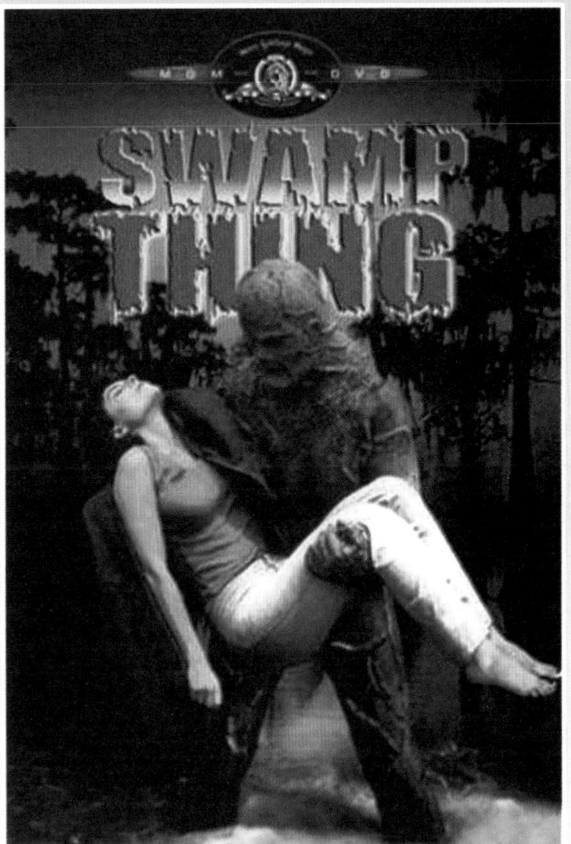

The classic comic inspired the 1982 film *Swamp Thing* by horror-flick director Wes Craven and a less successful sequel, *The Return of Swamp Thing*, not affiliated with Craven, in 1989. The Bayou State's original bad boy from the bog has also been celebrated in numerous muck-alike spin-offs like Parlangua, Le Bon Gumbo, Thunder-Petal, Megaclaw, The Jonesville Monster, The Swampster, Nutria Boy (or Man), and our very own fave, Sump Thing.

Honey Island's Swamp Thing

Louisianans living in the eastern part of the state have seen it—tall, hairy, bipedal with big feet, lurking around the swamps around Slidell and Pearl River. They call it the "Honey Island Swamp Monster," after the area where it was first seen, and where it continues to be observed more often than anywhere else.

According to Slidell native Dana Holyfield, her grandfather Harlan E. Ford and his friend Billy Mills were flying near Honey Island in 1963, over an uninhabited section of the vast swamps that extend along the Pearl River, when they spotted what appeared to be a "campsite" down in an artificially cleared opening in the dense canopy of trees. Noting the spot on their maps, they made their way overland a few weeks later to the site, which was in the western part of Pearl River Swamp above Bradley Slough.

Here they had a completely unexpected encounter. They were hauling an outboard motor to one of their boats when, about twenty yards away, a creature they later described as being somewhat "baboonlike," but bigger, more hairy, and standing on two legs, suddenly raised up, made eye contact with them, and then dashed off into the thick understory. The area where the creature had been lurking was found "disturbed." They saw broken branches and discovered a small nestlike structure, but there were no artifacts. Around the structure they found strange tracks with three principle toes, as well as some kind of vestigial toe, but since they had neither cameras nor plaster with them to make casts, they were unable to document the footprints other than by verbal descriptions and, later, by sketches drawn from their recollections.

In 1974, Mills and Ford were back in the same general area when they found several feral hogs whose throats had been ripped out. Nearby they heard a splashing sound.

Running toward it, they came upon a hog in its death throes, bleeding profusely at the neck. In the soft mud on the creek bank they found three-toed tracks like the ones they had seen a decade earlier. This time they alerted Wildlife and Fisheries officers, who came to take a look at the site. They made casts of the footprints that were subsequently studied by a zoologist who trained at Louisiana State University. Based on the size and depth of the casts, the creature who made the prints was estimated to be about seven feet tall and weigh 300 to 350 pounds.

Their 1963 encounter had been easily dismissed by officials as a case of mistaken identity of some "regular" animal like a bear or panther, or else it was blamed on a shared hallucination brought on by heat prostration, even though both men were lifelong swamp hunters and skilled outdoorsmen and both had seen enough bears and wild felines to know the difference. Both men also worked at the Federal Aviation Administration, where Ford was an air traffic controller, and risked losing their jobs if their claims made them seem mentally unstable. They had nothing to gain by making a false claim.

Because of this, their reports seemed reliable. As word of the discovery and its subsequent official confirmation leaked out, others began to come forward to describe their own sightings of the mysterious creatures. An elderly loner named Ted Williams admitted to having seen them on numerous occasions in the vicinity of Peach Lake but said that he'd always "regarded them as harmless." He also said he'd been able to get quite close to them by sitting in a hiding place at the edge of the lake and watching them swimming in pairs and "families." When "Old Man Williams" went missing several months later, it was widely believed that he had dared to approach the creatures more closely than he should have—and that they were not nearly as benign as he thought. While looking for his remains, searchers found more tracks around Peach Lake and its surroundings.

Reports of additional sightings continued to flood in. A mysterious beast that could obviously climb extensively damaged a hunting camp mounted on ten-foot stilts. The owners, Scott Bond and Mark Daniel, discovered claw marks that didn't match the kind left by bears, cats, or other known denizens of the swamp, and the hair and feces didn't look human, either.

Buddy Dean reported seeing a "six-foot hairy man with no clothes on" while he was squirrel hunting. Then Jim Hartzog was chased off a steep bluff by an unfamiliar bipedal creature after taking potshots at it with a shotgun. Jason Holburn saw a tall, hairy figure walking in a part of

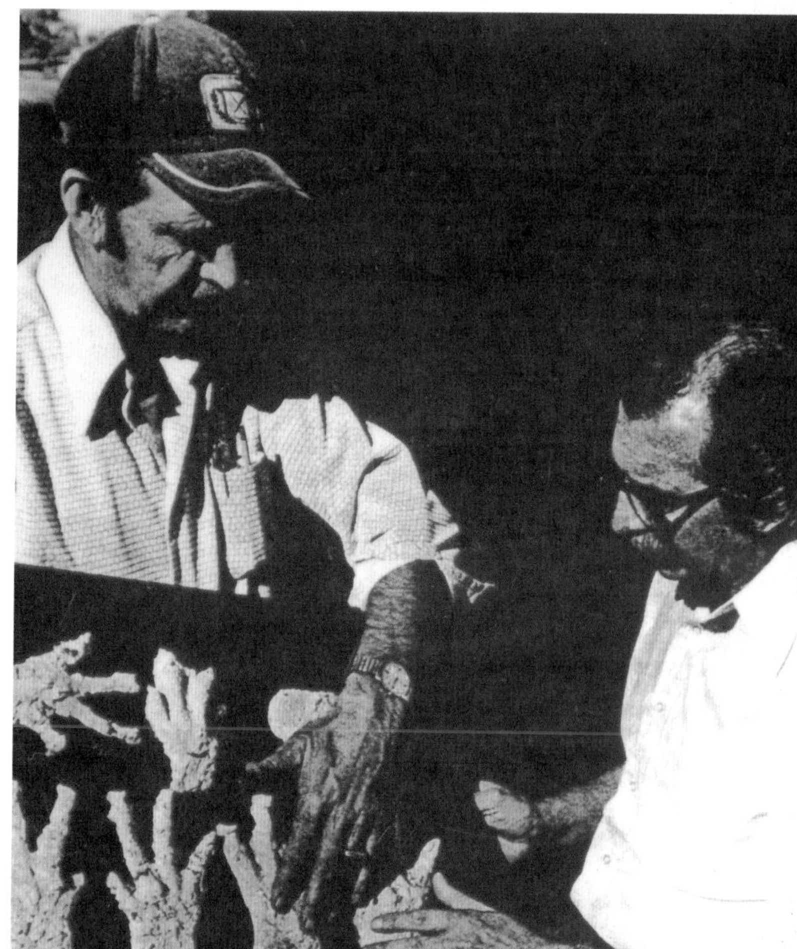

the swamp called Debbie's Ditch. Goat farmer and swamp man Denty Crawford came up behind a hairy creature roughly the size of an adult male human and knew right away it wasn't a bear. "A bear has a rounded back," he pointed out, "but this thing had a flat back like a man. It is not an 'it'—it's a 'them' or a 'they.'" Herman Broom had a chance to see one of them from the front, in daylight, and said that it "had a smooth face. He had a hairy body, but his face was smooth." At another site, dead feral hogs weighing several hundred pounds hung in the forks of trees, as if something had wedged them up there to prevent ants and legged scavengers from eating them.

Dana Holyfield recalls her grandfather Harlan as a serious man, not at all the kind to keep a story going for so long for the sake of a mere prank. In fact, she says, he went well out of his way to try to substantiate the existence of the "unidentified animals" (he didn't call them monsters), because he was continually frustrated by the ongoing doubt and occasional ridicule he had endured over the years. She tells of how he attempted to lure the beasts within capturing (or shooting) range with live goats as bait, and how, at night, he would firmly bind shut the doors of his own hunting camps with nylon ropes to keep the mysterious animals out. Harlan Ford was clearly shaken by his experiences and witnessed firsthand, as few others had, how deadly—or else desperate—the beasts could be.

To Be, or Not to Be, a Bigfoot

There are many theories about the origins of the Honey Island Swamp monster. Harlan Ford believed the creatures to be some kind of previously undocumented species that had somehow managed to elude detection in the vastness of the swampy lowlands. He shared this belief with researchers, who see the mysterious swamp monster as yet another kind of Bigfoot. Cryptozoologists like Lloyd Pye, who specialize in the study of legendary creatures, believe the animals witnessed by Ford and others in the region may be three-toed, web-footed, swamp-dwelling relatives of the elusive Bigfoot.

Another theory is that a circus train overturned in the area many years ago, releasing apes in the woods that mated with the local ape population and quickly evolved to adjust to swamp life. But folklorists have pointed out that the circus-wreck story is common throughout the country, wherever Bigfoot-type creatures are reported. Either dozens of circuses from Florida to Alaska lost their menageries or there's some better explanation.

Yet another theory suggests that the names for various swamps are only local terms or politically determined boundaries drawn for the convenience of various governmental purposes. There is no "natural" division between the Honey Island Swamp, the Pearl River Wildlife Management Area, the Bogue Chitto National Wildlife Refuge, or, for that matter, the Isobell Swamp, the Fritchie Marsh, or Big Branch Marsh National Wildlife Refuge—or any of the other low, wet, mostly uninhabited zones that extend for hundreds of thousands of acres in every direction. It's all one big, swampy place, much of it unmarked by human footprints.

There are as many theories about the Honey Island Swamp monster as there are sightings, and some of the tales are just too tall for us to retell here. One thing the locals do agree on—*something* is out there.

Fact or Science Fiction?

One theory on the origins of the Honey Island Swamp monster sounds an awful lot like a storyline from the *Swamp Thing* comic. Just beyond the Pearl River, on the Mississippi side of the Honey Island Swamp, is the forbidden territory of the Stennis Space Center, NASA's leading center for Earth science applications. According to the Web site, the center's goals include extending the ". . . discoveries, knowledge, technology, and data . . . to turn Earth science results and capabilities into practical tools for solving practical problems." Doesn't this sound like the kind of place that would synthesize Dr. Alec Holland's biorestorative formula? (See page 115 for more on Dr. Holland and the Swamp Thing phenomenon.)

Well, the Stennis Space Center was founded in 1961 as the Mississippi Test Facility. In January of that year, the first chimpanzee astronaut was launched into outer space. A handful of theorists suggest the government created an experimental animal, half human and half ape, for use in space travel simulations on Earth around this time. Could this ape-man have escaped into the swamp? Or maybe he was released once the experiments concluded? Is it mere coincidence that the experimentation with chimps in space was already well established in 1961 and just two years later the creature Harlan Ford and Billy Mills saw was wandering around not so far away?

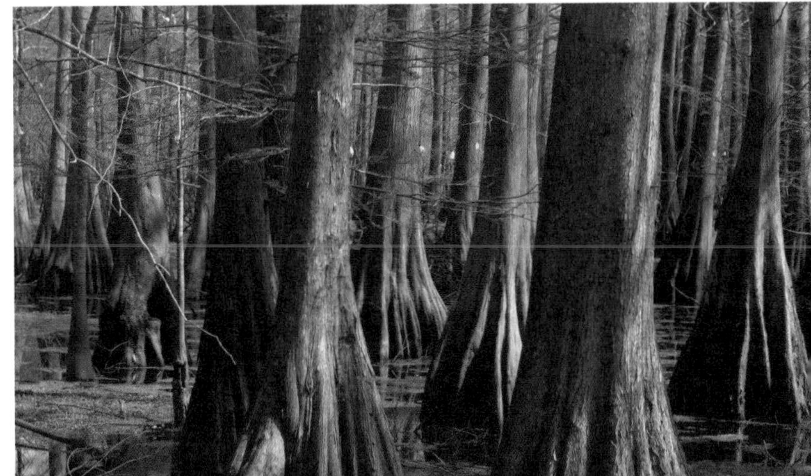

Louisiana Bigfoot

We've got to hand it to the old guy. Anyone who can stand to spend a sweltering Louisiana summer running around barefoot outdoors covered in thick fur is a force to be reckoned with. The mysterious monkey man has many aliases—Sasquatch, Yeti, the Abominable Snowman (in chillier regions), the Night Screamer, Skunk Ape, the Swampster, Nutria Man, and a host of other less savory names. We're talking about Bigfoot, of course.

Most often only fleetingly glimpsed in back swamps and piney woods, evidence of Bigfoot's existence is limited to a handful of blurry photos, broken tree branches suggestive of makeshift shelter, and a number of plaster casts of larger-than-life footprints. There are no skeletons in any museum collections, and there are no examples of artifacts that are undeniably Bigfootian in nature. Still, there have been more than a few eyewitnesses and many others who swear on their mortal souls that *he's out there.*

Boggy Bayou Bigfoot

On August 29, 2000, the *Alexandria Town Talk* reported a major sighting by two loggers near Cotton Island, east of Esler Regional Airport in northeast Rapides Parish. According to an article by Andrew Griffin, on August 22 log foreman Earl Whitstine was removing hardwood logs using a tree cutter when he spotted a mysterious creature he later referred to as a "booger." The beast, which he described as being about seven feet tall, covered in black hair, with big feet, appeared to be startled by the loud noise of the tree cutter. It leaped up and waded across the creek before disappearing into the woods. "After it jumped into the water, it looked back at me," he said.

A few days later, Whitstine was with saw-cutter Carl Michael Dubois when the pair spotted the large-footed beast as they were walking along Boggy Bayou at the edge of Mary Ward's wooded property. This time Whitstine shouted at it, but the creature ran away before they could approach. The men then discovered a series of huge four-toed tracks in the muddy bottom of the dry bayou. They measured the stride at about six and a half feet between tracks.

Mrs. Ward was alerted to the strange discovery on her land, and sheriff's deputies soon joined her at the edge of the bayou, where they could see giant footprints extending thirty feet before disappearing, thanks to the harder-packed soil in the woods.

As word of the sightings spread around town, curiosity seekers flocked to Ward's property. Bigfoot researcher Scott Kessler of Pineville arrived on the scene and made plaster casts of several of the Boggy Bayou tracks and collected a number of hair samples before the invasion of onlookers could destroy all the evidence. After several hundred visitors had swarmed

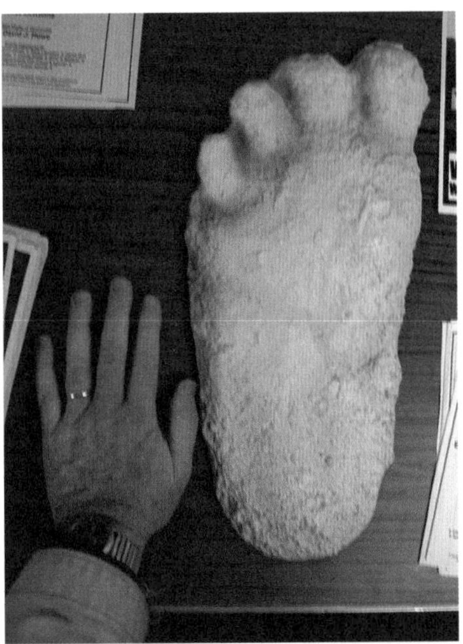

over the premises, Mrs. Ward erected a sign that read BIG FOOT PROTECTION AREA—ROAD IS CLOSED TO PUBLIC, although she continued to allow anyone without guns or dogs to explore her property as long as they agreed not to harm the beast. Eventually, according to a sheriff's report filed later, she even began selling T-shirts and tickets to visitors.

A few days later, fisherman Larry Satcher came forward with a story about a "hairy fella" he had seen a few months earlier while casting for bass at the Honey Hole Slough on another part of Ward's acreage. As Andrew Griffin's follow-up article in the *Town Talk* described it, Satcher detected a strong, pungent smell while fishing. As he waded out into the slough to cast his lure, he heard a noise and turned in time to see a pack of feral hogs on the bank. And then, he saw *it*—seven feet tall, covered with dark mottled hair, tucking a 150-pound hog under its arm as though it were a ladies' pocketbook.

"When I finally got out of the water, I started to run," he said, but when he looked back to see if it was gaining on him, the creature had already disappeared. Even so, he said, "I ran as fast as I could and even passed my truck. . . . I was scared so bad."

The Honey Hole Slough is only a few hundred yards from Boggy Bayou, so in all likelihood the three eyewitnesses had seen the same creature. "I don't know if it was a Bigfoot or whatever [but] if it had wanted to catch me, it could have caught me," Satcher said. "It'll definitely stay with me the rest of my life."

After Satcher's Honey Hole encounter, Mary Ward began avoiding the most thickly wooded parts of her land. Her faith in the existence of the animal remained unshaken even after forensic anthropologists and veterinary pathologists at Louisiana State University in Baton Rouge determined that the hair samples Scott Kessler had collected at the site had come from a horse. Another scientist at the Oregon National Primate Research Center reported the hair samples had come from a cow. Still, Ward didn't doubt the eyewitness accounts, and Bigfoot researcher Kessler was quick to point out that the presence of domestic livestock hair on the scene didn't mean that a Bigfoot hadn't also been there. So Ward continued to believe in the existence of her Boggy Bayou Bigfoot. "I'm a little uneasy," she said. "I don't think it'd hurt me, but I know it's there now."

That wasn't the year's last sighting, either. A hundred miles to the west, near Zwolle in Sabine Parish, seventy-four-year-old Hosea Remedies was mowing his lawn when a Bigfoot lurched out of the nearby woods. As Cain Burdeau, an Associated Press writer, reported in the (Baton Rouge) *Advocate*, it didn't take long for Zwolle assistant mayor Allen Rivers to connect the Remedies sighting with the hog-killing creature of Boggy Bayou, since some of his own hogs had been killed recently by something with "pretty big claws and pretty big teeth." Retiree Steve Malik was frustrated, because in all his years as a Sabine Parish game warden, he'd never caught a glimpse of a Bigfoot. "God dang, everyone has seen it," he said, "why can't I?"

The "hairy fella" sure does get around. Additional Bigfoot sightings have been reported from Rapides Parish (1967); Acadia Parish (1972); East Baton Rouge Parish (1977); near Riceville in Vermilion Parish, Crowley in Acadia Parish, and twice in an area close to Krotz Springs in St. Landry Parish (all in 1978); in Franklin Parish (1980); near Bastrop in Morehouse Parish (1983); in rural Vernon Parish (1986); near Houma (1988) and outside Alexandria (1994); in Claiborne Parish (1999); near Ville Platte in Evangeline Parish and near Gibsland in Bienville Parish (both in 2001); and a sighting in Sabine Parish (2003). You can find details of many of these encounters by visiting the Bigfoot Field Researchers Organization Web site at www.bfro.net.

Watchgators

For a number of years, the New Orleans offices of Julian Hillery, founder of World Ship Supply and author of *To Be or Not to Be a Successful Business Person*, were guarded by five patrolling "watchgators." "It's a great deterrent," the company's chief security professional explained. "Thieves have learned you can usually 'buy off' a watchdog with nothing but a raw pork chop, but a gator might not only take the meat, but the hand and arm holding it out, and *then* some. They don't bark ahead of time, either, so you never know what they might be about to do."

Coming or Going?

Larry Roberts of Chalmette owned a heifer with two tails. One was in the usual place and the other tail grew out of its head. Louisiana State University scientists speculated that this might be a natural evolutionary step in the development of "Louisiana cows of the future." According to their theory, traditional cow tails evolved many thousands of years ago as a way to keep flies away from mammalian back ends. But the tendency of love bugs to gather on the front ends of every moving object in the state may be triggering a new Darwinian development.

"You can think of it almost like a windshield wiper," one veterinary researcher suggested, "at least for now. As this thing gets passed down to generations to come, cattle might come up with all kinds of other uses for it. If it ever turns into something like an elephant's trunk, they might be able to pick up simple objects, operate self-feeding devices, and so on. I don't know if we can train them to milk themselves"—she smiled—"but that would be great, wouldn't it?"

Hitler's Horse

A few miles west of St. Rose in St. Charles Parish, near the old La Branche Plantation, is a plaque indicating the grave of Nordlicht, believed to be Adolf Hitler's horse.

Born in 1941, Nordlicht (meaning "northern light" or "Aurora borealis") quickly grew into a champion chestnut stallion. He had won both the Deutsches Derby in Germany and the Oesterreiches Derby in Austria before World War II ended in 1945. After the D-day invasion, when Allied forces and their convoys began to enter the part of Germany where Nordlicht had been stabled, his breeders spattered mud and dirt on his hide and attempted to conceal him in a crumbling barn, surrounded by a herd of ordinary farm animals. However, an American G.I. spotted Nordlicht among the common animals and pulled him aside. Supposedly his Nazi keeper then shamefacedly admitted, "Well, now you have the best. He is the finest horse in all of Europe."

Nordlicht was sent to the United States to be auctioned at Front Royal, Virginia, where he brought $20,300 in 1945 dollars. But he failed to perform as well in his new surroundings as he had for his former grooms. For whatever reasons, he won only a few minor races in the United States before being sold yet again and put out to pasture in St. Rose, Louisiana. Nordlicht, the former master racehorse of the self-styled master race, was buried at La Branche Plantation in 1968.

She's All Ears

We've all heard of cats with a few extra toes, but Lula Shell of Chatham, Jackson Parish, owned a cat with four ears, according to *Ripley's*. "Mice don't stand much a chance around here," she claimed. "My sweet Daisy can hear them coming and going!" Had the strange kitty been born a few years later, Mrs. Shell might have named her cat Radar, but in 1939 it hadn't quite been invented yet.

Mystery Monster or Devilish?

In November 1856, the *Thibodaux Minerva* ran a story about an unusual creature discovered in the warm Gulf waters near Grand Isle:

> *Mr. Martial Ogeron gives us the following description of a monster of the finny tribe lately killed by him off the mouth of the Lafourche, in the breakers: Length of the body from point of nose to the tail, 14 ft; length of tail, 6 ft; extreme width on the back, 20 ft; thickness from top of back to bottom of belly, 7 feet; width of mouth 3 feet 6 inches, with horns on either side, 3 feet long; cavity of brain, 9 by 16 inches.*
>
> *This huge monster, when killed, was lying with his mouth open catching small fish, on which it is supposed to subsist. It was shot through the head at the distance of about five paces, and immediately sunk to the bottom. It was then fastened to, and towed in to shore, where it was dissected for the purpose of being converted to oil; but a storm arising, the captor was forced to abandon the project and fly for safety. Its liver was the size of a rice cask. The exterior of this fish was covered with a skin resembling more that of an elephant than anything else to which we can compare it.*
>
> *Mr. Ogeron is a seafaring man, and says he has never before seen a fish of this description in our waters. What kind of a fish is it, and where did it come from? Let us hear from you, naturalists!*

On account of "horns on either side" in the description, some biologists suggested that the sea monster was a world-record-setting devil ray, a kind of manta ray with hornlike fins that project forward to help with feeding and locomotion. The *Minerva*'s main rival, the *Houma Ceres*, published soon after the previous article on November 22, 1856, came to the same conclusion:

> *We have not a doubt but this is the veritable devil fish, so common on the shores of our southern Atlantic States, and noted for his devilish pranks with boats' anchors, etc. There is a book somewhere entitled, we believe, "Devil Fishing on the Coast of the Carolinas." If you can find it, Miss Minerva, you may be thoroughly enlightened.*

But several things about the Ogeron story cast doubt on this theory. For one, devil rays are not all that rare in the Gulf of Mexico, as the *Ceres* editor himself points out. If Martial Ogeron was as experienced a seafaring man as the *Minerva* suggested, then why didn't he identify his catch as an unusually large devilfish or ray?

Also, the "monster" is described as having skin like an elephant—thick, bumpy, and wrinkly—and that doesn't agree with common descriptions of manta skin, which is typically thin, sandpapery, and streamlined. Because of this, some scientists have theorized that perhaps the mystery creature was a manatee instead, although manatees weren't completely unfamiliar animals either. Besides, a manatee that is even remotely close to twenty feet wide and seven feet thick would certainly be a sight to behold!

One other possibility is that it might have been an ocean sunfish, or Mola mola, as these do have wrinkly skin and two thick, almost rigid fins that may have been described as "horns on either side." Scientists have collected specimens more than fourteen feet wide and weighing upward of five thousand pounds—in fact, they are the largest bony fish known, outside the fossil record. At the same time they are rare enough in Gulf waters that it is no surprise an experienced fisherman like Ogeron might never have seen one. The dimensions that he gave make his fish quite a bit larger than the largest Mola mola reliably documented, but with a storm coming, no way to take accurate measurements other than stepping it off on the beach, and nothing in previous experience to compare it to, it would have been easy to make errors in gauging the size of his discovery. Besides, is there a fisherman in history who didn't exaggerate (at least a little) when describing the one that "got away"—as this one apparently did when that storm came up and he had to flee?

Still, none of these theories is certain. Because nothing quite like it has ever been caught again, the first Louisiana sea monster will forever remain a mystery.

„ZİTA"

Local Heroes and Villains

In Louisiana, colorful characters who make a splash historically go the distance. Just consider some of the folks who got elected to office in the mid-twentieth century. After Huey Long, the politician who proposed "Every man a king," there was O. K. Allen, said to be such a stooge that a leaf blew into his office one day and he signed it, thinking it was legislation from Long. Jimmie Davis and Earl Long executed allemandes in and out of the governor's mansion a few more times before Edwin Edwards cut in and spun around the political dance hall too, for four terms—until he whirled himself into prison. It's been nothing if not a wild hayride in the governor's mansion.

Although this chapter is called Heroes and Villains, we're not saying who's who—one person's chump is another person's champion, after all. Some of the worst crooks have been looked upon as Robin Hoods and some of the greatest citizens were, to some, avatars of the Devil. Curious to know more? We know you are!

Marie Laveau, the Voodoo Queen

Separating fact from fiction about Mme. Marie Laveau isn't easy. Almost everything known about the legendary lady is based on what others have said or written about her. She was illiterate, so there are no first-hand accounts of her extraordinary life. And Laveau did little to discourage others from believing or writing whatever they wanted about her—especially when it came to describing her spiritual abilities—since the legends and mystification only endowed her with more power.

But there was most definitely a real person named Marie Laveau, although there are conflicting records about the identities of her parents and the date of her birth. According to some accounts, she was born in New Orleans in September 1801, the daughter of a free mulatto woman named Marguerite D'Arcantel and Charles Laveaux, a successful plantation owner. Other records suggest she was born in Haiti in the 1790s and moved to New Orleans in the early 1800s.

Marie grew up and spent most of her life in a cottage that belonged to her maternal grandmother, located on the uptown side of St. Ann Street between Burgundy and Rampart. At eighteen, she married Jacques (in some records, referred to as Santiago or St. Yago) Paris, a mixed-race refugee from the Haitian Revolution who was well on his way to successfully establishing himself in Louisiana. The couple lived on Rampart Street where they had two children. Sadly, within a few years her husband and children died, most likely as a result of one of the yellow fever epidemics that had swept through the city.

Following her husband's death, Marie began calling herself the Widow Paris and took work as a hairdresser. As a hairdresser in the early 1820s, making house calls was part of the job, and so Marie was granted access to the parlors and bedrooms of the city's elite. While catering to her clients in the privacy of their boudoirs, Marie was privy to their most confidential affairs. She was an astute observer of the human condition, and the gossip she overheard helped her piece together information that would prove useful when people began asking for her advice. It was at some point during this same period that she began conducting ceremonies in her home and backyard, setting up altars in different rooms of the house, some for blessings and healings, others for cursing rituals.

In the late 1820s Laveau began a relationship with a white man named Capt. Christophe Glapion. They never officially married but had at least seven children together, all of whom assumed his last name. Glapion earned a living trading stocks, loaning money, and dealing in real estate and slaves. One of Captain Glapion's major investment deals went sour in the early 1850s, and when he died in 1855, Marie's house was put up for sale to recoup his debts. Friends bought it, however, and allowed her to continue living there. By that point, Marie Laveau was fifty-four and already gaining fame as Voodoo Queen. For the rest of her life her fame and the local belief in her near-magical powers continued to grow.

Voodoo Lady

Marie Laveau created and performed voodoo rites derived from animistic religions in West Africa that slaves introduced to Haiti (Saint-Domingue). In Haiti, the beliefs of slaves from numerous tribes mingled to create vodou, which also borrowed from the Catholicism of their French and Spanish masters. When vodou spread to Louisiana, it picked up additional Catholic and Native American customs. Despite voodoo being more Catholicized than its Haitian cousin, voodoo ceremonies in New Orleans, and Marie

Laveau's in particular, drew strong criticism from church members who compared it to witchcraft.

Witnesses said Laveau sometimes danced with a black snake in her trance ceremonies and kept black cats, black pigeons, and spiders in her house, although these may only be rumors. The biggest complaints involved annual voodoo activities carried out on Saint John's Eve, June 23, when Laveau and hundreds of other worshippers gathered along the shore of Lake Pontchartrain to light bonfires and immerse themselves in healing and purification ceremonies. These became popular annual events, drawing thousands of participants and curious onlookers.

Laveau was also known for her skills as a reader and advisor, and she'd manipulate situations for personal gain from time to time, especially with wealthier clients. But most of her ministry was not based on such chicanery, and she became well known as a minister to the condemned, visiting prisoners and helping them conduct predeath rituals that many psychologists would recognize as a form of reality therapy. These were especially effective with people who, like she, were unable to read a Bible or write down their thoughts.

Her work on behalf of prisoners wasn't limited to providing such comfort, however; she was also reportedly tireless in petitioning judges and officials to obtain pardons or commutations of sentences, too. But there were those who interpreted Laveau's appearance at hangings as a ghoulish fascination with death or a way to gather witchcraft materials, and they'd make up stories about her ability to thwart executions or to help prisoners to escape.

Laveau of Legend

Marie Laveau's fame continued to grow long after her death in 1881. She could walk on water. She kept a twenty-foot poisonous serpent in an alabaster casket and fed live children to it. She ran a brothel and conducted wild orgies in a shack/temple near Bayou St. John. She worshipped Satan and drank human blood from a black crystal chalice.

Laveau had two daughters and perhaps a younger understudy, all named Marie, which led to rumors that Marie Laveau used her powers to stay eternally young. When "Marie II" was seen walking around town long after the newspapers had announced Madame Laveau's funeral, word spread that she had come back to life. Add the tales that dozens of authors, songwriters, reporters, filmmakers, and tourism promoters have fabricated or embellished over time, and it's sometimes hard to tell if Marie Laveau was a real person or only a figure from folktales.

Whisper Your Wish to Madame Laveau

There's certainly no shortage of legends surrounding the life of Madame Laveau. In fact, there are even more stories about her afterlife and final resting place(s). It's believed that she occasionally comes to life and wanders around in St. Louis Cemetery No. 1 with her seven-pointed tignon tied atop her head. She's also been seen emerging from her other tomb—called the "Wishing Vault" and guarded by a raven—located on the uptown end of the middle section of St. Louis Cemetery No. 2. Still others maintain she was really buried in the Girod Street Cemetery, now covered by the Superdome.

Do you have a wish? Maybe Madame Laveau can help make it come true. Although the archdiocese strongly discourages the practice, hard-core believers often mark three *X*s on either tomb, knock three times, and then whisper your wish into the crack and wait for an answer. It may help to leave a little money on the ledge. Three nickels is the standard consultation fee.

The Bird Man of . . . ?

Schoolchildren from Audubon Elementary School in Kenner, visiting New Orleans's Audubon Zoo in Audubon Park and reading the inscription on the statue of bird painter John James Audubon, might be forgiven for believing that Audubon came from Louisiana. The engraving on the statue reads, JOHN JAMES AUDUBON OF LOUISIANA and includes the dates of his life as 1780–1851. This, however, only perpetuates a lie that Audubon told to gain entry into the United States.

Audubon fabricated and romanticized much of his own life story. He claimed to be a self-taught frontier artist, born on a plantation in Louisiana, although in fact, as a young man he had been tutored in a private school in Nantes, France. He also wrote that his mother was a Creole woman and his father a French admiral. The truth is that he was born in 1785 in Haiti and was originally named Jean Rabine. After his mother, Jeanne Rabin, passed away when he was six months old, he was taken to France. At the age of nine he was formally adopted by the captain his mother had served (and Jean's biological father) and given the name Jean-Jacques Fougère Audubon. In 1803, when Audubon was eighteen years old, his adopted father armed him with a fake passport and shipped him off to Pennsylvania to avoid conscription into Napoléon's military. The name on the passport was listed as John James Laforest Audubon (the name he kept for the rest of his life), and Louisiana was indicated as his place of birth.

After arriving in the United States, Audubon moved to a farm near Philadelphia where he spent his time hunting, studying taxidermy, and making drawings of birds he had shot. And then, some eighteen years later, when Audubon was thirty-six, he arrived in Louisiana *for the first time.* He lived briefly in a house on the corner of Conti and Dauphine (or Barracks) Streets in New Orleans, and then moved to a plantation in West Feliciana Parish between Jackson and St. Francisville. He continued drawing and painting birds (using dead birds as models), and though he has been immortalized as a naturalist, he often bragged: "I call birds few when I shoot less than one hundred per day."

After only four years in Louisiana, Audubon went to Europe in search of a publisher for his seminal work, *Birds of America.* There, he was memorialized by the statue in Audubon Park and became a hit! Once his book published, Audubon became an international celebrity and never returned to the Bayou State. He lived out his days in a Manhattan mansion.

Audubon's ruse continued until 1917, when biographer F. H. Herrick published the first exposé revealing the truth. Jean-Jacques Fougère Audubon may be exalted in New Orleans as "John James Audubon of Louisiana," but his enigmatic life is commemorated elsewhere with monuments to John James Audubon of Kentucky, Pennsylvania, New York, and France. There may even be a statue in Haiti.

Who Killed the Kingfish?

Sen. Huey Long, one of the most remarkable and controversial politicians in U.S. history, was assassinated on September 8, 1935, in Baton Rouge. What exactly happened and why remains a mystery to this day. Evidence remnants of the fateful event are preserved in the Louisiana State Capitol building, where actual bullet holes in the hallway where Long was shot can be still be seen and touched.

The Fateful Event

Long was in Baton Rouge to oversee a special weekend session of the state legislature. One of the bills on the agenda intended to gerrymander Judge Benjamin Pavy's Sixteenth Judicial District. Judge Pavy, from Opelousas, outraged Long when he sentenced some of Long's election officials to jail for election fraud. Long, in turn, outraged Pavy by pardoning them and then spreading the rumor that Pavy had "a taint of Negro blood." After Pavy forced him to retract that lie, Long made a point of being in the chamber of the State House of Representatives in person to make sure his anti-Pavy scheme was voted in.

At 9:21 P.M., Senator Long emerged from the House chamber and walked down the back hallway of the capitol to the governor's office, trailed by his Bureau of Criminal Identification (BCI) bodyguards—a band of secret police created to protect Long from his many enemies. As Long exited the office, a young man stepped from a shallow alcove toward Long. There was a momentary commotion, followed by a shot and a sudden hail of bullets that ricocheted off the hallway's polished marble walls. A few moments later, Long's shooter was dead, and Long was rushed a few blocks away to Our Lady of the Lake Hospital. Thirty hours later, Long died of internal bleeding.

Long's shooter was later identified as twenty-nine-year-old Carl Austin Weiss, M.D., Judge Pavy's son-in-law. According to most reports, Weiss was shot forty-eight times, although some estimates say that as many seventy .32 caliber bullets were fired.

Capitol Cover-up

The official version of the incident was quickly released before all the facts were in. Weiss was so enraged about the proposed bill to oust his father-in-law that he decided to kill Huey Long. Somehow he gained entry to the capitol building with a loaded gun and waited for Long to emerge from the governor's office. When he did, Weiss used a small handgun to shoot the senator at point-blank range before the bodyguards opened fire on Weiss. A .32 caliber murder weapon that was presumed to kill Huey Long, with one empty cartridge, was found next to Weiss's body, obviously implicating him.

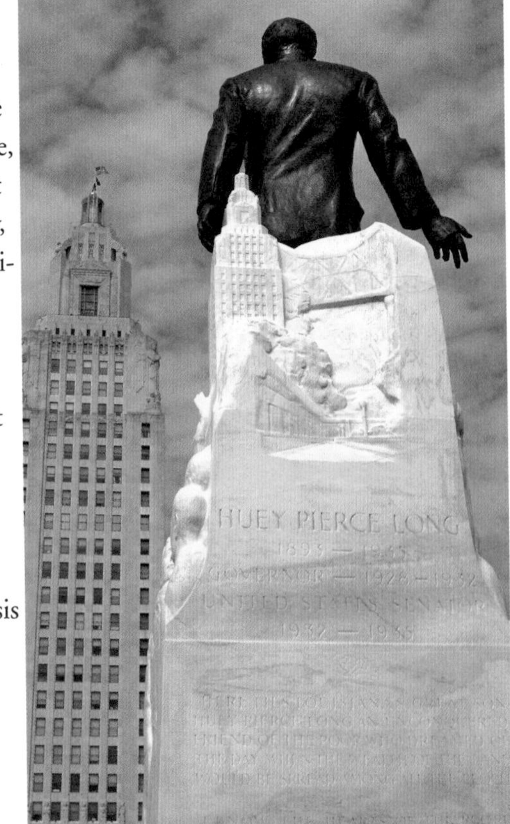

Gen. Louis Guerre, superintendent of the BCI, headed the assassination investigation. Guerre's analysis focused not on autopsies or ballistics, but only on promoting

Weiss as the culprit. In the following days, the BCI would reveal that besides his supposed outrage that his father-in-law was being gerrymandered out of his judgeship, Weiss was infuriated that Long impugned the Pavy family—his wife's family—by saying they had African blood. Guerre and others also claimed that Weiss was among a group who met at the DeSoto Hotel in New Orleans to plan Long's assassination (something that Long brought up a few months earlier on the floor of the U.S. Senate). Weiss, they said, had "drawn the short straw" to do the job.

Almost immediately after this evidence was announced, contradictory information began to surface. For one, Weiss had been nowhere near New Orleans during the alleged DeSoto Hotel planning session. Nor was he particularly concerned by the racist allegations toward his wife's family. Trained in New York, Vienna, and Paris, he'd had black teachers and associates and respected their abilities. In fact, Weiss—one of the city's best trained and most respected young physicians—was known for being even tempered, soft spoken, and uninterested in politics, although he was no fan of Huey Long and was well aware of Long's ongoing enmity toward his father-in-law.

An anonymous report from a state trooper suggested that the alleged murder weapon was planted. According to the trooper, when the crime scene was first examined, it was discovered that Weiss carried no weapon at all. Realizing this would automatically incriminate the bodyguards, a "throwdown" .25 caliber gun was placed in proximity to Weiss's body before anyone else was allowed to approach the scene. Later, when a .32 caliber bullet—the kind used by the bodyguards—was found in Long's body, General Guerre replaced the .25 caliber gun with a .32 caliber gun and confiscated the bullet found in Long's body.

The senator was buried in front of the capitol building on September 10, and tens of thousands gathered to pay their respects. But that's not the end of the story. When General Guerre retired in 1940, he cleaned out the files and evidence lockers and took the alleged murder weapon that Weiss supposedly used: a Belgian-made FN model 1910 Browning .32 caliber (some say .765 caliber) pistol, as well as a spent .32 caliber bullet. He put these in a safe-deposit box along with a number of files relating to the incident. Guerre also took the clothing that Long had been killed in, with its bullet holes indicating exactly where the senator had been shot.

Fifty Years Later . . .

In 1991, a Washington, D.C.–based forensic scientist learned about the safe-deposit box and hired a private eye to track it down. The investigator traced it to eighty-four-year-old Mabel Guerre Binnings, who inherited the evidence-crammed box from her father. Fifty-six years after the shooting, a custody battle ensued between Mrs. Binnings, the Louisiana State Police, the State Archives, and Carl Austin Weiss, Jr., who was just a baby when his father had been killed. The courts ruled in favor of the Weiss family, who then donated the gun and other items to the Center for Political and Governmental History in Baton Rouge.

But not before a ballistics test was finally performed on the weapon. When the gun was test-fired, experts from George Washington University and the Louisiana State Police found no connection between the spent bullet—supposedly taken from Long's body—and the weapon that once belonged to Dr. Weiss. Turned out, Weiss had bought the gun when he was studying medicine in France in 1930. The 1910 pistol cost $8, suggesting he may have picked it up at a flea market along with other items he listed on his customs voucher when he returned to the United States. Although the gun found at the scene was Carl Austin Weiss's, there was no evidence that it had been fired or even

Although the gun found on the scene was Carl Austin Weiss's, there was no evidence that it had been fired or even been in the building when Huey Long was shot.

been in the building when Long was shot.

In 1992, the state police officially closed its investigation into the death of Huey Long, although they ended it with a strangely inconclusive double-negative formulation, saying that they "had found no evidence that Weiss did not fire the shot that killed Huey Long," leaving the doctor still in the position of being considered guilty until proven innocent.

Cover-ups, outright lies, propaganda, and conspiracy theories have clouded so many of the facts that the truth will probably never be known. But the capitol is open to the public and you can visit the hallway where it all happened, so stop by sometime to look at the scene and see how you interpret it.

Not-So-Silent Statue

If you want an idea of what it may have been like to have seen Huey Long give a speech, don't miss the eerie talking statue of Long in the Old State Capitol Museum exhibit. The bronze-like robotic figure of the notorious politician moves and comes to life to deliver humorous moments from some of his speeches. In an adjacent room you can see the gun that belonged to Dr. Weiss, which may or may not have been a murder weapon.

Who Were Nita and Zita?

Some people march to the beat of a different drummer, it's true, but it's rare that two siblings march to the beat of the same different drummer. Sisters Nita and Zita, known to most New Orleanians only as the "Gypsy Ladies," were truly exotic dancers (not strippers) who writhed, twisted, and twirled to a mysterious beat all their own.

Flora and Piroska Gellert were born in Nagybánya, a Jewish village in Hungary, and arrived in New York in 1922 to make their debut on stage as Nita and Zita. For twenty years they traveled the world together, taking their unique act and elaborate costumes across the United States, Europe, Asia, and parts of Africa and South America. In 1947 they settled into a small house on Dauphine Street in the Marigny neighborhood and, apart from an occasional public appearance, the sisters became increasingly reclusive with age.

When they did put on shows, people watched them perform at a studio on Bourbon Street. Their act had an otherworldly flavor and they performed in decadent handmade costumes that they readapted regularly using beads, sequins, mirrors, and peacock feathers. Music and dance styles ranged from jungle and Hawaiian, to tango, rumba, and the waltz, with an occasional interlude of flamenco. So far as anyone can now recall, they danced only with each other; there was no male member of their troupe.

Flora (Nita) died in 1985 and Piroska (Zita) died in 1991. Neither ever married or had children, and no relatives attended their funerals. When Piroska died, she left behind hundreds of handmade beaded costumes, hats and headdresses trimmed with feathers and fur, and objects made from bottle caps, tin cans, and foil. A neighbor assumed responsibility for disposing of their belongings, and for several years a number of thrift shops in New Orleans were flooded with their inimitable clothing and the odd objects they had made. Eventually some of their costumes and creations made it into the collection of the Louisiana State Museum.

Flora and Piroska are buried next to each other in the portion of Hebrew's Rest Cemetery for paupers.

The Axeman Cometh

The most infamous serial killer in the Big Easy's history is, hands down, the Axeman of New Orleans. The Axeman's killing spree starting as early as 1911 and continued until 1919, when the slayings ceased just as mysteriously as they began. The notorious killer's reign of terror claimed the lives of twelve victims, many of them Italian grocers, and left at least five others seriously wounded. The Axeman's identity was never discovered.

Details of early killings attributed to the Axeman are somewhat sketchy. In 1911, an Italian grocer named Cruti was found dead, hacked to pieces with an ax. Before the year was out, another Italian grocer named Rosetti and his wife were also killed with an ax. Then in May 1912, an Italian grocer named Tony Schiambra and his wife were killed in their home in the Lower Ninth Ward. Mrs. Schiambra died, but her husband survived and spoke to reporters. Someone named Momfre was mentioned in the newspapers as a suspect, but there's no follow-up to say whether he was ever arrested or taken in for questioning. There are no records of these murders in NOPD files, even though the victims were well known in the Italian community at the time.

The Axeman was dormant for about six years, until the night of May 22, 1918, when grocer Joseph Maggio and his wife, Catherine, were axed to death in their bedroom on the corner of Magnolia and Upperline Streets. This time the killer left something behind. A bloody ax, partly rinsed off, was found in the Maggios' bathtub. An abandoned ax at the scene of the crime went on to become something of a calling card for the Axeman, a way of alerting officials that he had been there. Two weeks later, the Axeman attacked grocer Louis Besumer and his common-law wife, Anna Lowe, while they were sleeping. Once again, the ax was left behind. Anna died, but Besumer survived and became a suspect. He was tried but found innocent when a coroner proved his wounds couldn't have been self-inflicted.

The killings continued on through the summer. On August 5, Mrs. Edward Schneider was attacked by the Axeman while asleep in bed and miraculously survived. She later described the assailant as a dark, shadowy figure. Five days later Pauline Romano awakened to see a tall figure in a black hat standing over her, but when she screamed he ran off into the dark. Her uncle, Joseph Romano, hadn't been so lucky—he was found dead in his bedroom. After these attacks, the city finally went on full alert. Citizen patrols formed, people barricaded doors and windows, and family members took turns sleeping and standing guard over one another with loaded firearms.

The Axeman waited seven months before striking again, this time across the river in Gretna. Grocer Charles Cortimiglia and his wife Rosie survived the attack, but their two-year-old daughter, Mary, who had been asleep in her mother's arms, died as the result of an ax blow to the back of her neck. Soon after this attack, the editor of the *Times-Picayune* received a bizarre letter dated March 13, 1919, with the return address listed as "Hell." The writer claimed to be inhuman "a spirit and fell demon . . . what you Orleanians and your foolish police call the Axeman." He wrote that he would claim more victims as he saw fit, and the police should not try to discover who he was, lest they "incur the wrath of the Axeman." He even boldly gave another time and date in which he'd "visit" the city again: "12:15 (earthly time) on next Tuesday night," but he proposed a way in which its citizens could save themselves from his ax: play jazz music. So on Tuesday of the following week, March 19, every home that could afford to hire musicians did so—and those who didn't commandeer a band made sure to visit friends who did. Some chanced it with gramophones, and the entire city jazzed all night long.

And although no one was killed on this evening, the Axeman's sojourn didn't last. On August 10, 1919, the Axeman attacked Steven Boca, injuring but not killing the grocer. Three weeks later, nineteen-year-old Sarah Laumann was killed. On the evening of October 27, Mike Pepitone was attacked in his home and died the following morning from his injuries.

After Pepitone's killing, the Axeman murders stopped, but it took a while for people to believe the nightmare was over. According to urban legend, Mrs. Pepitone hunted down a man named Joseph Mumfre and shot him to death in Los Angeles in December 1920. The story said she was sentenced to ten years in prison (of which she served only three) because the jury shared her belief that Mumfre was involved in her husband's murder. When authorities compared Mumfre's known whereabouts with the calendar of killings, they saw that the hiatus between the 1911 killings and the resumption of murders in 1918 exactly coincided with time Mumfre supposedly spent in Angola Prison. Historical research never revealed a trial in either New Orleans or Los Angeles having to do with a Joe or Joseph Mumfre (or Momfre, Mimfrey, and Momefrei), nor is there any record of a widow of Mike Pepitone ever being tried in or visiting California.

All of which points to an alternative outcome that is far more likely to be true: The most feared serial killer in New Orleans history got away with it, probably thanks to a more pressing concern in late 1918: the Spanish flu pandemic. It's likely that Mumfre—if indeed he was the killer—was one of the estimated 80 million people who died during that flu season.

When the Grim Reaper takes on the Axeman, the scythe beats the ax every time.

Bonnie and Clyde

Sometimes it's difficult to picture the events being memorialized at a particular historic site. Once in a while, however, you'll come across a place that seems virtually unaffected by the passage of time. The Bonnie and Clyde ambush site, on a lonely stretch of Highway 154, seven miles south of Gibsland in Bienville Parish is such a place. The place is exactly as it was on the morning of May 23, 1934—apart from a single battered place marker and the fact that the gravel road is now paved—when Bonnie and Clyde's ongoing crime spree came to an abrupt end.

By the time they reached this particular rise in the road, Bonnie Parker and Clyde Barrow had been together for four years. They had avoided eleven police traps and killed thirteen people—two civilians and eleven law officers. Their ability to elude capture kept them in the national news, but after Clyde pulled off a successful prison break for a number of his captured cronies, the government had had enough. Texas brought legendary manhunter Frank Hamer out of retirement for one last *Mission Impossible*–style assignment: Hunt down Bonnie and Clyde by any means necessary.

Hamer assembled a team of seasoned Texas and Louisiana law officers and planned an ambush. Studying the pattern of the Barrow Gang's movements across several Midwestern states, Hamer concluded that they would stop in Bienville Parish, where gang member Henry Methvin's parents lived. Meanwhile, Hamer gathered weapons, including shotguns, pistols, and a number of Browning automatic rifles with magazines full of armor-piercing bullets. After tracking the two outlaws for several months, Hamer calculated they would arrive in the Gibsland area around May 22.

Hamer, who interpreted his "take any and all necessary actions" mandate broadly, realized he needed a human decoy to lure Bonnie and Clyde to his ambush and decided to kidnap Henry Methvin's father for that purpose. On May 21, Hamer's team took Ivy Methvin into custody, parked his truck on the side of Ringgold Road (Highway 154) south of Gibsland, and then removed a wheel so it looked like Methvin had stopped to fix a flat. Across the road, they arranged their weapons so each man could quickly retrieve whatever he'd need when the time came. By nine P.M. the trap was set, and Hamer waited through the next day and evening with no sign of the outlaws. To make sure the elder Methvin couldn't attempt an escape to warn the gang, they handcuffed him to a tree when night fell.

The following morning Hamer's posse heard a car. They ordered Ivy Methvin to stand by the truck and threatened to shoot him if he tried to thwart the ambush. They hid in the underbrush and raised their rifles when the spotter gave the signal.

Clyde Barrow recognized his friend's dad and slowed to ask if he needed help. But Bonnie saw some movement in the bushes across the road and yelled. Clyde seized a rifle and tried to shoot, but before he could aim, the officers opened fire. Clyde was killed almost instantly, followed by Bonnie's horrifyingly long, drawn-out scream as the posse emptied every weapon they had.

With Clyde dead at the wheel, his foot slipped off the brakes and the car rolled slowly into a ditch about 150 feet beyond the ambush site, almost tipping over. The officers kept firing even after the car stopped. The coroner's report later described fifty-three bullet holes in Bonnie Parker's body and fifty-one in Clyde Barrow.

Inside the bullet-riddled car were dozens of stolen firearms, thousands of rounds of ammunition, and multiple stolen license tags from six states. On the front seat were a half-eaten sandwich, a blood-spattered map of Louisiana, and a copy of *Police Gazette* magazine. Frank Hamer and the others left the scene to phone in reports of their success, and when they returned with the coroner a few hours later, a throng of souvenir collectors were combing through the wreckage with the two dead outlaws still slumped in it. Blood-soaked pieces of clothing and hair had been taken from their bodies, and one man was cutting off Clyde's left ear with a pocketknife when the coroner stopped him. Hamer ordered his men to take charge of the scene.

Gibsland now stages an annual Bonnie and Clyde festival on the Friday and Saturday closest to May 23, complete with reenactments of a bank robbery, hostage scene, and ambush, as well as guest appearances by surviving siblings and relatives of the outlaws. At other times you can visit two Bonnie and Clyde museums in town, one of which is run by the son of one of the lawmen who participated in the ambush. History doesn't "come back to life" much more directly than this, and you might even hear the echoes of gunfire down on Ringgold Road.

Pick Your Battles

As Michael Smith of Baton Rouge likes to say, "It's the little bitty things in life that make the difference." And he should know, since he's been recognized by both the *Guinness Book of Records* and *Ripley's Believe It Or Not!* as the creator of the world's largest sculpture to have been made from one of the world's smallest and most mundane media: the toothpick.

Born in White Castle in 1959, by age thirteen Smith had lost his mother and was addicted to drugs. He stayed that way for more than two decades, through moves first to Port Allen and then to Baton Rouge, in 1986. Often homeless, sometimes reduced to eating food scrounged from garbage cans, he finally overdosed and was hospitalized and then committed to a detox center. He's now managed to stay clean for more than a decade, thanks to toothpick sculpting, a task demanding creativity as well as intense focus. Smith found that through gluing one toothpick to another and then another, and slowly building up a solid form, he could create anything from a working saxophone to the sixteen-foot Louisiana bull gator that got him into *Guinness*. He sees this as analogous to the task of reforming himself. "To make something this way, you have to do it one step at a time, one toothpick at a time. Every day you just do what you *can* do, no matter how small or insignificant it seems. Just like life. You've got to deal with life on life's terms and face it one day at a time. My life was in lots of pieces, so I had to pick it all back up," he says, smiling ruefully at his own pun.

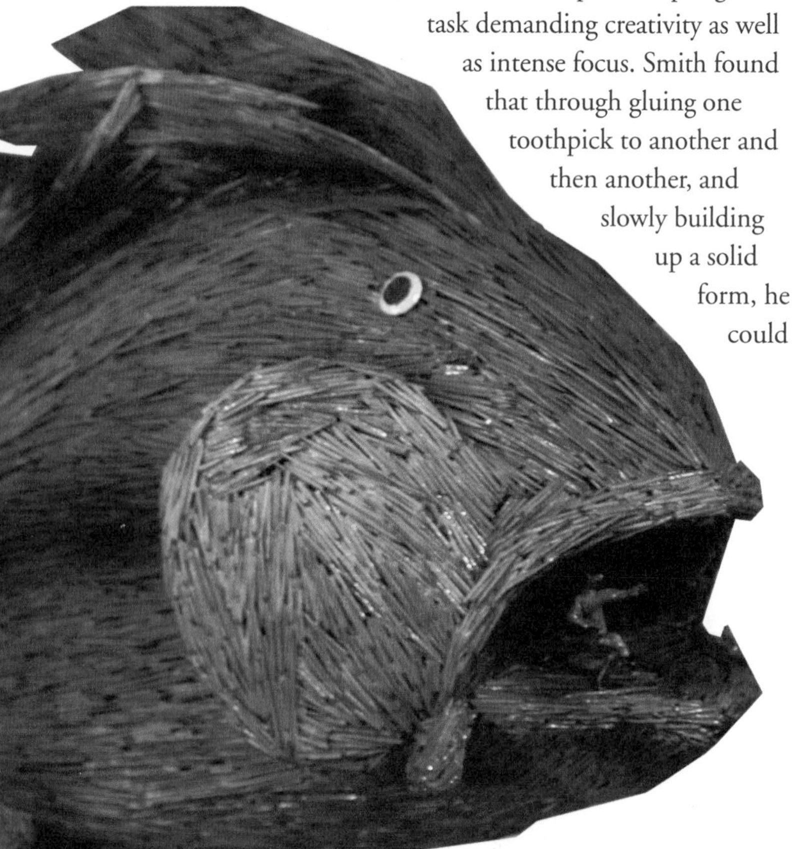

Along with significantly improved self-esteem, Smith's toothpick talent gained him a share of recognition as well. He's now regularly called upon to do demonstrations in school classrooms, using toothpicks to build simple birds or fish with remarkable speed. He's made fifteen-foot model ships, life-sized pelicans, gators of various sizes, bracelets and jewelry, and practical items like baskets and lampshades. He's also created a "Jonah and the Giant Fish" biblical scene—a reference to his own sense of having once felt trapped and desperately lost in "the belly of the beast" while addicted to drugs.

"Jonah finally got out, and so did I," Smith says, "and now everything I do is my way of being glad about it. Just one toothpick at a time. Toothpicks made me who I am today."

Edwin Edwards's Head of State

On Grand Isle, the state's only barrier island inhabited year-round, there is an imposing, partially carved granite boulder—a crude monument to one of the more colorful characters in Louisiana politics in recent years. He is one of the state's most popular governors, even though he's presently serving the second half of a ten-year sentence in federal prison for racketeering and corruption.

Edwin Edwards, who's been called the Cajun King, served four terms as governor—the longest run in the state's political history. As governor, he was nothing if not a witty communicator, and it's too bad that some of his more famous zingers weren't carved in stone with the pharaonic monument. During his race against incumbent governor David Treen, for example, Edwards said, "If we don't get [him] out of office, there won't be anything left to steal." He later described his opponent as being "so slow that he takes an hour and a half to watch *60 Minutes*." When Treen fired back, "How come you talk out of both sides of your mouth?" Edwards replied, "So people like you with only half a brain can understand me."

When asked to comment on his own corruption trial, Edwards said, "I never speak ill of dead people or live judges." Commenting on a campaign, he said, "Advertising is a valuable economic factor because it is the cheapest way of selling goods, particularly if the goods are worthless." His most famous remark, made just before Election Day in 1983, was, "I could not lose unless I was caught in bed with a dead girl or a live boy."

Strangely, however, the monument on Grand Isle isn't a tribute to the Cajun King's eloquence. Supposedly it was carved in recognition of Edwards's activities on behalf of preventing coastal erosion. This is a big deal because Louisiana loses a football field–sized chunk of land to erosion every thirty minutes—that's about 36 square miles per year or 17,520 football fields. At this rate, the state will be washed away entirely in little more than 1,400 years. Naturally folks in Grand Isle are worried since they'll be among the first to go.

Ironically if some of Edwards's environmental policies are reinstated, the inhabitants of the island may need to abandon it long before it gets washed into the sea. During his time in office, Edwards actively campaigned to promote the use of south Louisiana's bayous for hazardous waste disposal, and he encouraged oil companies to build chemical dumps in areas that could make places like Grand Isle uninhabitable health nightmares.

Nevertheless, when the Louisiana Political Museum and Hall of Fame opened in Winnfield in 1993 (on the hundredth anniversary of the birth of Huey Long), Governor Edwards was one of its very first inductees, along with Hale Boggs, William C. C. Claiborne, James "Jimmie" Davis, P. A. "Pap" Dean, Dudley LeBlanc, Earl K. Long, Huey P. Long, Russell B. Long, John J. McKeithen, Ernest "Dutch" Morial, and B. B. "Sixty" Rayburn. Five years later Edwards was indicted and eventually convicted of extorting kickbacks from riverboat gambling casinos (which he had encouraged to develop in Louisiana). He is reportedly working on his memoirs as inmate #03128-095 of the Federal Detention Center in Oakdale (Allen Parish), with a scheduled release date of July 6, 2011, when Edwards will be 84. If his writing is anywhere near as colorful as his speeches, it should be quite a read!

Saints of South Louisiana

Some of the most beautiful churches in the country are located in southern Louisiana along River Road, Bayou Lafourche and Bayou Teche. Many can easily hold their steeples up with pride among the churches and cathedrals of Europe, and the decorative stained glass, statuary, and paintings express the deep faith and commitment of their parishioners. Back when the old bayou churches were first built, however, members almost certainly realized that all the Gothic tracery and gilded decor was inauthentic. The sacred structures lacked a sense of history.

When Fr. Charles Menard was in Rome in 1867 to celebrate the anniversary of the martyrdom of Saint Peter the Apostle, he saw countless frenzied worshippers fawning over saints' relics—bones and other objects resting in their reliquaries. It occurred to him that he could bestow a sense of history to his church, St. Joseph Co-Cathedral in Thibodaux, by displaying a few blessed relics for the community. He met with Cardinal Patrizzi, legate of the pope, and negotiated a price for a piece of Saint Valérie's arm bone and a fragment of Saint Faustine's, as well.

Who was Saint Valérie? Often referred to as a virgin martyr, she lived during the second century A.D. and, according to some scholars, was the wife of Saint Vitalis of Milan and mother of Saint Gervais and Saint Protase. She was a member of a team of early Christians who made regular stops at the Coliseum and other sites in Rome to pick up the remains of fellow believers who had been martyred the day before, to give them a decent burial. She was captured by Roman soldiers who tortured and publicly beheaded her after she admitted she was a Christian. Despite the authorities making an example of her, other Christians retrieved her body the following day and placed her remains in the catacombs of Saint Sebastian. There her remains sat for the next 1,300 years or so, until pieces began to circulate in the late Middle Ages, and at least one arm bone finally wound up in Cardinal Patrizzi's possession. Less was known about Saint Faustine, but according to the cardinal she, too, was a virgin martyr who had been beheaded.

Father Menard headed back to St. Joseph in Thibodaux ahead of the shipment to prepare for the arrival of the relics. Meanwhile, each piece was placed in a cardboard box sealed with the cardinal's signet pressed into red wax to guarantee its authenticity, and then each box was placed inside its own lifelike wax statue, which in turn was dressed appropriately and placed in a glass coffin and then crated up for the sea voyage.

In early spring 1868, the two crates containing the coffin-shaped reliquaries of the two saints reached New Orleans. Father Menard went down to New Orleans to arrange an appropriate form of transportation. This is

when he discovered a minor complication: The wax statues containing the relics of the two unrelated saints looked uncomfortably similar. Each depicted a young woman with her head thrown back in the same expression of rapturous ecstasy, and other than Faustine being a redhead and Valérie a brunette, the statues could have been twins. It would be difficult to exhibit both relics in the same church without counteracting the very spirit of piety that they were intended to encourage. Luckily Fr. Jules Boucher, at the Église Assomption in Plattenville, was eager to acquire a relic for his church as well, so Saint Faustine would go there. Plattenville is about twenty miles northwest of Thibodaux, so it was unlikely that people would visit both on the same day—and if they did, maybe nobody would notice the similarities.

Feast days for the two saints were celebrated in similar ways, but it's hard to believe that Father Menard didn't choreograph things to play down the association. Saint Valérie arrived in Thibodaux on April 18, 1868, the feast day for Saint Faustine (thus preventing her relics from being feted in Plattenville yet). The coffin containing Saint Valérie's bone was carried to St. Joseph Church amidst a ceremony with four thousand people on hand. Meanwhile, the crate containing Saint Faustine was quietly forwarded up the river to Plattenville. Ten days later, on April 28, Thibodaux celebrated the feast day for Saint Valérie, and she became the patroness of the city. Many still invoke her protection during storms and floods, and she's credited with preserving the community from the worst of Hurricane Katrina's damage in 2005.

Saint Faustine—A Fraud?

The town of Plattenville first celebrated Saint Faustine's feast day on April 18, 1872, and did so annually thereafter, even opening her reliquary each year to comb her hair and freshen her clothing for the event. But in the early 1960s, church officials sent word from Rome that there was no record of there ever having been a Saint Faustine—or if someone by that name had existed, she was never canonized. After that, Saint Faustine's celebration was quietly discontinued.

Blessed Bits and Pieces

Father Menard considered Saint Valérie's arm bone quite a coup, since her relics were rare. By contrast, 3 churches had holy umbilical cords, 3 had crowns of thorns, 4 had the spears that pierced Jesus' side, 3 had the arms of Saint Francis Xavier, 3 had heads of Saint John the Baptist, 14 had a portion of flesh removed from Christ at his circumcision, and there were at least 204 shrines with pieces of the babies Herod had ordered massacred, not to mention all the nails and pieces of the true cross in circulation.

Until Death Do Us Not Part

Ernie K-Doe (see chapter 4) passed away in 2001, but that hasn't stopped him from attending concerts, riding in parade floats, or hosting parties—he even ran for mayor of New Orleans in 2006! Ernie also attends his own annual All Saints Day get-together at his grave site. He doesn't say much these days, but you can still hear him singing regularly on oldies R&B shows, especially his hit "Mother-in-Law," which rocketed to number one on the *Billboard* Hot 100 charts in 1961.

A lot of people, of course, are more than ready to retire when they die, but then they probably didn't have a go-getter helpmeet like Antoinette Fox K-Doe. She was willing to drive the star-spangled hearse he likes to ride in, push his wheelchair, and help her late husband get dressed in whatever outfit the occasion may demand. "He was *always* late anyway," she says.

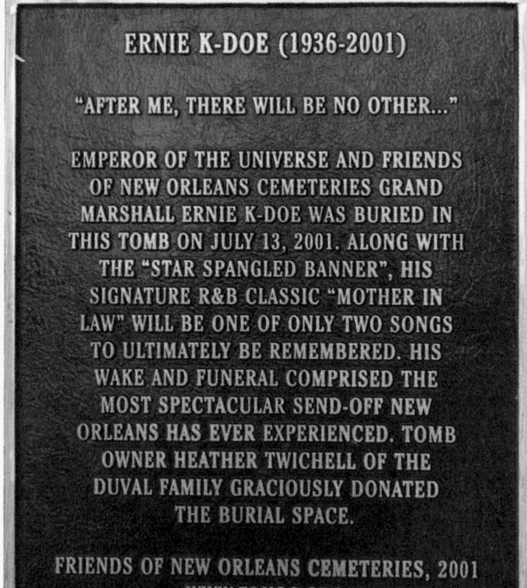

ERNIE K-DOE (1936-2001)
"AFTER ME, THERE WILL BE NO OTHER..."
EMPEROR OF THE UNIVERSE AND FRIENDS OF NEW ORLEANS CEMETERIES GRAND MARSHALL ERNIE K-DOE WAS BURIED IN THIS TOMB ON JULY 13, 2001. ALONG WITH THE "STAR SPANGLED BANNER", HIS SIGNATURE R&B CLASSIC "MOTHER IN LAW" WILL BE ONE OF ONLY TWO SONGS TO ULTIMATELY BE REMEMBERED. HIS WAKE AND FUNERAL COMPRISED THE MOST SPECTACULAR SEND-OFF NEW ORLEANS HAS EVER EXPERIENCED. TOMB OWNER HEATHER TWICHELL OF THE DUVAL FAMILY GRACIOUSLY DONATED THE BURIAL SPACE.
FRIENDS OF NEW ORLEANS CEMETERIES, 2001
WWW.FONOC.ORG

Antoinette's beloved K-Doe had a tremendous presence in her life, in body—courtesy of sculptor Jason Poirier, who created an Ernie look-alike soon after he passed away on July 5, 2001—and in spirit. K-Doe had a larger-than-life personality and referred to himself as "Emperor of the Universe, the One, the Only, the Baddest Motor Scooter and the Greatest Boy-Child Ever Conceived at Charity Hospital in New Orleans, Louisiana" and solemnly maintained that a thousand years from now, only two songs will still be remembered from the current epoch: "The Star Spangled Banner" and "Mother-in-Law," "because someone is always going to get married."

K-Doe, born Ernest Kador Jr. in 1936, grew up singing in his church choir and, later, with gospel groups like the Golden Choir Jubilees and Divine Traveler. Always a dynamic singer, he learned early on the power he could wield over audiences by physical moves like collapsing to the stage and sometimes even diving off the stage—a move punk bands later rediscovered. After his recording career took off in his mid-twenties with "Mother-in-Law," he and his band performed numerous times at the Apollo in New York, the Howard in Washington, D.C., the Uptown in Philadelphia, the Regal in Chicago, and even at Carnegie Hall. His other major recordings included "Here Come the Girls," "A Certain Girl," "T'ain't It the Truth," "Come on Home," "Hello My Lover," "Te-Ta-Te-Ta-Ta," "Later for Tomorrow," and, late in life, "White Boy / Black Boy."

As the years wore on, however, he slipped into alcoholism and by the late 1980s was, in his own words, "living in an alcoholic haze," dressing in capes and outlandish costumes and referring to himself as "Mr. Manawgahide." He was, in other words, turning into yet another New Orleans eccentric. But a key influence in turning him around and bringing him back to sobriety was his relationship with the indefatigable Antoinette Fox, who cofounded the Ernie K-Doe Mother-in-Law Lounge in 1994 (see chapter 4). The couple married in 1996 and enjoyed five years of living matrimony before she became the sole partner with a pulse.

Ernie K-Doe's memorial service is still talked about as one of the all-time great New Orleans–style jazz funerals. His remains were placed in the Duval family mausoleum in the central section of St. Louis Cemetery No. 2, where they joined those of his second mother-in-law and Earl King, his best friend. For the next eight years his artificial avatar continued to accompany Antoinette on all her rounds. After weathering Katrina, Antoinette went out in style as well, dying on Mardi Gras morning, February 24, 2009.

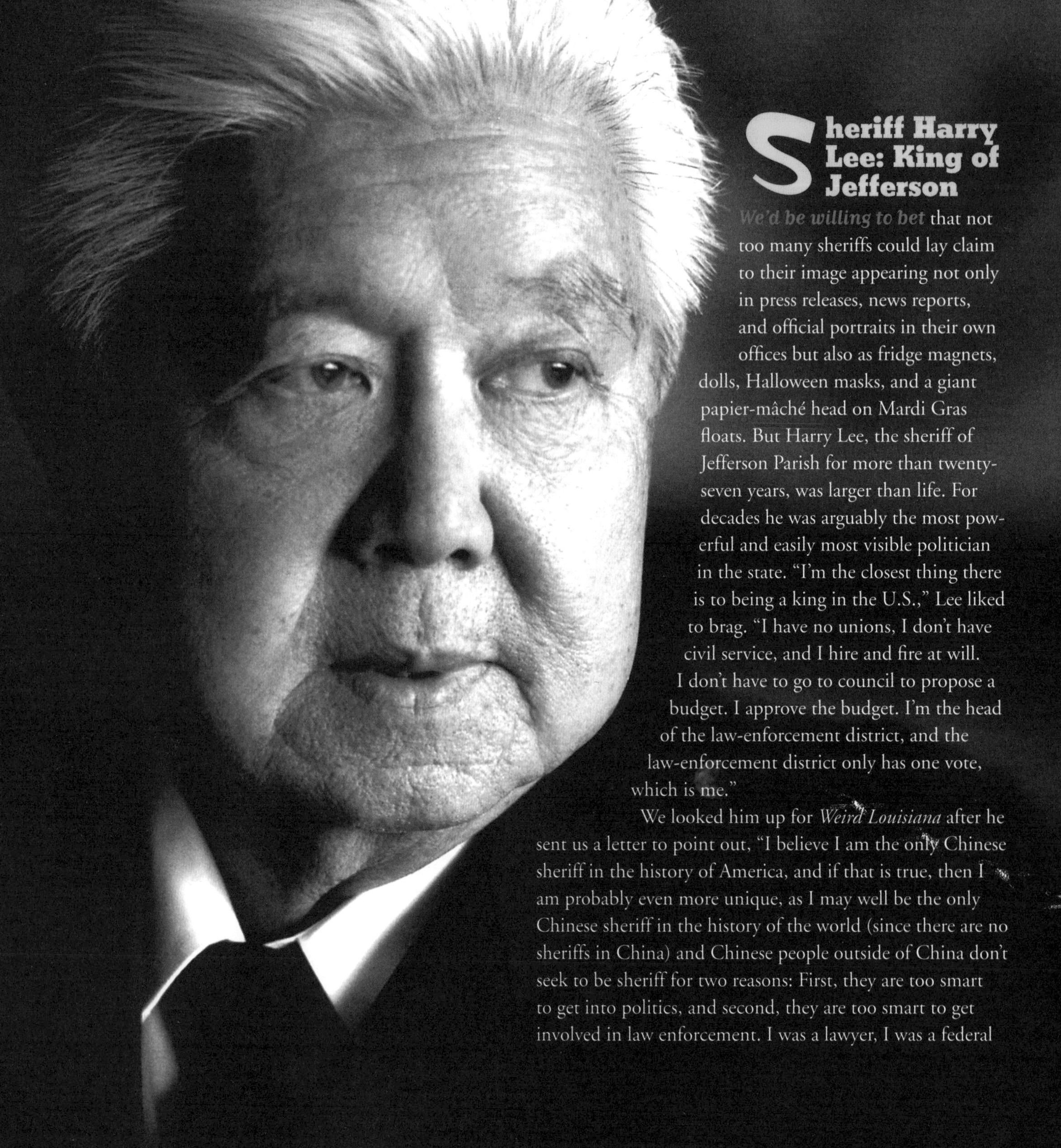

Sheriff Harry Lee: King of Jefferson

We'd be willing to bet that not too many sheriffs could lay claim to their image appearing not only in press releases, news reports, and official portraits in their own offices but also as fridge magnets, dolls, Halloween masks, and a giant papier-mâché head on Mardi Gras floats. But Harry Lee, the sheriff of Jefferson Parish for more than twenty-seven years, was larger than life. For decades he was arguably the most powerful and easily most visible politician in the state. "I'm the closest thing there is to being a king in the U.S.," Lee liked to brag. "I have no unions, I don't have civil service, and I hire and fire at will. I don't have to go to council to propose a budget. I approve the budget. I'm the head of the law-enforcement district, and the law-enforcement district only has one vote, which is me."

We looked him up for *Weird Louisiana* after he sent us a letter to point out, "I believe I am the only Chinese sheriff in the history of America, and if that is true, then I am probably even more unique, as I may well be the only Chinese sheriff in the history of the world (since there are no sheriffs in China) and Chinese people outside of China don't seek to be sheriff for two reasons: First, they are too smart to get into politics, and second, they are too smart to get involved in law enforcement. I was a lawyer, I was a federal magistrate and I was dumb enough to give up a law practice and a Federal Judgeship to chase crooks! On April 2, 2008, I will be the longest serving sheriff in the history of Jefferson Parish."

Unfortunately he didn't live long enough to break that record. We met him just three days before he passed away (he died October 1, 2007), but even then he was still making plans for the future, including erecting a giant flag memorial to the World Trade Center victims of 9/11, to be offered by Greater New Orleans (including money from his own political war chest, which he raised at his annual "Chinese Cajun Cowboy Fais Do Do"—the biggest political party event in the state). He wanted to do it because "New Orleans and New York are the only two cities in the country to experience such tragic loss of life in the twenty-first century so far." Had he lived, he stood to win an eighth term in office.

"If my choice is lying to you or offending you, I'm going to offend you, because you can forgive me for offending you, but you cannot forgive me for lying to you." —Sheriff Harry Lee

Lee's outspoken leadership style was controversial—Lee was pro-choice and a staunch supporter of gay rights—leading some to find his positions too liberal. Others thought he was "to the right of Attila the Hun," especially after encouraging his officers to practice racial profiling by stopping blacks who were seen driving through predominantly white neighborhoods. He eventually managed to overcome the calls for his resignation by saying, "It's difficult for somebody to accuse me of being a racist. When I was a kid, I was called a chink."

Despite stepping on toes on both sides of the political divide, Lee handily won reelection time and time again, because he spoke his mind. He could often be offensive but was so candid the public never had to guess where he stood, even making his last will and testament a public document. "If my choice is lying to you or offending you, I'm going to offend you," he liked to say, "because you can forgive me for offending you, but you cannot forgive me for lying to you." Sheriff Lee never let his high-profile job determine who he could be a friend with, preferring outspoken or reckless people like himself—from Mafia bosses to Willie Nelson—over more careful politicos. "I told Willie not to smoke pot around me, that's all."

Lee was born in 1932 in the back room of his family's laundry on Carondelet Street in New Orleans and grew up working in the laundry and, later, in his father's Chinese restaurant. After high school he was an oil-field roustabout, then majored in geology at LSU. Eleven years later he attended law school and launched a career in law and politics. As a politician, he maintained the highest approval rating of any officeholder in the history of the state. When recent polls showed him still holding an 87 percent rating, he muttered, "How did I piss off 13 percent?"

Ho Lotta Shakin' Going On

After little more than a century in existence, the town of Ferriday in Concordia Parish has grown from a railroad stop in 1903 to 3,700 people today and still covers less than two square miles. But a sign on the edge of town states the proud claim that more famous people per square mile have come from Ferriday than any other town in the country.

These include 1963 number-one recording artist Dale Houston; renowned trombone player Leon "Pee Wee" Whittaker; TV journalists Howard K. Smith and Campbell Brown; Brown's dad, former State Sen. Jim Brown; State Sen. Dan Richey; and former Louisiana Secretary of State Al Ater. Also from Ferriday are state Superintendent of Education Shelby M. Jackson, as well as Louisiana House Rep. Rickey L. Nowlin, agribusiness magnate Pete Vegas, and politician Troyce Guice.

The list goes on, but perhaps the best known sons of Ferriday are three talented piano players whose mothers were sisters. Country-and-western star Mickey Gilley, rock-and-roll star Jerry Lee Lewis, and Pentecostal televangelist Jimmy Swaggart are all first cousins and all nearly the same age.

Fate hasn't always been easy on the three cousins, and sometimes it's become star-crossed. While Mickey Gilley may have been spared—he was born just across the river in Natchez, Mississippi—scandal seems to have dogged both Lewis and Swaggart. Lewis was still technically married to his first wife when he married his second (the divorce only became final two weeks later), and later, when the news broke that his third wife was not only a cousin (first cousin once removed) but also just thirteen when they married, it almost derailed his career.

Jimmy Swaggart was riding a tidal wave of success as the nation's leading television preacher. After nearly thirty years in the pancake-makeup pulpit, Swaggart commanded an evangelistic empire that was one of Baton Rouge's largest employers, producing an eponymous TV show carried on hundreds of stations and seen by millions of viewers worldwide. A church with a four-thousand-member congregation, a religious tract factory, a music-recording studio, a film and television facility, and the Jimmy Swaggart Bible College (JSBC) were all part of the enterprise, which generated income of some $500,000 a day.

Not long after JSBC opened, Swaggart attacked some of his rival ministers in the Assemblies of God, accusing one of a sexual entanglement with a member of his congregation and the other of paying off a woman to keep secret her allegations of rape. In retaliation, one of them hired a detective to track Swaggart, who was photographed in the incriminating company of a prostitute at the Texas Motel in Metairie. When the photos reached the leaders of the Assemblies of God, and then the media, Swaggart's broadcasting empire began to implode. After he was suspended from appearing on his regular programs, he delivered a tearful apology to the world from the studios in his worship center.

Even with the suspension and apology, he was soon back on TV. The Assemblies of God revoked his credentials and ministerial license, but he continued to preach. Despite his pleas of penitence, however, it was not long before he was caught in another indiscretion with another prostitute, this time in California, by the California Highway Patrol. His son Donnie, also a televangelist, then announced that Swaggart would be taking a break from his televised ministries to focus on "healing and counseling," although his salary would continue to be roughly $350,000 a year.

The Swaggarts' broadcasting activities continue today and remain highly profitable, although they are much diminished from their heyday in the late 1980s. Meanwhile the famed Texas Motel seems to be doing as well as it ever did at the junction of Metairie Road and Airline Highway in Metairie.

Blonde Bombshell

You won't find any historic markers, but if you're lucky you may find a treasure if you drive out Chef Menteur Highway or Gentilly Road east of New Orleans and then take old Highway 90 beyond Greens Ditch toward Fort Pike. Roughly in the vicinity of the fort, where the road swerves twice, is the site where thirty-four-year-old movie star Jayne Mansfield met her grisly end at 2:25 A.M. the morning of June 29, 1967.

Early reports said that Mansfield's head had been "crushed," but she'd actually been decapitated when her long blond hair got tangled in the folding mechanism of the convertible's windshield. According to some reports, it took a few days before the actress's head was located, and there had been some fear meanwhile that rubberneckers arriving early on the scene might have found it and kept it as a bizarre souvenir.

She was on her way to New Orleans from an appearance at the Gus Stevens Supper Club on the beach in Biloxi, where she'd put on an eleven P.M. show, when the driver of Gus Stevens's 1966 Buick Electra was momentarily blinded by insecticide fog from a mosquito spray truck. The car slammed into the back of an eighteen-wheeler. Mansfield, her boyfriend/attorney Samuel Brody, and twenty-year-old driver Ronald Harrison were all killed. Her three children and three of the four Chihuahuas traveling with them survived the crash because they were lying down asleep on the backseat.

A few souvenirs from the crash may still be worth finding. Parts of a diamond bracelet worth $10,000 (in 1967 dollars) that Mansfield had been wearing were found wedged in the engine block of the wrecked car, although not all of the diamonds were recovered. Also, the earrings she had been seen wearing were never found and may still be lurking among the shards of broken glass along the highway or lost in the muck on the bottom of the canal.

Personalized Properties

Four-leaf clovers are thought to be lucky because they're so unusual compared to the typical three-leaf type. Some coin collectors value mis-strikes more than perfect coins because they're rare, and certain stamp collectors pay big money for misprinted stamps because they're different. It's their differences that make them special.

In Louisiana, there are individuals who stand out because of their differences, too. People who aren't satisfied to follow the herd but had to take things a few steps farther—and sometimes quite a few steps farther! People who covered their houses in painted concrete, surrounded themselves with driftwood, built their dreams out of chicken wire. . . . Take a look at this chapter and maybe you'll start to see what we mean—to each his own.

Folk Art Zone

At Algiers Point, facing the levee just across the Mississippi River from New Orleans's Lower Ninth Ward, is a fenced-in cluster of houses and a trailer collectively known as Charles Gillam Sr.'s "Folk Art Zone." Murals, concrete head sculptures, paintings, carvings in driftwood and tree stumps, assemblages of found objects, bas-reliefs of corrugated metal—taken together, they suggest a man whose creative spirit knows no limits.

Gillam's art is organic, a natural outgrowth of the way he's lived his life. Born in the mid-1940s just outside Alexandria, when he was five years old, his large family moved to the Lower Ninth Ward. By the age of ten he was shining shoes in the French Quarter and spending what free time he had on Dryades Street. It was there that young Gillam was inaugurated into the local folk art scene. He watched artist Willie White draw bold compositions with paints and markers on poster boards and learned how to cast plaster from a Dutch immigrant named Johnny Cash. Inspired by their ability to create art from readily available materials, Gillam realized he could earn money by making jewelry from scrap metal and other found objects, so he continued scouring the streets for items to use in small assemblages he could sell. Fights and arguments often interrupted what little time he spent at home with his father, who drank, womanized, and lived the kind of life celebrated in songs by bluesmen like Robert Johnson and Roosevelt Sykes.

At eighteen, Gillam joined the army and went to Vietnam, returning to the United States barely in time to try to reconcile with his father before he passed away. For years after his father's death, Gillam struggled to find balance in his life. He drifted into associations with the Black Panthers and the Rastafari movement and also tried and failed at marriage. It was only when he rediscovered his art that he started to settle down. In his forties he remarried, bought a small house at 207 LeBoeuf Street in Algiers, and began transforming it into what he calls The House

of Bluesmen. Lining the walls of the house are painted bas-relief portraits of musical heroes like W. C. Handy, Smiley Lewis, Scott Joplin, and Ernie K-Doe, while decorations made from Mardi Gras beads, vinyl record albums, and painted driftwood pepper the areas around the house. The yard is filled with more statues and monuments dedicated to the musicians he admired, from Son House and T-Bone Walker to Louis Armstrong and Professor Long Hair.

Gillam's inspiration knew no bounds, but unfortunately, he ran out of space long before running out of ideas. There was only one thing to do: He acquired buildings around his house. Charles Smith, a friend and fellow artist, bought an adjacent house and together they began calling the site the Folk Art Zone, created for the purpose of generating positive creative experiences in what was then a violent and drug-ridden neighborhood. And it looks like Gillam's efforts have paid off.

The Doctor Is Finally In

The Rev. Dr. Charles Smith's life has finally come full circle. It took well over thirty years and more than a few relocations—but Smith has settled happily in his Hammond home, about an hour or so north of New Orleans, where he was born in 1940. He moved with his family to Illinois in 1955 after his father's death and married in 1964. After working a few odd jobs, he was drafted into the U.S. Marine Corps to fight in Vietnam from 1966 to 1968. Many of his friends didn't return from the war, but Smith made it back to the United States with a Purple Heart for a battlefield injury, chronic illness due to toxic exposure to Agent Orange, and a major case of post-traumatic stress disorder. After struggling through several difficult years that included a divorce, Smith eventually retrained to become a rehab counselor for the visually impaired and successfully pursued that career until a 1985 back injury forced him into unemployment.

It was then that he discovered his true calling. "God led me to art," he says. A year later he began building an environment in Aurora, Illinois, called the African American Heritage Museum and Black Veterans Archive. The first of several such environments he has built, the museum included hundreds of painted concrete sculptures surrounding a small building and illustrating the history of the African diaspora in the New World. Scenes depicted the institution of slavery, the heroes of emancipation and civil rights (from Dred Scott to Emmett Till and Rodney King), and eventually his experiences in Vietnam. When a feud with the local government forced his museum to close in 1999, the John Michael Kohler Foundation acquired 448 of the more than 600 sculptures in the site but moved them to Sheboygan, Wisconsin, effectively saving the works but failing to save their environment.

Smith then had the idea of spreading the story of Afro-America down the Interstate 55 corridor that stretches from Chicago to New Orleans. This vision included contributing works to museums and cultural institutions along the way but eventually led to collaboration with fellow self-taught artist Charles Gillam on the construction of Gillam's Folk Art Zone in Algiers. However, in time, Smith felt a more urgent need to expand beyond Gillam's localized focus on the music and traditions of Greater New Orleans and decided to build another personal environment that could better express his own interests in the larger sweep of the entire African American experience. He headed across Lake Pontchartrain, bought a piece of property near Hammond, and began building another massive collection of sculptures. Unfortunately more problems with neighbors eventually forced yet another relocation, which he hopes will be the last. Smith has recently disassembled the entire new environment, has moved all the sculptures to another site within Hammond, and has begun the task of reorganizing the scenes and events to fit their new location. So far, his presence seems to be welcomed by his latest neighbors.

Smith remains cheerful and philosophical about the relocations. "Anyway, each time I rebuild the place, it gets better," he says. "I get a better understanding of how one thing led to another in our African history, and then I get better at how to tell the story, too. I know this is God's way of making my dream come true, and His way of helping me, through all these trials and tribulations, to make what I'm doing a lot more effective each time I do it. But I sure do hope He's getting satisfied now, because I really don't know if I want to do it all over yet again!"

The latest incarnation of Dr. Smith's museum is in East Hammond, on the corner of Walnut and Louisiana Streets. Visitors are very welcomed and, while there is no charge, donations are accepted.

Black Magic

When we asked Craig Black if he minded whether we took any pictures of his private home, he said, "Are you kidding? Be my guest!"

He was right; the house definitely takes a walk on the wild side. In fact, locals refer to it as "that House on 44" whenever they give directions. On Highway 44 a mile or so north of Gonzales in Ascension Parish, Black's house is a landmark you can't possibly miss, and more than a few vehicles have gone into a full skid after coming upon it unexpectedly for the first time. Giant dragonflies, owls, wood spirits, rabbits, and mermaids morph through a swirl of colors into tree roots, spiraling stars, vibrant vegetation, and even the occasional Kilroy (a face peeping over a fence as in, "Kilroy was here"). A self-portrait of Black as the wizard Merlin (or Gandalf) stands in the midst of the chaos. The sculpture represents the artist conjuring up a scene that brings to mind Alice's Wonderland or the enchanted forest of Oz. And if that's not enough, Black keeps things fresh by changing his public exhibits from time to time—the waterfall streaming from the side of the house may be dyed different colors, or the yard may be marked off in gridiron patterns to celebrate major football games.

Born in Gary, Indiana, in 1953, Black had an unassuming upbringing as the son of a chemical plant employee. In his early teens, his family moved to Baton Rouge where his father helped start a polystyrene plant. After marrying at age nineteen, he followed his father into the work, loading trucks and chemicals for BASF Wyandotte. But he hated it, and after his wife, Linda, found work as a secretary in an architect's office, Craig began devoting his spare time to art. Unable to afford canvas or other fine-arts supplies, his first paintings were done on discarded bed sheets stretched over homemade frames.

Linda's father was a tree surgeon who had been hired to treat the old oaks at Houmas House Plantation, several miles south of Gonzales in Darrow. Thanks to connections there, the couple was able to step into the role of caretakers at the plantation, moving into a small dwelling on what was then a run-down estate. (Their residence is now used by visitors as the Bridal Cottage at Houmas House.) In time they managed to set aside just enough money to share the cost of a down payment on what was then another bland roadside bungalow.

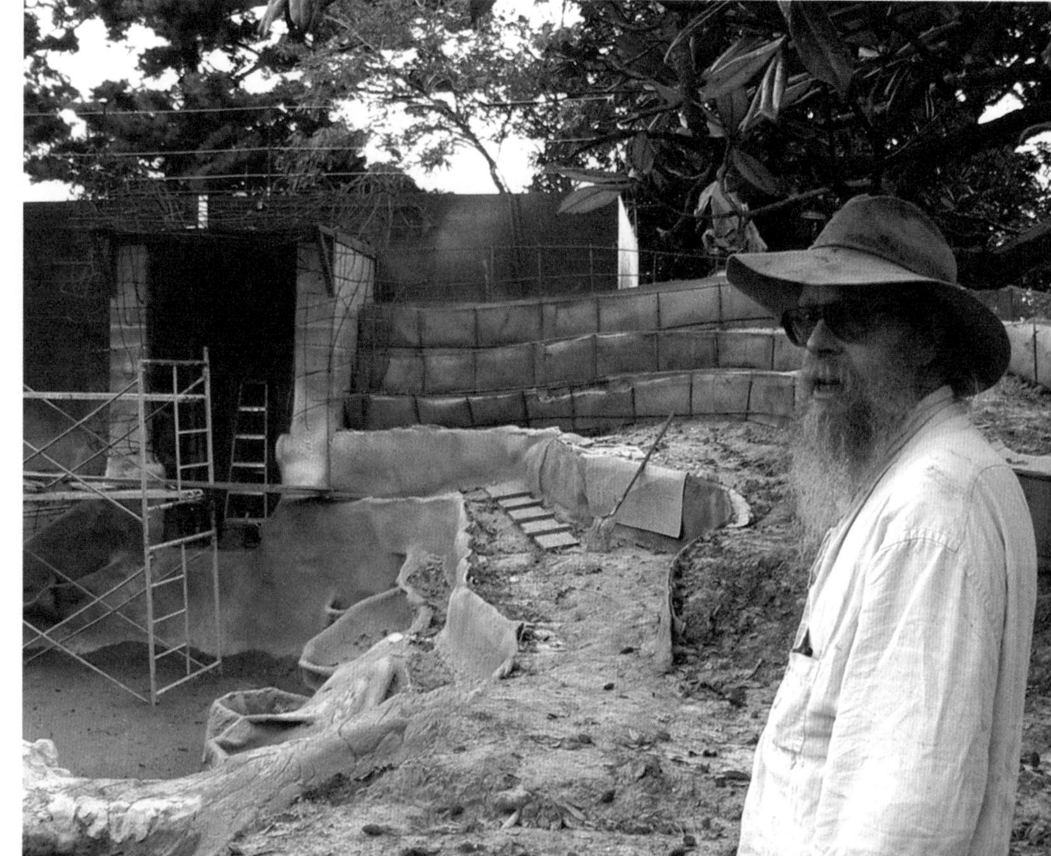

Craig's skills as a natural artist caught the attention of new owners of Houmas House, who offered him a job as chief landscape artist. His first task was to renovate the grounds into a unique wonderland. The job provided a good balance for his artistic bent: At home, Craig can give full vent to his wildest fantasies, experimenting with pigmented concrete and playful figures however he likes, albeit on a small scale, while at the plantation he can work with a much larger budget and grand scale, but in a somewhat more refined way.

Still, the elaborate waterfalls, fountains, pools, temples, pergolas, and other garden features he's been making for Houmas House for the past several years are scarcely out of step with the flamboyant displays created 150 years ago for the great Creole plantations that stretched along the Mississippi. Amazing as his public works at Houmas House already are, Craig still has a way to go before his work catches up with the pagodas, Roman temples, and mock fortresses found in older places like Valcour Aime's Refinery, or before weddings at Houmas House outdo those at Durand's of St. Martinville in terms of sheer ostentation. But at the rate he's going, it won't be long.

Driftwood Patriot

Head all the way down along the bayou toward the dead end of South Bay Road in Pierre Part in Assumption Parish, and you'll eventually come to Adam Morales's property. And how will you know you've arrived? Weirdly shaped cypress knees and eroded fallen branches alongside hundreds of birds, reptiles, soldiers, monsters, religious icons, and political monuments—all fashioned out of driftwood.

Adam has spent his entire life here, never more than fifty feet from water on either side of his property. And since his early retirement about a decade ago, he's been building an artistic empire, expressing his feelings and deeply held beliefs in the form of gray, swirling driftwood. He's got a yard full of the evocative stuff. It spills across the road around his makeshift workshop (also made of driftwood) and in the other direction, out into the swamp that begins just a few yards behind his house. In the front yard a small-scale Noah's ark seems to be guarded by (or else threatened by) an enraged *Tyrannosaurus rex*. A dour-looking Statue of Liberty raises her torch near a flotilla of half-submerged gators, while a scale model of New York's twin-towered World Trade Center stands belatedly protected by driftwood National Guardsmen. A wood replica of the granite Ten Commandments sculpture that Alabama Chief Court Justice Roy Moore installed in the Alabama judicial building (and that got him removed by the federal courts) is prominently displayed as well. Across the road, driftwood marines raise a driftwood flag on Iwo Jima while beyond them Loch Ness–like sea monsters lift out of the water as convincingly authentic looking as some of the photos people claim to have shot in Scotland. Behind the house, seeming to emerge from the swamp under a driftwood arch, are a Spanish-moss-bearded Bigfoot and his equally shaggy mate.

Adam began dabbling in driftwood relatively late in life. For many years he worked as a carpenter until a degenerative arthritic condition developed in his knees and hands. When physicians told him he could no longer pursue his trade, he entered a deep depression. It was during that dark period in his life that Adam discovered his ability to recognize forms and suggestive shapes in pieces of

weathered swamp wood. His spirits and his energy soon returned and the dark cloud began to lift. Adam felt as if his desperate prayers had finally been answered, although in a most unusual way.

When the Mississippi River starts to rise in late February each year and the water level markers in Baton Rouge indicate a depth of twenty-five feet or more, the lakes and swamps around Pierre Part become their most accessible—at least by boat. Adam can shove off from his own dock and go nearly anywhere in the whole Atchafalaya flood zone in search of driftwood. And now that he's been at it for more than a decade, Adam is no longer completely dependent on chance to determine what to make. "Now I know what kind of knot it takes to make a bird head or maybe a fish tail, so if I'm working on a bird and don't have his head or if I need something to finish my fish, I can go out and find just exactly the pieces I need." He especially enjoys heading into the flooded woods at night, "when it's just me, God, and nature all by ourselves. With nothing but my boat and my sealed-beam light in all that dark, I feel closer to God."

Salvation Garden

In 1988 an itinerant brickmason arrived in the tiny Terrebonne Parish town of Chauvin and set up camp in a tent on a rented lot fronting the Bayou Petit Caillou. Quiet and reclusive, Kenny Hill took on short-term bricklaying jobs while building a modest cottage beside his tent. Two years later, additional structures appeared on the property: a garden arranged around nine circular platforms, planted with rosebushes, vines, and banana trees. Concrete angels were soon seen hovering above the shrubbery and statues of Jesus were erected, indicating some kind of religious theme. Then came a four-story lighthouse, covered with full-relief statues of cowboys hoisting a horse, marines raising the flag on Iwo Jima, jazz musicians, slaves, Indians, angels, and eagles.

Everyone in town wondered what was going on, but the brickmason kept mostly to himself. He never entered the local eateries and didn't participate in any community social activities. While he seemed willing enough to ramble on about what each of the more than one hundred figures represented, he offered only the briefest of explanations whenever anyone tried to probe deeper into his motivations. "It's about life," was about all Hill was willing to say about why he felt compelled to sculpt. In time, most folks in Chauvin just shrugged it off with a live-and-let-live attitude. It seemed harmless, or even inspiring.

Delicate slender angels made of painted concrete formed over wire armatures seemed to float effortlessly above figures of suffering people, gently guiding and helping them toward salvation. People collapsing beneath the burdens of their lives were lifted up while their sins were washed away. Figures of Kenny Hill himself could be found among them, on horseback, bearing his own cross, or sometimes blinded or painted half black and half white to suggest a deep, personal conflict. Images of nine disks, representing planets or constellations, seemed to refer both to the universe and to the nine circular scenes of the garden itself, but no one knew for sure what they meant.

By late 1999, as the end of the millennium approached, the formerly quiet and self-sufficient brickmason showed signs of distress. Neighbors witnessed fits of anger and erratic behavior. Hill quit working, owed money for the first time, and allowed rampant weeds to overtake the property. Landlords came to collect rent and Hill refused to pay, threatening violence when he was told he'd soon have to come up with the money or leave. In January of 2000, Hill knocked the head off one of the Jesus figures, walked out of town, and disappeared. He hasn't been seen since.

Some locals think Hill is living in the woods in Arkansas, while others say he hopped freights to head west. There have been reports that he suffered from medical problems that left him with amnesia and that he may be languishing somewhere in a mental institution. Authorities finally entered his cottage in search of clues relating to his whereabouts and found these words, painted in red letters over the kitchen sink: HELL IS HERE. WELCOME.

Very little is known about Hill's life before he moved to Chauvin, although a few facts did emerge following his disappearance. He was born about sixty miles away in Patterson in 1950. When he was twenty, he married a fourteen-year-old girl who gave birth to three children while he worked as a bricklayer. There is no record that he ever attended school in Patterson, and the spelling that appears on some of the circular bases of his figures suggests that his education was limited. One of several self-portraits standing in the garden is mounted on a base that reads, IT IS EMTY. The figure is of Hill, clutching his own bleeding heart.

When it became clear that Hill had left town for good, the lot was put up for sale. The sculptures and their environment remained in danger of demolition until Dennis Siporski, the chair of the art department at Nicholls State University (about thirty miles north of Chauvin), brought the site to the attention of the Kohler Foundation of Wisconsin, dedicated to art preservation. Purchasing and preserving Hill's environment was the foundation's first major project outside its home state. In partnership with the university, Kohler made it possible to stabilize the site, and clean and seal all the figures. The foundation funded a reinforced wall along the bayou banks to reduce erosion and constructed a new building across the road to host visiting artists, scholars, and art conservators.

What Kenny Hill would make of all this is anyone's guess. When he still lived there, he avoided social interaction so much that most of the locals never spoke with him. He rarely allowed anyone to photograph the site and shunned attention so much, they say, that once when a magazine ran a picture of a boat he'd built, he destroyed it. No one seems to know where he went, whether he'll ever return, or even if he's still alive.

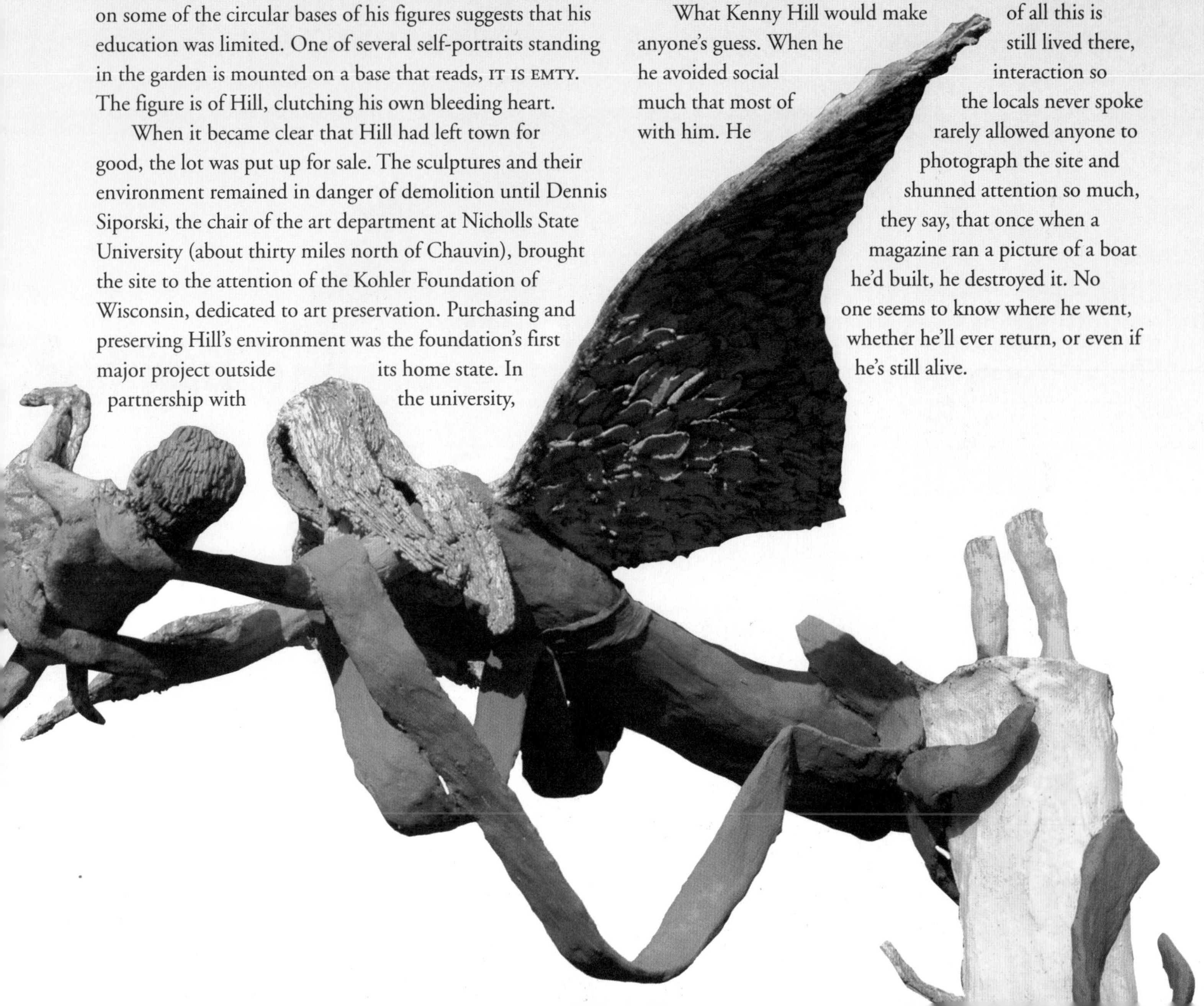

Mr. Rogers's New Sanctum

We've all heard the old saying that one person's trash is another person's treasure, right? Well, in the case of Frank Rogers, his penchant for finding treasures in other people's trash ultimately landed him in court engaged in a long, heated debate with his former neighbors near Arnaudville.

Rogers transformed his quarter-acre property into what admirers dubbed "Mr. Rogers's Outer Sanctum." The lot was divided up into outdoor "rooms" or activity areas where items like milk jugs, bottles, toys, old computers, abandoned television sets, bones, plants, and beads were carefully arranged and organized to highlight themes of special interest to Rogers. It was a kind of open-air time capsule,

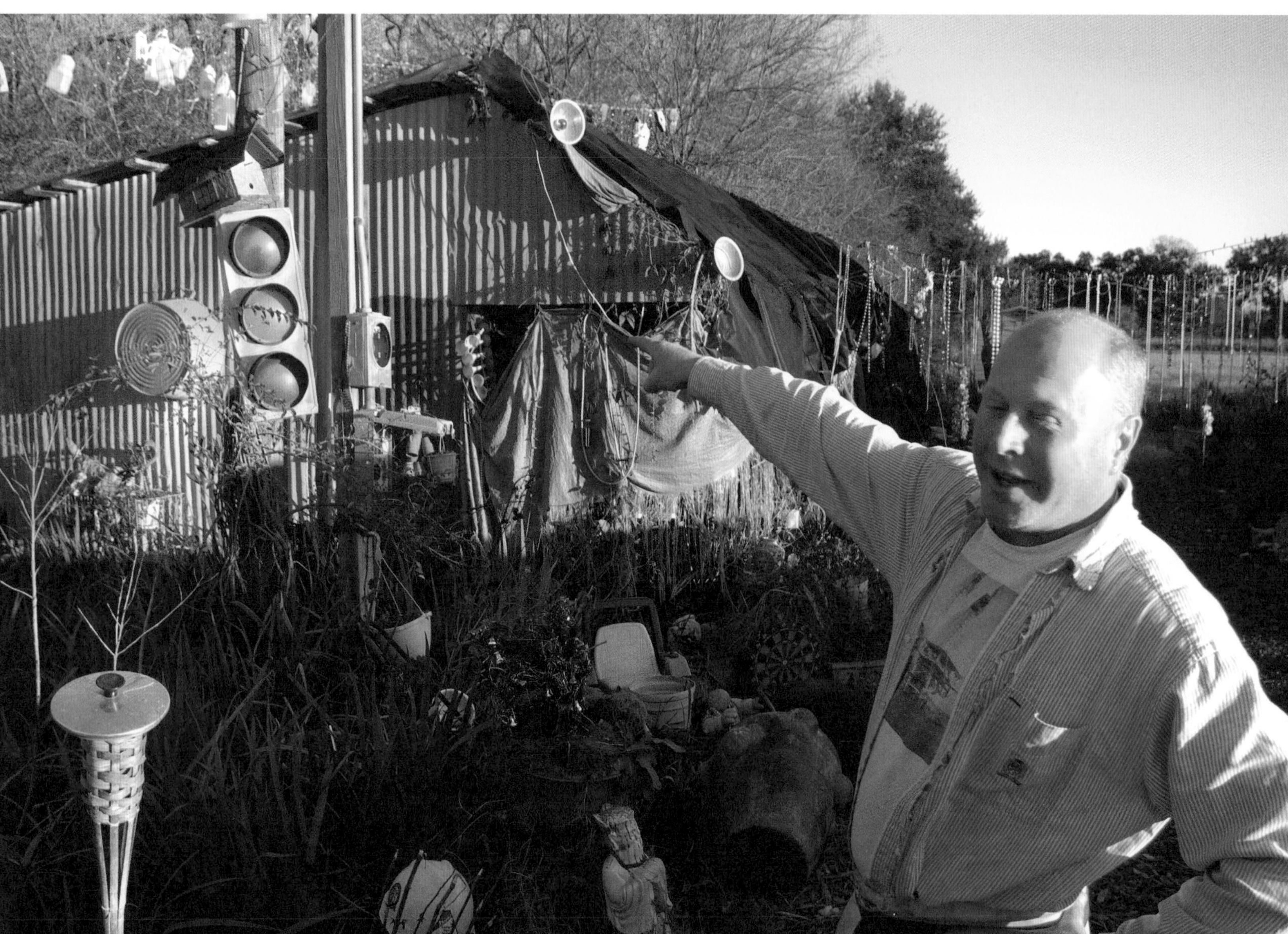

the kind of place that archaeologists of the future would dream of stumbling upon. Sadly, neighbors who bought into what subsequently became a "gated community" were less than thrilled to find themselves living next door to such a curious collector—TVs, computers, lawnmowers, kitchen appliances, and various other items were displayed prominently in Rogers's front yard. And although he was one of the first people to build in the area, money talked, and eventually he was served with a court order to downsize his collection. He had no interest in trashing his treasures, so he relocated instead.

Rogers's new sanctum is far away from his nearest neighbors, out in the country between Pitreville and Savoy. He's just getting started on the reconstruction, and although he wasn't able to move everything to the new site before the dump trucks arrived, he promises one day the new sanctum will be every bit as grand as his former digs. Serendipitously, he discovered that the new property is along the route of a major flight corridor, so plans are already afoot to create a display that will boggle the minds of airline passengers who happen to look down at just the right moment. Rogers has already sketched off (with a mower) the patterns and layout; what remains now is only to fill them in. "It'll be a gift to the sky," he says.

Before beginning the original Outer Sanctum, Rogers had worked for a number of years as a long-line commercial fisherman, shrimper, crabber, truck driver, and, until a work-related back injury forced him into early retirement, a supplier servicing offshore drilling rigs. The walls of his house are lined with snapshots of the rigs he used to visit. Some day, he hopes, a museum like the Smithsonian will acquire his photos and curious collection of the stuff of modern life. But for now, he's happy fulfilling his own version of the American Dream as a living example of "more is more."

Peniston Street's Mysterious Artist

Walking on Peniston Street in New Orleans between Loyola and Saratoga it's hard not to notice the pair of lavishly decorated houses. An embellished tree growing out of the sidewalk between the two homes—dubbed a "Mississippi Pine Tree"—holds bird decoys, bottles, and Mardi Gras beads. Chimney vents have been turned into dazzling crowns that spin in the wind to provide a bit of movement among the many linear feet of architectural ironwork.

The houses stand side by side and the cohesiveness of the designs suggests the same artist worked on both, and yet, none of the locals we spoke with was willing to divulge the artist's identity. It could be that several artists contributed decorative elements, but we just don't know. When the *Weird Louisiana* team tried calling the owners of the houses, we were told, "No one painted them, no one decorated them. They've always been the way they are now." Perhaps they thought we were from a municipal commission, bent only on making everyone conform to some kind of strict building code. Meanwhile, neighbors eyed us suspiciously. One man responded to our inquiries with, "I know who did it, but I won't tell you. This is New Orleans. You can't be asking something like that."

"No one painted them, no one decorated them. They've always been the way they are now."

We're unable to thank and credit the artist in these pages, but at least we're left with the exuberant and playful work itself, which provides a bright dash of gold and glitter in the midst of a neighborhood that clearly suffered during the Katrina disaster. We can only hope that if enough people admire these brilliant additions to the city's eye candy, eventually the artist will come out of hiding. Such spirited creators deserve our deepest appreciation, whoever they are.

Artistico

The "Libra Patriarch Prophet Lord Archbishop Apostle Visionary Mystic Saint" Royal Robertson and Adell Brent were married for nineteen years and had eleven children together before their relationship soured and the couple separated in the mid 1970s. The breakup apparently pushed Robertson, who was rather eccentric to begin with, over the edge. With paintbrush and plywood he turned his entire front yard, along with all the exterior and interior surfaces of his house, into one massive cry of blame, warning, and protest—a bitter blast of fury that eventually reached near-biblical proportions in an environment he labeled "Artistico." The former professional sign painter turned his lettering skills to the task of making sure that all who passed his property in Baldwin (St. Mary Parish) knew his feelings about his former beloved, in no uncertain terms. Women like Adell, he claimed, were vipers, demons, harlots, and monsters who deserved only to be consumed in tidal waves of fire. Apparently hell hath no fury like a prophet scorned in his own land.

Over time, the content of Robertson's signs crossed over into the realm of science fiction. Imagining himself the focus of an interplanetary female conspiracy, Robertson claimed to have gotten in touch with alien beings that supported his misogynistic campaign against adultery, fornication, lust, and the women who made such sins possible. He painted highly detailed scenes of futuristic cities filled with Amazon women (Adell among them) warring with spaceships and flying saucers, created calendars and numerological charts that merged personal events from the marriage with predictions of the end-time, and drew diagrams connecting deception, faithlessness, and treacherous female behaviors with patterns revealed by astrology and prophecy. In due time, he predicted, the hurricanes of hell would exact their revenge on such evildoers as his ex-wife.

Unfortunately the hurricanes of reality struck first. In 1992 Hurricane Andrew flattened his home and all its signage. After that, Robertson was a calmer, more chastened man, much less consumed by blame and anger as he focused only on rebuilding and recovery. He had even begun reconciling with some of his estranged children when, in 1997, he suddenly died. We don't know how the news struck Adell, or even if she was still alive when he passed away—but if she was, she probably breathed a sigh of relief, knowing that the storm was finally over.

Steamboat Style

Two of the oddest houses in New Orleans stand near the levee at the end of Egania Street in the Lower Ninth Ward. Locally known as the old "Steamboat Houses," they were built by retired riverboat captain Milton P. Doullut. The first was erected between 1905 and 1913 and the second, for his son Paul, soon followed. Each sits on a small mound of earth intended to compensate for their position below the water level of the nearby Mississippi River. In fact, they are best seen from midriver, where the portholes, cupolas, and smokestacks sticking up over the levee provide the illusion of two old paddle wheelers docked on the far side. Like many of the self-taught artists mentioned elsewhere in this book, Captain Doullut only wanted to create a place where he could feel "at home." After decades spent in tiny pilothouses atop big steamboats, Doullut built his home at the top of the vessel, where he could look out for what was coming around the next bend.

Beadmobile

Crowds lining the streets along Mardi Gras parade routes often get caught up in what some have referred to as "bead greed." People clamber up on ladders, wave signs and flags, or even occasionally offer a quick glimpse of forbidden flesh to elicit plastic beads or other "throws" from float riders.

Once the parades have passed, you'll often spot partied-out revelers staggering home bearing volumes of colorful trinkets. This begs the question: What in the world do they plan to do with all of that shiny stuff? Some of it will end up draped over fences, gates, and shrubbery for that inimitable yearlong Mardi Gras look. Some will find its way to the bottom of fish tanks as a substitute for aquarium gravel, and some will be thriftily redistributed at next year's pre-Lenten debaucheries. But most of the bits and bobs, we suspect, are headed for the local landfill.

Alton Osborn of New Orleans has found a crafty way to recycle those tossed-away trinkets. A few years' worth of hard-earned catches covers his older-model Caddy in a dazzling display of mosaic mastery. Silicone caulk is the secret, and since the molded-on-thread beading comes already spaced at the appropriate intervals, it's a relatively easy technique to lay down a strip of caulk and then press the beads into it as desired. The difficulty is in coming up with a good design and choosing the colors—but jazz and Mardi Gras themes are always appropriate to the material.

Giving your old beater a face-lift using discarded Mardi Gras beads isn't just fun, it's also eco-friendly! You're not only helping keep beads out of landfills, you're also preventing rust (and the need for repainting), and the shiny surfaces and trapped air inside the individual beads actually helps insulate your vehicle. This means it'll need less air-conditioning in the summer and less heat in winter, which translates into a big savings on gas. With all that extra mileage, anyone who takes up auto body beading will be able to ride in style farther and longer in their shiny new beadmobile—while giving a new meaning to the old expression, "I'll be there in a flash."

The Unifier

Percy Taplet's Unifiers barbershop, at the corner of Pauger Street and North Claiborne Avenue in New Orleans, is a shrine to African-American history. Inside the shop, clippings, paintings, and old photographs documenting the African diaspora cover nearly every available surface, vying for any remaining space with price lists for, and drawings of, the various kinds of cuts that Taplet offers along with his spoken philosophy.

Outside, his paintings put an African spin on subjects like scenes from the life of Christ, the construction of the pyramids, and daily living with a kinder, gentler attitude toward one's brothers. That's pretty important in the part of town where he's situated: The little barbershop is a visual/historical vortex as well as an island of relative calm in what can, at times, be a rough neighborhood. By offering his steady, unifying voice to both clients and the street, Taplet has become one of the many unsung heroes of our country.

ALL TOURIST GET 1 FREE MARDI GRAS BEADS
FREE BEADS FOR TOURISTS
BROCHURES
192 LA 74 807
LOUISIANA 73

Roadside Oddities

Roadside Americana can be a trip, especially when you know where to look! We're not talking about the beaten path, where six or eight national fast-food franchises, Big Oil outlets, and the same old rest stops break up the highway scenery. *Weird Louisiana* is here to remind you that the journey *is* the trip. Off the main roads, away from heavily trafficked multilane thruways, the journey gets a whole lot trippy-er. So come wander on the weird side and let us point out a few diversions that will help make your next trip a little . . . different.

Airheaded Justice

In front of the new federal courthouse in downtown Lafayette are two colossal heads representing the spirit of justice. Often depicted as a blindfolded toga-clad woman wielding a sword (for punishment and retribution) in one hand and scales (for weighing evidence and seeking balance) in the other, the sculptures are usually assumed to be the ancient goddess of justice.

However, the ancient symbols of jurisprudence were never depicted or described as blindfolded or even vision impaired. The blindfold was reserved for Fortuna, the Roman goddess of luck. There were almost never any swords or scales, either. The Greeks often portrayed the concept of justice by showing the beautiful goddess Dike (Fairness) choking and beating her unattractive counterpart Adikia (Unfairness) with a large stick, while the Roman goddess of justice, Iustitia, held an olive twig, a scepter, and a ceremonial wine cup; she was also bare breasted. It's not so hard to see why some of our more puritanical forebears had a little trouble with these depictions and decided to come up with something new. Cobbling together a new image with different gear and a higher neckline, they created a symbol that better reflected their own worldview.

The new giant heads in Lafayette suggest that images of justice and power are still evolving and that they are androgynous, blind, and brainless.

Gossiping Gator

Ponchatoula's roadside gator, Old Blue Eyes, has the gift of gab—and he's got a weekly column in the *Ponchatoula Times* to prove it. That's right, the gossiping gator observes town residents from the comfort of his cage in the heart of downtown, and then his reports are published in the town's newspaper.

Camp Street Lighthouse

A lighthouse stands proudly on Camp Street in downtown New Orleans, near the intersection with Julia Street. Far from any shoals, rocky promontories, or coastal hazards, the tower was built in 1922 as the headquarters of Lighthouse for the Blind, a nonprofit serving the blind and visually impaired. Although the organization has since relocated and a company dealing in glass now occupies the unusual structure, it still attracts attention, at least from anyone who can see it.

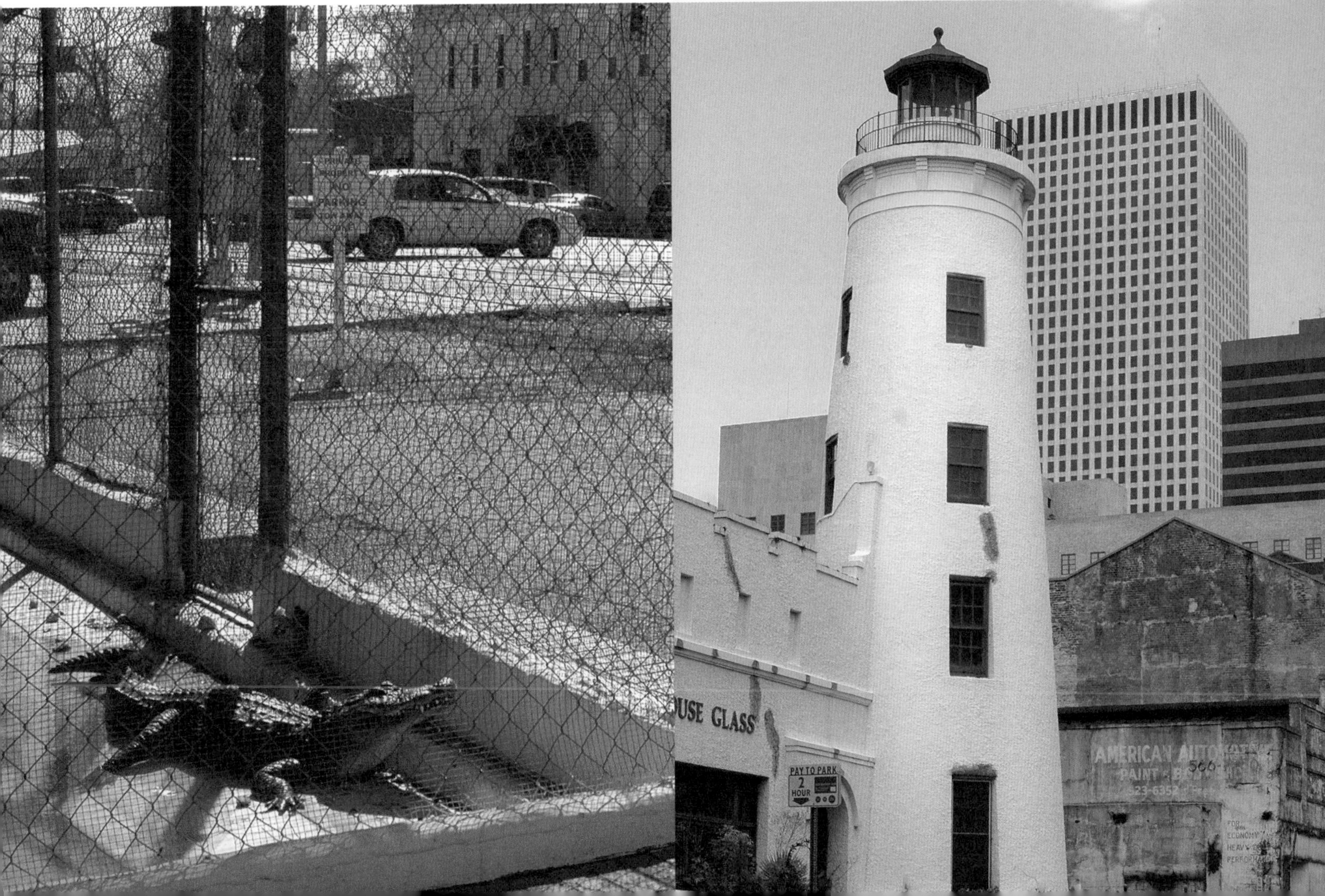

Greener Grass, Yum!

Sometimes the grass really *is* greener, taller, and tastier on the other side of the fence. At least that's what this bull, mounted at the entrance to a farm near the village of Longstreet, seems to suggest.

Sign of the Past

According to locals we spoke with, at one time the forbidding message embedded in the sidewalk along St. Claude Avenue in New Orleans near the bridge over to the Lower Ninth Ward read STOP! DON'T GO ANY FURTHER. They explained that this was the site of a ballroom that allowed only whites inside for dancing. A vestige from the painful days of segregation, the sign set a strict limit on how close blacks could get to the ballroom's doors.

Car Parts Critters

If you're in the New Orleans area, head to 4031 St. Claude Avenue. Just across the bridge from the hardest-hit part of the Ninth Ward stands a group of welded metal creatures that survived the worst of Hurricane Katrina.

Moulton's Mammoth Instruments

Music, as anyone can tell you, is a really big deal throughout Cajun country. And it doesn't get much bigger than the supersized structures in front of Mouton's Accordions. About four miles north of Crowley on Highway 13 heading toward Eunice, amidst the crawfish and rice fields, are two mammoth musical instruments: a bright red accordion and an electric guitar dressed up in red, white, and blue. Mouton's has been crafting authentic Cajun accordions for more than forty years, and the store also sells traditional Cajun gifts and music.

Colossal Cans of Syrup

The world's largest cans of cane syrup—a staple of Cajun and Creole cooking—are lined up on Main Street in downtown Abbeville. Each is a replica of the C. S. Steen Syrup Mill's regular twenty-five-ounce can but holds 85,412 times as much of the sugary solution. Together, the three giant cans contain enough syrup to generously slather more than eight and a half million pancakes.

Sometimes there can be too much of a good thing, though. In mid-September 1911, a tank filled with molasses (cane syrup from which the sugar crystals have been extracted) burst in New Orleans, flooding the area around Market Street with 600,000 gallons of goo three feet deep. For weeks afterward, clouds of flies plagued the city, and citizens reported feeling nauseated by the sickeningly sweet smell.

The problem only got worse when millions of fish, shrimp, and crabs died after the syrup reached Lake Pontchartrain. The lake was described by the *New York Times* as looking "like a great sheet of white paper" as a result of the pale, densely packed corpses of fish floating belly-up in the lake, while residents along the shore found the stench unbearable.

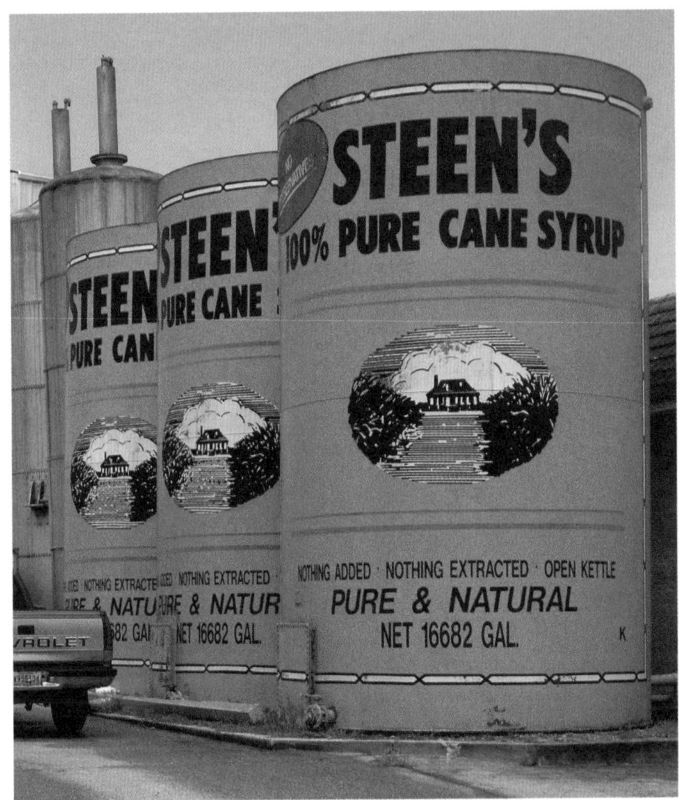

Death by Molasses

The spill in New Orleans is nothing compared to the Great Boston Molasses Disaster that took place just after World War 1 and devastated a large part of the city. A tank in Boston's North End neighborhood burst on January 15, 1919, sending a fifteen-foot wave of Louisiana molasses roaring through the streets at 35 mph, sweeping buildings, bridges, and trains out of its path and drowning twenty-one people, along with numerous horses and domestic pets. The waist-deep gunk took months to clean up and stained the harbor brown for most of the rest of the year. North End residents claim you can still smell molasses at the site of the spill on hot summer afternoons.

Man Bites Gator

Driving on the east side of Highway 1 a few miles northwest of Natchitoches, it's hard to miss the sign for Bayou Pierre Alligator Park—a retired yellow schoolbus painted to look like an alligator, complete with teeth under the hood. The sign points the way to the five-acre park that's home to hundreds of gators.

Watch as park staff entices a thousand-pound gator to catch its dinner in midair during Big Al's Feeding Show, or take a stroll through the Marsh, a natural alligator habitat with four half-acre ponds. If you're in the mood to get up close and personal, you can even pet and feed some of the smaller gators. Of course it goes without saying (but we'll say it anyway), touching or feeding the gators is only allowed under the supervision of the park's specially trained staff.

But wait, there's more. The park is also an authentic Cajun countryside hangout offering up local music and plenty of Cajun fare. After a long day of gator gazing, head over to the Gator Bites Snack Shop and sample some of the finest in alligator cuisine. Menu offerings include alligator kabobs, spicy alligator sausage, and alligator crunch pie. If you're not game for gator meat, try the Natchitoches meat pies, a favorite among locals.

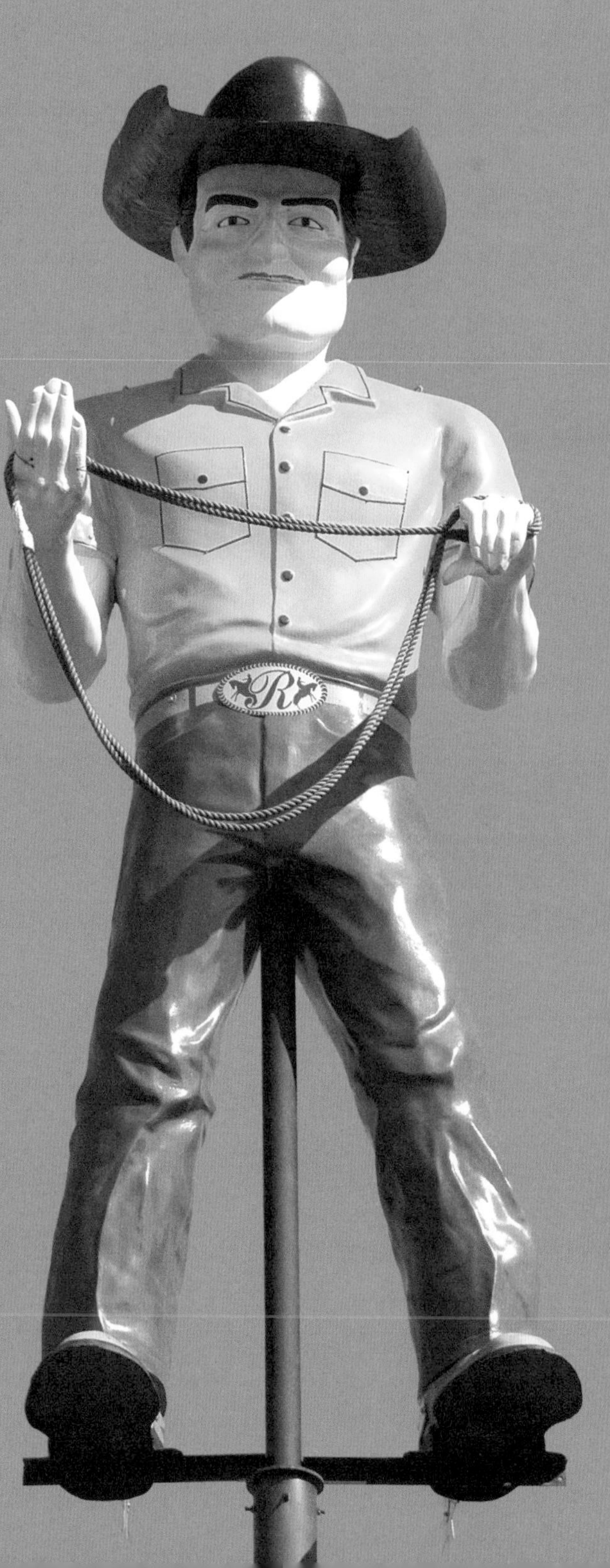

Giant Cowpoke

A tall, lean, lantern-jawed cowboy hulks over the Industrial Boulevard exit off I-20 in Bossier City. It's hard to tell whether he's smiling or just gritting his teeth, and he holds his rope like he's planning to garrote the first city slicker who gets in his way. Don't cross him. It doesn't look like he's the kind to take prisoners.

Many Curiosities

The famed Robert Gentry Museum in downtown Many (Sabine Parish) is no longer a tourist destination now that Mr. Gentry and his wife, Marsha, have parted ways. After the separation, he kept the *Sabine Index* newspaper and its Sweet Dreams Publishing Company spin-off, while she was awarded the former family pawnshop directly across the street. The odd collection of artifacts that once filled the museum was divided between them.

If you drop by Many Pawn & Jewelry when things aren't too busy, maybe they'll let you go upstairs to marvel at the remaining treasures: a life-sized figure of P. T. Barnum's famous midget General Tom Thumb, decked out in original clothing; a model of a split-tongued woman who was able to whistle like a nightingale; Elvis souvenirs; baseball memorabilia; piles of Indian artifacts; and our personal favorite, a weasel-eyed mannequin of John Wesley Hardin, the notorious gunslinging Texan outlaw who killed upward of thirty men between 1868 and 1878. There's also a curious collection of famous (and not-so-famous) people's belongings, including an outfit that once belonged to Chris Owens, the "international singing and dancing sensation," mounted on a replica of the performer. The wonderfully weird relics still cram the upstairs, although the infamous albino bats have disappeared.

Giant Root Beer

A giant mug of root beer on the corner of Government Street and St. Ferdinand Street in Baton Rouge dates back to the early 1960s. If it were full, it would hold the equivalent of almost five thousand thirty-two-ounce drinks!

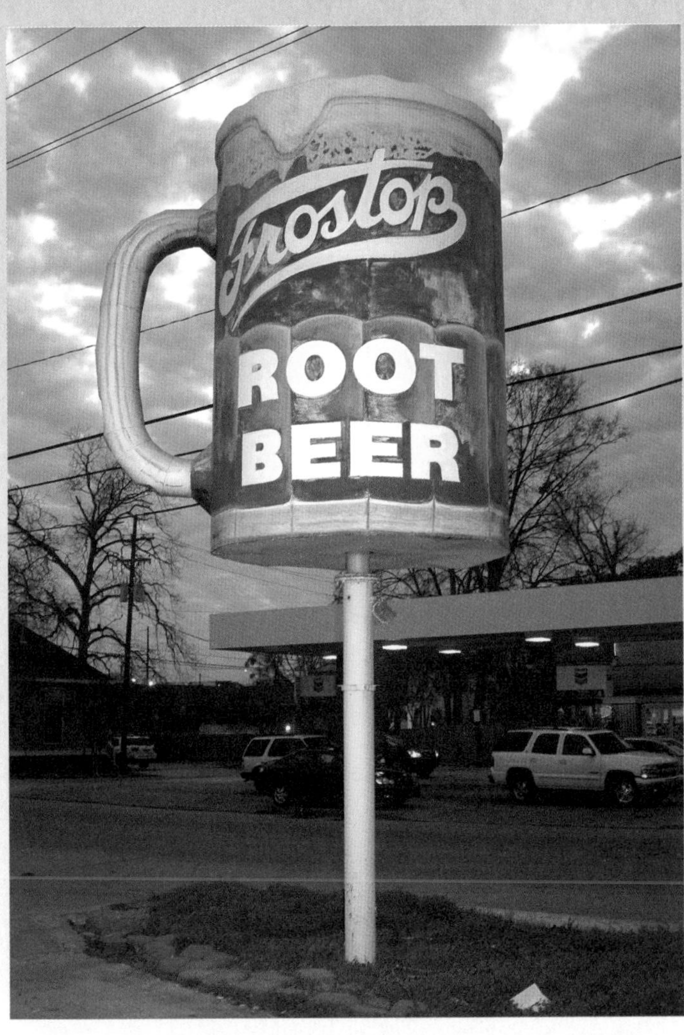

Burnside's Big Box

On the east side of Highway 65 a few miles north of Newellton in Tensas Parish is the largest rural mailbox we've come across during our Weird travels. We have no idea why Ben Burnside Sr. decided to build such a big box—at five feet tall and eight feet deep, it can hold nearly thirty regular bags of mail—but whatever the reason, his design is solid. Despite the worst that nature or local pranksters have managed to hurl at it, the mailbox has survived intact since the mid-1950s. And speaking of pranks, we suggest you don't make any attempts to climb the post or gain access to the inside of the box. If you need more convincing that it's a really bad idea, note the scattering of old bullet holes perforating the sides of Burnside's mega mailbox.

World's Smallest Church

Near Bayou Goula in Iberville Parish, directly across the Mississippi from St. Gabriel, is a tiny structure that locals proudly claim is the world's smallest church. Services are held once a year at the Madonna Chapel, on August 15, and the vigil light candle burns year-round. But it has no seats or pews. In fact, during the annual mass only the priest and an altar boy or two can cram inside to stand before the altar, while the congregation and participants remain outside.

The chapel was built to fulfill a pledge that immigrant Italian sugar farmer Anthony Gullo (also spelled Goula or Goullo) made in 1890 when he prayed to the Blessed Virgin to cure an illness that threatened the life of his eldest son. When the son recovered, Gullo donated land for a churchyard and members of the community began constructing the tiny church in 1903. When the levee was enlarged in the mid-1920s, the church had to be moved and rebuilt and was enlarged to its current size of eight feet by six feet.

They felt it was the least they could do.

Roadside Religious Experiences

The small town of Golden Meadow is home to an unusual roadside shrine that's a popular destination among devout Catholics seeking healing. The shrine was built according to the instructions of Joffery Cochennic after he experienced a vision at the nearby church of Our Lady of Prompt Succor in 1974. Bishop Warren L. Boudreaux blessed the shrine in April 1981 and since then, a number of mysterious healings have occurred at the holy site. Golden Meadow Police Capt. Chet Louivere describes his experience, which is typical of other healings that have occurred at the shrine:

> *It was about the time of September 11, 2001, that I injured my back on my job and I was unable to work. . . . I had constant pain. The doctors couldn't do a thing for me because nothing was broken; it was a pinched nerve. After about a week, I couldn't take the pain anymore so I told God, "God, if you can't cure me then take me. I can't take the pain anymore."*
>
> *Well, moments after, Mr. Joffery Cochennic Sr. came to mind. I gave him a call and told him what was going on. Mr. Cochennic advised me that he would begin praying for me right away and that, if I could, to come over to his place where he had built the shrine to the Blessed Mother, the Holy Mary shrine. I was able to get a ride over there and we sat at the shrine. Mr. Cochennic prayed over my back and I could smell a strong odor of flowers of some type. Soon after that, my back started feeling better. Finally, some relief from the pain. I was soon able to return to work and my back has been feeling good ever since that day.*

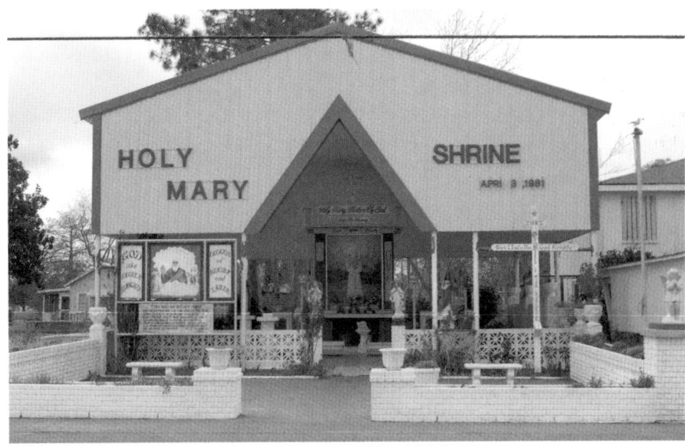

Now in his midnineties, Cochennic is no longer at the shrine on a daily basis, but by calling the city hall and police department, you may be able to arrange a meeting.

Wall's Wall in West Monroe

Stretching for more than a mile along Trenton Street in West Monroe, a levee is reinforced with a concrete flood-detention wall painted to resemble stone masonry. A few decades ago Louisiana State Rep. Shady R. Wall had an idea to help deter local students from vandalizing the West Monroe levee. The idea was simple: Wall reasoned that if, as a community service, local high school students painted the entire length of gray concrete to resemble a stone wall—complete with faux gates, arched windows, and fake doorways—they'd exorcise future urges to deface that wall with graffiti. "Let 'em go ahead and get it out of their systems," Wall said. "After they do that, they'll never feel like putting paint on another wall again—and they sure won't let anyone else touch this one, either."

It looks like Wall was on to something. The 43,929 faux limestone blocks that pretend to hold back the floodwaters of the Ouachita River have yet to be defaced with a single mark.

Lake Arthur Rocket

You wouldn't think launching a rocket would be such a great idea in the midst of a yard full of tanks loaded with flammable gases, but it looks like they're ready to do just that in Lake Arthur. It's eye catching, anyway.

Crawfish Culture

Louisianans are fixated on crawfish. The little crustaceans turn up everywhere, and we're not just talking about swamps and bayous. You'll see their likeness on everything from signs, logos, and blankets to leather folds of Cajun accordion bellows and parade floats. Crawfish loom large in the collective consciousness of Louisianans. And sometimes they just loom large, period, like this huge critter we found on a back street in the small town of Lake Arthur in Jefferson Davis Parish. As far as we've been able to determine, it's the largest permanent, outdoor three-dimensional representation in the state, though we could be wrong.

By the way, if you're not from Louisiana, there are a few things you should know. Don't call them crayfish, even if it's spelled that way on the menu—and don't bother to ask why *cray* is pronounced *craw* or next thing you know you'll be asking why *Natchitoches* is pronounced *NACK-a-dish*, and there's no real explanation for that, either. Don't call them *crawdads* or *mudbugs*, either, as both terms are no longer in use. Oh, and don't be alarmed if someone insists that you "suck the head." They're actually encouraging you to sample the best part of the crawfish—the fat parked in the back end of the crustacean's head. The fat is mostly unsaturated, so all you calorie counters can dig in with a clear conscience.

Mike's "Repair"

A sign outside an Abbeville workshop makes us wonder if appliances brought in for "repair" really come out "fixed."

Pipe Wrench Girl

The sign on the side of South Claiborne Hardware, at the intersection of Napoleon Avenue and South Claiborne Street in New Orleans, is clearly designed to induce male shoppers to acquire new tools!

Mother Cabrini on the Lookout

An austere, nearly life-sized figure of Saint Frances Xavier Cabrini, known better as Mother Cabrini, keeps watch from a porch on Hillary Street in New Orleans. Canonized in 1946, she was the first American saint. She founded a New Orleans orphanage in 1892 for children who had lost parents to one of the many yellow fever epidemics that periodically swept through the region. The former orphanage is now Cabrini High School for girls, at 3400 Esplanade Avenue.

The door to the house now has the code markings spray-painted by officials on nearly all city dwellings after the Hurricane Katrina evacuation.

Mysterious Metal Menageries

Across the street from the Bossier Arts Council's offices in Bossier City is a strange collection of insects, snails, arthropods, and other creatures cobbled together from parts of old cars, farm equipment, abandoned tools, and industrial castoffs. It took the *Weird Louisiana* team several months to uncover the identity of the mysterious metalloid artists. We questioned everybody—staff at the Bossier Arts Council, local libraries, tourist centers, police departments, and historical societies, and even a few dozen passersby at the site—but came up empty-handed. And then, after we stopped looking, the artists' identities were revealed: Carolyn Hughes and Charlie Wilson, two self-taught artists from Texas. Wilson, a former barbecue grill welder, began making sculptures after developing health issues, and Hughes sanded and painted them.

Neutral Ground

Other cities around the country use the terms *median strip* or *traffic divider* when referring to the narrow patch of land running between two opposing lanes of traffic. In New Orleans, the divide is called *neutral ground,* a term originally used to describe the strip of land bisecting Canal Street. In the past, the Canal Street strip separated the American part of the city, Faubourg St. Mary, from the French Vieux Carré. Because neither side could legally claim the dividing strip, it was considered neutral. Similar strips soon appeared elsewhere in the city as immigrants set up their own ethnic neighborhoods.

In New Orleans today, neutral ground serves as a kind of no-man's-land separating rival gang territories. In calmer parts of the city, the strip can accommodate overflow parking, neighborhood cookouts, and an occasional football field. Neutral grounds are also the obvious place to erect political signs, ad hoc artworks, roadside accident shrines, or homemade monuments.

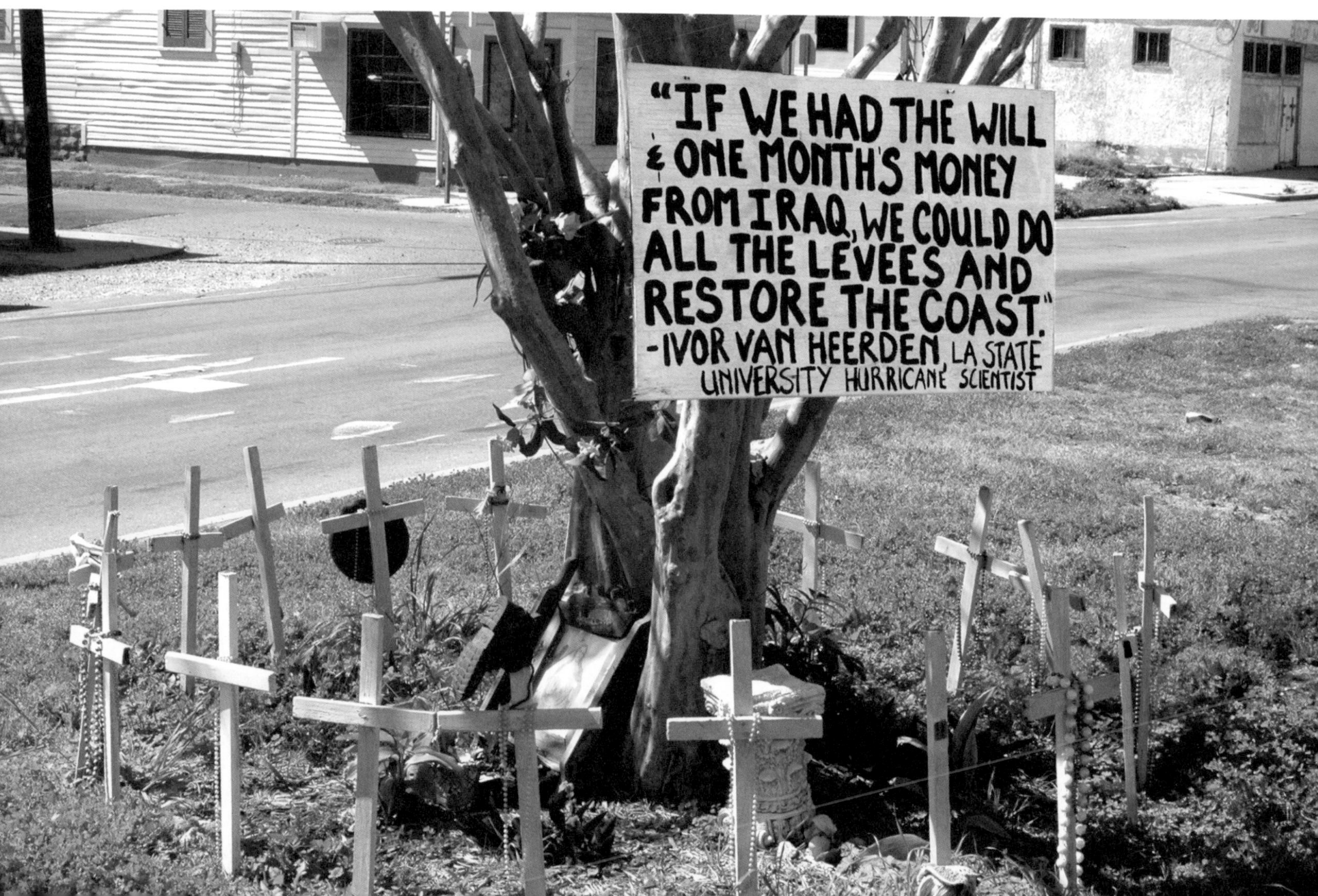

Fun-Loving Gorilla

The life-sized gorilla jovially guarding the walkway leading up to a house in Plaquemine dresses appropriately for whatever holiday season is at hand. Around Christmas, for example, he's been known to sport a red, white, and green Santa's helper outfit, and at Halloween he may dress up in a scary ape costume. We found him at Mardi Gras time, decked out in the traditional purple, green, and gold and looking about as ready to get on with the hearty partying as any die-hard krewe member.

Muffler Man of Raceland

Have you heard about Raceland's Muffler Man? Most people haven't, as it seems the muffler-made man is Raceland's best-kept secret—and town locals want to keep it that way. The *Weird Louisiana* team asked about a dozen passersby where we could find the statue made of mufflers and other car parts. We were told that no such thing existed anywhere in the community. Sometime later, we finally we spotted it about fifteen feet behind the last person we asked, in plain view next to the main street through town.

Roto-Spheres in Shreveport

Roto-Sphere signs are perhaps the biggest and most dramatic neon signs ever mass-produced. Warren Milks created and produced around 230 signs from 1960 to 1971. Sixteen or so of the original spheres still exist, and of these, only seven are still fully operational. Nicknamed "Sputniks," they were promoted as sign add-ons and distributed nationwide; a few were sent outside the country.

Roto-Spheres feature sixteen aluminum spikes outlined in neon. The eight-foot-long multicolored spikes are mounted on a ball that spins in three directions. Not only does the sign rotate on its pole, but the ball itself is composed of two counter-rotating hemispheres.

Restoring and maintaining Roto-Spheres can be tricky and costly because of their size, mechanics, and the amount of neon used. I believe the original sign cost about $2,000 with shipping. To fully restore one today costs around $15,000. The Shreveport Roto-Sphere on Barton Drive was restored in 2007 and is usually lit at night, although you might want to call ahead of time to avoid making a wasted trip. I believe it's always spinning. The sign came from the long-gone Holiday Manor Motel in Bossier City. This was the second Roto-Sphere that Warren Milks created. The first was installed in front of NESCO, his sign shop, in Bossier City. *—Debra Jane Seltzer, www.agilitynut.com*

Transylvania, LA

The small town of Transylvania sure is proud of its infamous moniker. Don't believe us? Well, next time you're on Highway 65 about twenty miles north of Tallulah, take a small detour and check out the giant bat that adorns its water tower. Then pay a visit to the town's general store, which boasts a painting of bloodthirsty Count Dracula and sells bat-related items—bats made of black rubber, bat T-shirts, and ashtrays shaped like bats and skulls. Although there's not all that much to do in Transylvania, town residents are quite welcoming to tourists. As the general store's proprietor likes to joke grimly, "We're always glad when new blood comes to town."

All kidding aside, there may be more to all this than just the spooky name. Highway 65 has been the site of numerous paranormal sightings. Locals and visitors have reported seeing strange bearded ghosts riding by on bicycles, bloody hitchhikers, and other otherworldly apparitions. Meanwhile, some paranormal researchers claim that more than seven hundred other members of the "undead" stalk the community, inhabit its dwellings, water its lawns, and lay in wait for unsuspecting passersby.

If you do decide to visit Transylvania, best to play it safe. When darkness falls, seek lodging outside the town limits. The closest motels are about eight miles north, in Lake Providence.

Can't Take It with You?

The huge bronze doors of St. Jean Vianney Catholic Church in eastern Baton Rouge are covered with castings of objects that had special significance to members of the church congregation, from screwdrivers, scissors, and piano-tuning wrenches to toys, bones, perfume bottles, trophy fish, military medals, and even a rodeo belt buckle.

Tree of Soles

It had to happen sooner or later: Someone managed to get a pair of shoes stuck in a tree, looked up and saw the soles, and then a lightbulb appeared, as if hovering above them. The Tree of Soles, a.k.a. the Tree of Souls, was born. Others soon began tossing their own shoes skyward, and a tradition began. Before long, somebody put up a sign and made it official.

To visit the Tree of Soles, take Exit 97 off Interstate 10 (northwest of Scott, in Lafayette Parish) and head north on Highway 93 about 2.5 miles. Keep a lookout for Cocodril Road. When you find it, turn left (west), and when the pavement gives way to gravel after about a mile, you're almost there.

Abita Mystery House

In the mood for something weird? Head about an hour north of New Orleans to Abita Springs and spend some quality time at the Abita Mystery House. Formerly known as the UCM Museum, the mystery house is the brainchild of artist John Preble and offers up a most enjoyable way to safely immerse in weirdness for the better part of an afternoon.

The mystery house looks like a little old 1930s-era gas station from the outside, but if you step inside you'll soon discover you've entered into a much larger, stranger realm. You'll pass the service station, home to an awesomely eclectic gift shop full of whoopee cushions, chattering teeth, letter openers made from alligator bones, and X-ray sunglasses.

Beyond the gift shop you enter the main exhibit hall, which features several mechanically activated miniature dioramas. Press a button to see a tornado spin through a trailer park in a scene called "Tragedy on Dog Pound Road." Another button revs up a miniature jazz band playing "Muskrat Ramble" for a funeral at New Orleans's St. Louis Cemetery No. 1, while tombs creak open, skeletons pop out, and spirits flutter overhead.

"Martians Come to Mardi Gras" asks some of those key questions that occur to all Louisianans from time to time: What would happen if we were invaded by space aliens during Carnival? Would anybody notice? And would they have a good time? The answer, of course, lies in that old Cajun saying, *Laissez les soucoupes volantes roulez* (Let the flying saucers roll)!

Your attention is then drawn to a thirty-foot-long scene called "River Road," inspired by some of the funkier elements on the back roads between New Orleans and Baton Rouge. From Pinky's What-All

Store and Lil' Dubs BBQ & Gas Station (motto: "Eat Here and Get Gas") to Rudy's Over-the-Rainbow Hotel and Wild Will's Catfish Barn & Buffet ("If You Can See It You Can Eat It"), the "River Road" scene that presents Louisiana in miniature, all of it is operated by the pull of hidden strings and the turning of invisible gears. A row of buttons makes everything happen: The door to the "Cajun library" pops open, dancers jump to Doug Clark and the Hot Nuts at Rudy's Rainbow Lounge, the swamp monster looms ominously, and the windmill spins in the Putt-Putt golf course while old Donna hawks her vegetables next to the refinery, which includes a sign that says CHEMICALS FOR A NEW TOMORROW. These are glimpses of real Bayou State life, and none of it is made up.

It feels good to step out of the exhibit hall into the bright light of day to marvel at the House of Shards (an old horse barn covered with more than fifteen thousand pieces of broken crockery) and then enter to see still more wonders, like a largemouth bass (complete with a set of false teeth), a Feejee Mermaid, and a homemade helicopter with a belt-driven power train.

Beyond the House of Shards is the Shed of Revelations, a UFO crash site, and Buford the Giant Bassigator—a half-gator, half-fish horror more than twenty feet long that would have sent a shiver through Jaws.

We could go on describing Darrel the Dogigator, the Gator Girl, and the Gatorcycle, but it would spoil the fun to list all the surprises in store for you at the Abita Mystery House. Just take our word for it: It's worth the side trip and the small entry fee. The UCM Museum and Abita Mystery House, located one block east of the only traffic light in Abita Springs, is open every day from ten A.M. to five P.M. Don't miss it.

Making a Mystery House 101

John Preble's inspiration for the Abita Mystery House came during a 1995 vacation, when he pulled off the road outside Albuquerque and dragged his family into a roadside attraction called Tinkertown, built by a guy named Ross Ward. Part miniature western town and part snake zoo, Ward's creation struck a nerve, and Preble returned home determined to do something like it in Abita Springs. As a lifelong junk collector, he'd unconsciously been preparing himself for decades to launch something like the UCM (You See 'Em) Museum, but seeing Tinkertown finally brought the dream into sharper focus. Five years later the doors opened, and it's been in business ever since. See lots more at http://www.ucmmusuem.com/.

IN MEMORY OF

Roads Less Traveled

If life is a highway (according to singer Tom Cochrane), then we have to make choices each time we come to a fork in the road, find ourselves at a crossroads, or reach a dead end. American popular culture is full of road references. "Let's not go down that road," we'll say to a colleague or friend who's on the verge of overstepping, or, "It's time to hit the road," whenever things are coming to a close. We'd all rather be on the road to riches than the road to perdition—and certainly not on the highway to hell, even if some heavy metal bands do manage to make it sound like a fun trip. Our most primitive jokes include those about chickens crossing roads, and one of America's most beloved films has a yellow brick road as its central plot device.

If you're wondering where we're going with this, here's the deal: There's a whole world full of roads out there, and if life is, in fact, a highway, we could all use some help navigating through its rough terrain, dark alleys, slick spots, and all the things that don't show up in the headlights or on standard road maps.

Okay, so we can't actually help you plot a course for your life's journey. What we can do is tell you about a handful of haunted highways and roads around the bend in the Bayou State that you may not know about. Ready? Buckle up and get ready for a bumpy ride!

The Crossett Light

A mysterious light has been spotted along the railroad tracks in the town of Crossett, Arkansas, since the early 1900s. Some say the eerie spectacle is the ghost of a headless train brakeman—decapitated after slipping on a patch of ice and falling under the train—who prowls the tracks at night in search of his lost head.

But why are we talking about an otherworldly light show in Arkansas in a book about Louisiana? Because citizens in Morehouse Parish in northeastern Louisiana have been observing the Crossett Light from across the state line—only about ten miles away—since the days of Prohibition. The light show *could* be an electrical phenomenon. Or it could be a reminder of an Arkansas bootlegger and the flammable cargo that lit up the skies in the roaring twenties.

According to the story, the bootlegger's car was so overloaded with carboys of popskull corn liquor—barrels of poorly made moonshine—that he had a hard time steering. It wasn't long before law officers spotted him speeding toward the state line. Just after the bootlegger crossed from Arkansas into Louisiana, frustrated deputies fired a shot that ignited the bootlegger's liquid load. The liquor began pouring onto the road, leaving a trail of flames and fireballs. The bootlegger drove as fast as he could to outrun the flames, hoping the moonshine would run out before the gas in his tank ran dry. Sadly for him, his luck ran out first. An armadillo darted out in front of him, he swerved and crashed. The fireball could be seen for miles.

Unlike the tales of a headless brakeman, the bootlegger's story squares with the supernatural spectacle described by those who say they've seen the Crossett Light: a bright trail of light that shoots down the road low to the ground and then weaves quickly along until it is clear out of sight, followed by a brilliant flash.

Railroad Crossing Railroad

East of Lake Charles, Railroad Avenue rounds a bend, comes out from behind a stand of trees, crosses the tracks, and continues toward some abandoned rice mills. In the 1950s, a family of four was killed here when their car was struck by an oncoming train. In those days, before automatic warning lights were installed at railroad crossings, such tragedies were all too common.

There was something unusual about this particular event. The eldest daughter had a premonition about the family's demise. Neighbors who attended the funeral said she didn't want to get in the car on that fateful day; they'd overheard her arguing with her parents and then crying, "We can't do this! We can't! We're going to die!" Her father insisted her fears were unfounded and that the premonition was just a bad dream. When the family didn't return from the afternoon trip, neighbors began to worry. Sadly the daughter's foresight turned out to be spot-on.

Since then, paranormal phenomena have been observed regularly at this crossing and near the junction of East Opelousas Street and Shane Road. If you're looking for an otherworldly encounter, head to the tracks just after sunset. In the light of an oncoming train you may see an apparition of the girl, four orbs (or points of light), and sometimes both. However, not everyone is able to see supernatural entities.

Paranormalresearchers point out that in a randomly selected group of observers, only 50 percent are typically able to see an apparition or orbs. And this isn't surprising; just as some people are colorblind or unable to hear high-pitched sound frequencies, not everyone has the ability to observe paranormal events. Among the members of this ill-fated family, for example, only the eldest daughter could see that it would be their last trip—but no one else would listen.

So-Low of Wilson Point Road

Wilson Point Road fizzles out into a driveway leading to the last house twenty miles southeast of Pineville. Surrounded on three sides by the Red River, the little Rapides Parish enclave is effectively cut off from the rest of the state. Highway 1 may be only a mile across the river as the crow flies, but it takes almost half an hour to get there by car. And back when roads weren't paved and cars traveled at slower speeds, it could take almost half a day. As one elderly resident put it, "We was so far from everything out here no one could even hear us if we screamed." Screaming, in fact, would probably have only made matters worse, since the bow in the river that loops around the point is famous for its echo, and your screams would only have been joined by others sounding just like yours.

Living in this isolated enclave meant that whenever problems came along, locals were forced to face them alone. One such problem: a particularly pesky phantom hell-bent on terrorizing the community. The consensus on the ghost's identity is that in life he was a Confederate soldier who returned home after fighting on the losing side in the Civil War. Most of the Wilson Point folks were former slaves from the Grimes and Wilson plantations who had intermarried with Native Americans and, learning of the great emancipation, weren't about to revert to subjugation. Upon returning home, the soldier tried to order the liberated slaves back to the fields. They responded by attacking him and then stringing him up on a nearby tree limb.

"We was so far from everything out here no one could even hear us if we screamed."

Whether because of the soldier's rage or the collective guilt of the murderers, his spirit grew restless. Before long, his vengeful ghost returned and began regularly pestering the community from beyond his shallow, unmarked grave. And over time, locals have learned that there is only one way to deal with the spiteful spirit—be prepared.

Shape Shifter Shenanigans

Old So-Low, as locals call him, is a shape-shifter and dealing with his antics can be tricky. In a July 1982 article in *Alexandria Town Talk*, ninety-year-old Rollie Lipscomb told about his first after-dark encounter with the ghost more than forty years earlier. So-Low suddenly appeared on a sandy path as Lipscomb and his wife were coming home from visiting a sick friend. "I heard something fall out of a tree like a sack of dirt into the water. I says . . . 'Old feller, don't start nothing.'" Something with horns like a billy goat appeared in the road. "His eyes looked like balls o' fire. . . . I then stepped aside and let him pass. He had martingales on, just like a little dog. . . . He was grunting with every jump he made. . . . I ain't never seen nothing like that in my life."

So-Low's antics were unpredictable. The ghost didn't merely jump out of the bushes or run down the path. Instead he was often seen dragging heavy objects like washtubs or pieces of furniture through the woods. The furniture left long gouges in the soft ground, but no accompanying footprints were ever found. Locals soon took to carrying stout clubs to fend So-Low off at night, and although no one was ever physically harmed, the spirit's spiteful acts certainly made life more frustrating.

"Others met old So-Low in every shape, fashion, or form that he can be met," said Lipscomb, although in the late 1940s, after automobiles started rumbling down the country lanes, the sightings waned. Still, Lipscomb was convinced that "So-Low is still out there somewhere—waiting." The ghost has also appeared as a bright light moving through the trees and as a shadowy figure easily detected by dogs or horses but difficult for people to see. Once in a while, if it's still early enough in the evening, blood is visible on the ghost's neck where presumably the martingale collar had cut into him.

To get to Wilson Point, take Harris Ferry Road west off Highway 454 a few miles south of Ruby. Turn left onto Wilson Point Road, which forks south.

Tunnel to Nowhere

Back before most roads were surfaced with asphalt and concrete, the biggest problem that Louisiana travelers faced was dealing with mud. When it was wet and fresh after a rainstorm, there was the constant danger of getting bogged down in it, and then after it dried and hardened, the ruts became like permanent ditches that made steering almost impossible. In the early 1880s Judge John Watkins came up with a unique solution by building Louisiana's strangest toll road, which stretched for nine miles from the Red River near Bossier City to Red Chute, passing near Ferguson along the way. The roof-covered roadway that gave the Great Shed Road its name not only provided shade but also kept the rain off, so it remained relatively smooth, hard, and flat. But when the railroad from Bossier City to Minden was built ten years later, the Shed Road that paralleled it quickly went out of business.

Legend of Mary's Bridge

Follow Rue Bayou Tortue (Turtle Bayou Road) in Broussard west to the Lafayette Parish line and you'll find a small bridge crossing over Bayou Tortue. Tall cypress trees line the banks of the bayou, with Spanish moss draping down from the branches. Alligators and water moccasins can be seen teeming in the waters, but there's more to this bayou than meets the eye.

According to the legend of Bayou Tortue, a Cajun girl named Mary was dating an "Americain" (an outsider who wasn't Cajun or Creole) boy against the wishes of her parents. Mary, being a good Catholic girl, refused to give in to her boyfriend's sexual advances. One night just before midnight the young couple was driving through the country. Mary's boyfriend had been drinking, and his advances became violent; he threatened to throw her into the bayou if she continued to resist him. When she tried to flee, he bludgeoned her with a whiskey bottle and then dumped her body in the bayou. Despite an intense search effort, the body was never recovered; and about a week after the incident, Mary's boyfriend disappeared.

They say if you go to the bridge at midnight, turn off your car, and say, "Mary . . . Mary . . . Mary," your car won't start up again and you'll have to push it to the road so it's not on the bridge in order to start the engine. Every year at midnight on the anniversary of her death, you can see Mary's ghost on the bridge. Dressed in a long white dress, she roams around the bayou where her life was tragically cut short. —*Tim Westcott*

Headless Horror at Greenwood Cemetery

Once construction on Interstate 20 west of Shreveport was complete, the old Greenwood Cemetery became more or less cut off from the rest of the community. Located just north of the town of Greenwood, the cemetery used to be just across the tracks. These days, you have to cross an overpass, the tracks, and a small bridge to get there, so it's unlikely that you'll find anybody out there after dark. Still, young pranksters and thrill seekers sometimes head to the cemetery for after-hours high jinks only to have the bejesus scared out of them by a headless figure in dark clothes roaming the grounds. There haven't been any reports of the mysterious figure harming or killing anyone, although the entity has been known to chase folks who visit the cemetery at night. Maybe the headless entity is just having some fun . . . but why chance it? If you're interested in visiting Greenwood Cemetery, plan on doing so during daylight hours.

Hook Man of Highway 810

According to a local legend, a man was hanged from meat hooks inside the now dilapidated barn by the roadside on Highway 810, south of Caney Creek Reservoir in Jackson Parish. His body was then disposed of in the woods.

Behind the barn, there's a trail leading into the woods. Locals swear that if you park on this trail at night, turn your headlights off, and wait in perfect silence (with the doors *locked*) for twenty or thirty minutes, you'll have an otherworldly encounter with the ghost of the hook man. First you'll hear the sound of something dragging its way toward your car. Then the car will shake, as if someone is trying to break in. At this point, you should start the car and get out of there.

Of course, we don't recommend that you drive out there to mess with the mysterious entity. Local legends often preserve a core of truth, and we're reluctant to dismiss this one as a myth because of some interesting facts that came to light while we were doing our research. We learned that over the years a great many lynchings took place in the nearby parishes of Ouachita, Caddo, and Bossier. With 423 known "informal executions" in the state's history, the story of the hook man's hanging is likely based more on fact than fiction, as disquieting as that may be.

Haunts of Highway 80

Highway 80 between Tallulah and Quebec in Madison Parish takes some surprisingly sharp turns on seemingly flat terrain. The winding road catches many first-time visitors by surprise, often sending them careening into the countryside and face-to-face with fields of indigenous plant life. Sometimes, however, it's not just snaky turns that lead to sudden swerves off the road.

In 1984, an ambulance driver was racing west on this zigzagging stretch of highway to the hospital in Monroe when a white horse suddenly appeared in middle of the road, emerging from what looked like a large white cloud. The driver veered onto the shoulder of the road to avoid hitting the mysterious white steed. As he swerved, he saw the truck's sideview mirror pass directly through the horse, as if nothing were there.

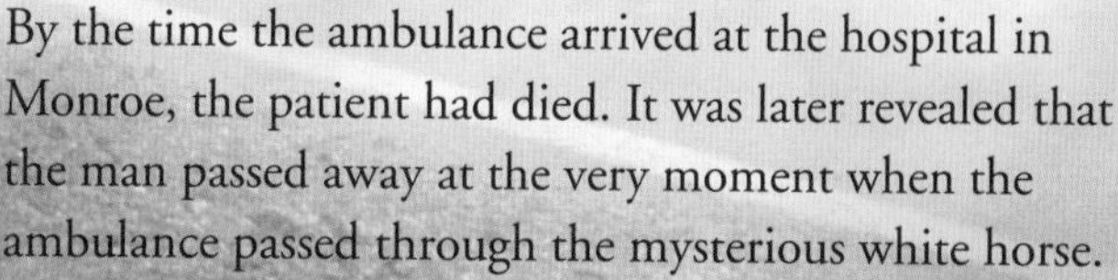

By the time the ambulance arrived at the hospital in Monroe, the patient had died. It was later revealed that the man passed away at the very moment when the ambulance passed through the mysterious white horse.

A few months later, another strange encounter occurred on the same stretch of highway. A woman from Texas saw a man dressed in a black cape and top hat standing by the side of the road, his hands stretched out toward her in warning to slow down. A few seconds later, she neared one of sharp curves for which the road is famous and saw a flash of bright light. She rounded the bend just in time to see an oncoming car overturn. The driver was killed instantly, and had she not slowed down at the sight of the caped stranger, she would have collided with the other car.

Ghost Car of Highway 167

A ghost car has been spotted with some regularity on the stretch of Highway 167 between Lafayette and Abbeville. Witnesses say the black 1940s sedan appears for a few moments and then suddenly vanishes. A woman driving with a child in the passenger seat—both dressed in 1940s clothing—appear in the car, which has been seen during the daytime and in the evenings traveling in either direction on the highway. Occasionally the woman pulls up alongside another car on the highway and waves to drivers as if she wants them to pull over. Then the car disappears.

The most famous of these sightings occurred on October 20, 1969, when a driver on the highway spotted the old black sedan pulling up beside a vehicle ahead of it. The driver watched as the two cars headed toward the shoulder of the road and, once again, the car vanished. No one knows who the woman is, what she wants, or why she's condemned to an eternity of driving on this stretch of highway. Maybe you can help solve the mystery. If you catch a glimpse of the license plate, maybe some old Louisiana Department of Motor Vehicles records can help shed some light on Highway 167's famed ghost car.

Highway 105: Easy Rider Death Road

Okay, we're going to be upfront with you. The fabled *Easy Rider* Death Road isn't really all that frightening anymore. But we do realize that some of our readers may have fond memories of *Easy Rider* as the movie that introduced them to backcountry Louisiana. The film is a unique, nostalgic slice of Americana; and for that reason alone, there's a certain allure to tracking down some of the sites where it was shot.

One of the most famous sites is the stretch of Highway 105 between Melville and Krotz Springs in St. Landry Parish, about forty miles west of Baton Rouge, where Billy (Dennis Hopper) and Wyatt (Peter Fonda) met their filmic demise. The road has grown more suburban since the film was shot in the late 1960s, though if you face the levee and avoid looking across the road at all the brick ranchettes, you can still picture the scene pretty well. If you stop to take pictures, some scary-looking local guys in a pickup may even pull up next to you. But the next sound you hear is more likely to be Garrison Keillor on National Public Radio pumping out of their dash than the sound of a pump shotgun. Don't say we didn't warn you; 1969 was a long time ago.

Headless, with a Twist

Headless brakemen stories are a dime a dozen, and frankly, we at *Weird Louisiana* have had our fill. So here's a tale we heard with a twist.

In the 1920s, a woman (who didn't work for the railroad) was riding the train from Coushatta to Natchitoches. Her destination: a speakeasy far from the town she lived in where she could consume an illegal amount of alcohol—of course, in those days of Prohibition, *any* amount of alcohol was illegal. Our heroine spent the larger part of the evening at the speakeasy, and after throwing back the lioness's share of homemade gin, she boarded the train to return home. She never did make it back. Soon after boarding, she fell off the platform at the rear of the car and had her head torn off. Ever since that evening, the ghost of the ill-fated flapper has been spotted on Highway 480 between Coushatta and Campti.

The Walker Road Walker

Highway 147 southeast of Jonesboro in Jackson Parish has been the setting for a number of unexplained events. Walker Road, historians assure us, was named for a local family, but a handful of locals who live along the road tell a different story. They refer to a strange figure often seen walking along the road as "the Walker," describing him as unusually tall, dressed in dark clothing, and wearing either a pointed or stovepipe hat. Two of the people we spoke with mentioned that the mysterious man is able to pass through the walls of homes along the road and sometimes starts fires in them. Although we don't know if the tall man is just a tall tale, we did notice the charred remains of several burned-down homes on Walker Road when we visited the area.

Other people have described odd sounds—trainlike rumbles, vibrations, distant muffled whines like metal grinding into metal—emanating underground in areas around Walker Road. In nearby regions the strange sounds and even an occasional house fire might be attributed to underground natural gas deposits building up pressure, but as far as we know, there aren't any such deposits in the immediate area. Whether caused by *the* Walker or just *on* Walker Road, our best advice to offset combustion: Avoid smoking in these areas, keep moving, and in case of emergency stop, drop, and roll!

Front and Center

Front Street in downtown Natchitoches is a pretty happening place when it comes to paranormal activity. According to *Old Natchitoches Parish Magazine*, town residents report seeing a man dressed in Civil War clothing wandering around the area in the evening after the shops close. Some say he's decked out in a Confederate uniform, but from what we've learned, it's almost certain that he's a Yankee—Brevet Brig. Gen. Napoleon McLaughlin, who was gunned down on Front Street around 1872.

McLaughlin was part of the Union occupation forces left behind to keep local citizenry under control after the war ended. The West-Kimbrel gang had set itself up as a group of insurgent warlords in the largely lawless country just across the Red River from Natchitoches. McLaughlin had been sent from Washington with express orders to bring the gang under control.

According to historian Jack Peeples, McLaughlin's techniques were brave but also somewhat simpleminded. After one of his officers was killed by a member of the West-Kimbrel gang, the relatively inexperienced general took only an orderly and set out on a search-and-destroy mission without any other backup. He crossed the river and rode up to the Kimbrel house and dismounted. He knocked on the door and Ma Kimbrel stepped out. When McLaughlin asked her where the boys were, she lied, saying they had fled to Texas.

On the way back to Natchitoches, McLaughlin ran into Billy Kimbrel. The general shot him down and decided to make an example out of him by dragging Billy's corpse to Ma Kimbrel's house and draping it over the fence alongside her drying laundry. McLaughlin didn't know it at the time, but he had just made a fatal mistake.

Some time later, General McLaughlin was strolling along Front Street when he was killed by a single gunshot fired from the darkness. He was lying facedown when his body was found the next morning by local shopkeepers. No one knows whether it was Billy's brother Laws Kimbrel, another member of the gang, or even Ma Kimbrel—whose infamous bloodlust rivaled that of her sons—who fired the shot that ended McLaughlin's life.

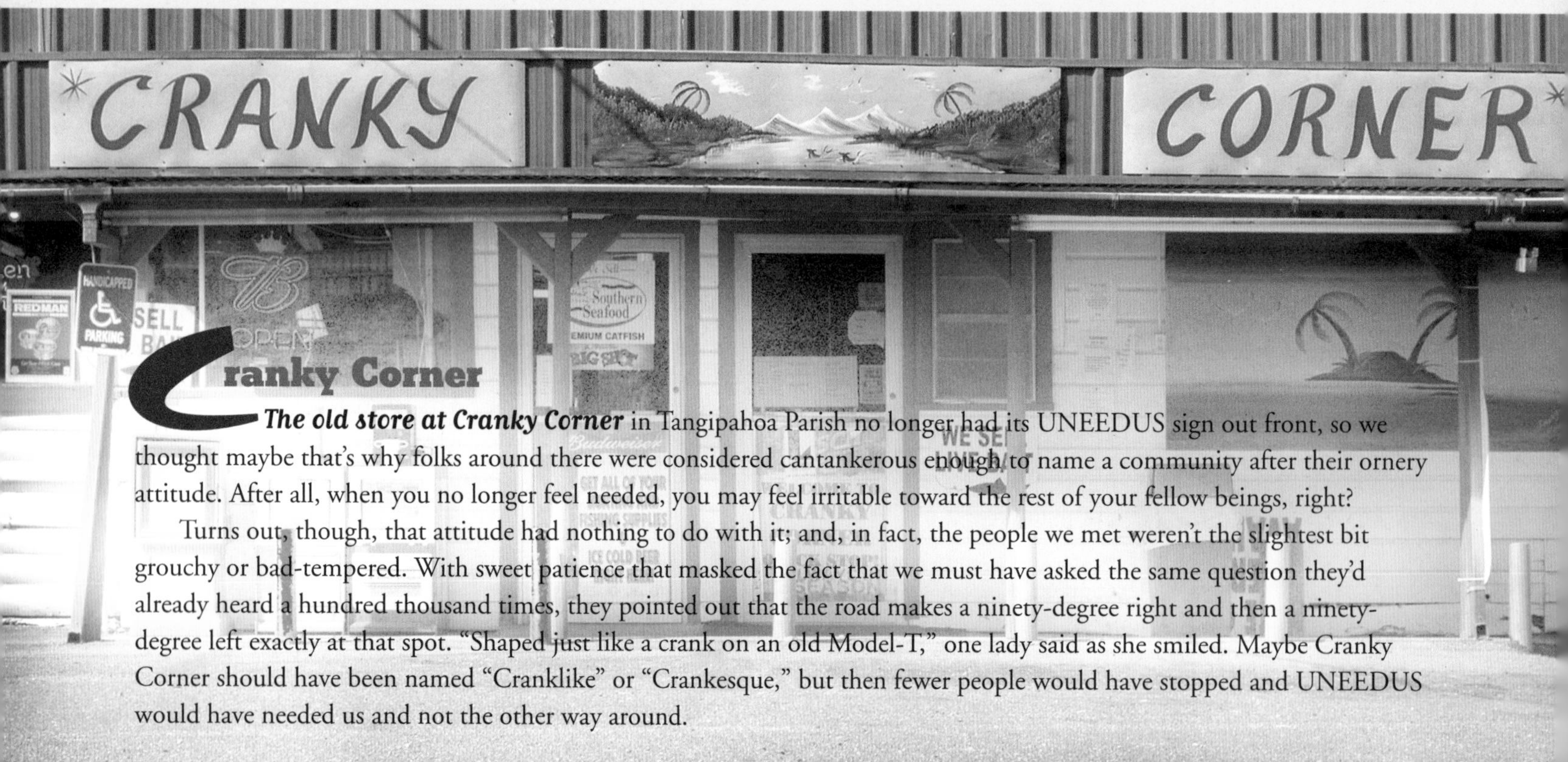

Cranky Corner

The old store at Cranky Corner in Tangipahoa Parish no longer had its UNEEDUS sign out front, so we thought maybe that's why folks around there were considered cantankerous enough to name a community after their ornery attitude. After all, when you no longer feel needed, you may feel irritable toward the rest of your fellow beings, right?

Turns out, though, that attitude had nothing to do with it; and, in fact, the people we met weren't the slightest bit grouchy or bad-tempered. With sweet patience that masked the fact that we must have asked the same question they'd already heard a hundred thousand times, they pointed out that the road makes a ninety-degree right and then a ninety-degree left exactly at that spot. "Shaped just like a crank on an old Model-T," one lady said as she smiled. Maybe Cranky Corner should have been named "Cranklike" or "Crankesque," but then fewer people would have stopped and UNEEDUS would have needed us and not the other way around.

Green Light Bridge

Roads aren't often named after paranormal phenomena, but if you look on any detailed map of Franklin Parish, west of Chase between Winnsboro and Jigger, you'll find Green Light Road. And where the road crosses Turkey Creek is Green Light Bridge, named for the green light that hundreds of people have seen emerging from the thick growth along the creek to hover silently over the bridge. If the light begins approaching your vehicle, locals say it's a good idea to keep the car running—it may not start again if you turn it off. Cars with electric ignitions are most likely to break down on the bridge in the presence of the lights, and electrical mechanisms like door locks, windows, and radios may also go caput.

Our advice about the Green Light Bridge? Remember green means "go," so if you see the light, push the pedal to the metal and get out of there. As far as we know, there is no legend or explanation for the light—at least no one we asked seemed to know anything about it. "It's just there," as one older man said, "so what more do you want from it?"

Pirates Alley Specters

Pirates Alley is a small passageway in the French Quarter of New Orleans. It runs right next to the St. Louis Cathedral, which is one of the oldest operating cathedrals in America. The alley is sometimes the location of strange sightings. Countless people have spotted someone who appears to be a pirate walking up and down in it—hence the name. After a short amount of time, the figure simply vanishes into thin air. Some believe it's the ghost of the famous pirate Jean Lafitte, who frequented the French Quarter and whose headquarters were located only a few blocks away. Others believe it is the ghost of one of Lafitte's loyal pirates, who was killed in the Battle of New Orleans and is trying to find his way home. Either way, too many people have witnessed this scene for it to simply be ignored. —*Matthew Muller*

Old Columbia Road

Old Columbia Road in western Franklin Parish cuts the corner off the junction of Highways 4 and 135 to form an equilateral triangle with Fort Necessity at one of its three points. A cemetery by the Boeuf Prairie Methodist Church in Fort Necessity is thought to be the cause of some of the psychic disturbances in the area, since not long after the church was built in 1833 it was commandeered for use as a courthouse. When a place supposedly consecrated to forgiveness and "turning the other cheek" is turned instead into a place of legal retribution, it's just asking for trouble, they say.

Confederate colonel Lemuel Bowden, who helped build the church, killed the infamous outlaw John Word and buried him in the cemetery there. For years afterward there were reports of Word's ghost chasing after anyone who dared to ride a horse around the back of the building. The only way to shake the ghost was to gallop around the circuit of the three roads—Old Columbia crosses Goose Creek and Lower Eagle Creek over two small bridges—because the ghost can't follow over running water.

The Moaning House

One of the most forbidding points along Old Columbia Road is a place locally known as the "Moaning House," although there's no actual house on the site anymore. What used to be the Eagle Creek Schoolhouse is now a patch of overgrown shrubs, a few fragments of foundations, and some stern warnings from the sheriff's department to stay away from the place, nailed to all the surrounding trees.

Ground fog collects around the Moaning House and animal life seems to avoid the site altogether. We don't know if there's a crack in the ground leading to a vast subterranean cavity or if the site is a portal to another dimension, as many locals, including Lee Erwin, believe. He points out, "You never see any roadkill of critters along the roadsides . . . no dead possums, coons, armadillos, no nothing . . . and looking out over the pastureland of stunted weeds, you never see any songbirds flitting about . . . no fire-ant mounds, no mice, no rabbits, no nothing . . ." The area is strangely unnaturally silent—apart from that eerie moaning sound for which the place is named. If our theory about a cave is correct, maybe odorless natural gas slowly escaping from the deep cavern through a small hidden crevice to cause that deep, shuddering moan. It sounds as if the earth itself were grieving.

According to local lore, a man was hanged at the old Eagle Creek Schoolhouse and the killers cut his throat when they grew tired of waiting for him to stop kicking. The trapped air escaping from his severed larynx made a distinct moaning sound, which reverberates at the abandoned site to this day. We can't say what the cause is for the sounds, but we can say that Old Columbia Road is a stretch of rough asphalt that you don't want to find yourself broken down on, on any night of the week.

Don't Pull Over!

There are two roads in the nearby towns of Moss Bluff and Gillis that have similar legends attached to them. In Moss Bluff, the road's name is Coffey Road, and in Gillis the road is Welcome Road. Several years ago, local police found a headless horse on Coffey Road. It was assumed that mean-spirited teens killed the horse, but then people in the area started reporting more animals being killed in a ritualistic manner and sightings of men in black robes running around the forested areas. Reports stopped after a housing development was built on Coffey Road; however, reports about cults started on Welcome Road. Stories spread around that cultists would pose as stranded motorists and try to get people to pull over. They would then ambush the unknowing drivers when they got out of their cars. —*Clifton Knight*

Ghosts of Louisiana

Our Louisiana guide pointed at an old plantation house in the distance and said, "Now *that* old place is extremely strange, even for Louisiana. In fact, I don't know that I've ever heard of another place quite like it . . . but as far as I can tell, there's absolutely no ghost whatsoever attached to that place. Isn't that the strangest thing you ever heard? It just doesn't make any sense at all."

We knew exactly what he meant. After a full day visiting half a dozen plantations, we'd seen ample evidence of eerie encounters—blood stains, ax marks, quilts with bayonet holes, bullets embedded in window sashes. In every case, something horrible had happened and supernatural spirits lingered. We listened attentively to story after story and soon realized that in Louisiana a home without a ghost is sometimes scarier that a home with a familiar haunt.

Lalaurie Mansion in New Orleans

Ask a Crescent City native if there are any haunted houses around, and he'll likely poke fun at your ignorance. After all, nearly every house built before the turn of the last century is considered to have some unquiet spirit wandering about its premises. But if you ask a local where *the* haunted house of New Orleans is, they'll point you in the direction of old Lalaurie Mansion, hulking on the corner of Royal and Governor Nicholls (formerly Hospital) Streets. The place has been considered haunted since at least April 10, 1834, when the *New Orleans Bee / L'Abeille de la Nouvelle-Orléans* announced the discovery of a dark secret that had been kept hidden within its walls for years.

Doctor and Madame Lalaurie

Madame Lalaurie, born Delphine de Macarty, was the daughter of a Scottish nobleman who had been exiled to France and knighted by King Louis XV. Her uncle was the Spanish governor of Louisiana. Dr. Louis Lalaurie, a member of the French Academy of Science in Paris, was her third husband.

Doctor and Madame Lalaurie purchased the mansion in 1831 and quickly became the toast of the city's well-to-do French Creole society. After selling their vast property in Haiti, the couple used the earnings to outfit the forty-room house for the finest social events the city had yet seen. Marble-floored double parlors welcomed guests toward a ballroom with fourteen-foot ceilings held up by fluted Corinthian columns, and a dining room surrounded by a frieze of winged angels and lighted by a giant crystal chandelier. On the second floor, huge French windows led onto a 130-foot wraparound balcony where guests could step out for fresh air or a smoke during the crowded parties frequently held there. Formal invitations to the masques, balls, sumptuous dinners, and musical soirées held at the grand Lalaurie place were among the most sought-after endorsements of acceptance into the good life that New Orleans could offer.

Suspicious Socialites

In 1833, one of the Lalauries' neighbors witnessed an uncharacteristic display from the well-regarded lady of the house that culminated in tragedy—and controversy. From a top floor window of his house overlooking the enclosed yard behind the mansion, Monsieur Montreuil saw a whip-wielding Delphine Lalaurie chasing a young enslaved female house servant along the railed balconies of the house. He watched as the terrified girl ran up to the rooftop cupola, with Madame Lalaurie just a few steps behind her, and then leaped off the roof, falling three stories to her death. According to the report filed by the neighbor, he later saw the Lalaurie couple burying the girl's body by lantern light in a shallow grave in the garden.

Did the girl jump, or was she pushed? Speculative whispers circulated around the city, although when the incident was investigated, Madame Lalaurie and her husband were more or less exonerated. They paid a fine when the body was uncovered, but the death was ruled accidental, since authorities had only the neighbor's account to contradict the Lalauries' story that the girl had fallen onto the marble floor of the central stairwell while playing on a banister. Besides, Monsieur Montreuil's report wasn't entirely reliable. There had been bad blood between Montreuil and Madame Lalaurie ever since she had been revealed as the de facto executor of an estate that he thought rightfully belonged to him.

Doctor and Madame Lalaurie's good standing among the city's elite didn't suffer as a result of the young girl's death, and life at the mansion soon returned to business as usual. The stylish soirées resumed and continued in full swing for about another year, until Madame Lalaurie's dark secret was revealed.

Sinister Secrets Revealed

The fire started in the kitchen of Lalaurie Mansion. Some say it was the cook's doing and that he did it intentionally. After dense smoke began pouring from the kitchen windows, the Lalauries were seen frantically hauling furniture out onto the street. Someone sounded an alarm. While waiting for the fire brigade to arrive, neighbors pitched in to help rescue the Lalauries' belongings. Before long, someone noticed that none of the house servants was helping with the frenzied task and realized that they might still be trapped inside the mansion.

Despite strong protests from Madame Lalaurie and her husband, several men ran into the burning building to rescue the missing household staff. They climbed to the upper floors, and, hearing muffled screams from behind a battened portal, the men broke down the thick door. According to the *Bee* story that ran on Friday, April 11, 1834, ". . . the most appalling spectacle met their eyes. Seven slaves more or less horribly mutilated . . . Language is powerless and inadequate to give a proper conception of the horror . . . confined by her [Madame Lalaurie] for several months in the situation from which they had thus providentially been rescued, and had been merely kept in existence to prolong their suffering and to make them taste all that the most refined cruelty could inflict."

After the mutilated slaves were carried from the burning house, some with the iron rings still locked tight around their necks, the crowd that had gathered to help save the building and its contents turned almost immediately into an angry mob. They began smashing furniture, looting, and destroying everything in sight.

The details of what happened next remain unclear to this day. According to a report that came out some years later, Doctor and Madame Lalaurie managed to get away during the chaotic melee that took place as the looters swarmed through their mansion. They fled to France a few weeks later, where they lived out the rest of their lives in relative obscurity. Delphine Lalaurie is thought to have died in Paris on December 7, 1842, but she may not have been buried there. A 1941 *Times-Picayune* article mentions that in the mid-1930s a cemetery worker discovered a corroded copper "epitaph plate" with Madame Lalaurie's name on it in Alley No. 4 of the old St. Louis Cemetery No. 1. This suggests that her family had welcomed her remains back home to New Orleans, perhaps nearly a century earlier.

A History of Hauntings

Despite her veneer of culture and refinement, Madame Lalaurie did, in fact, keep a torture chamber at 1140 Royal Street. Whether or not there's truth to some of the more fantastic stories that have emerged over the years—that she and her husband performed weird medical experiments on their victims or that a mass grave full of skeletons had been uncovered beneath the floorboards—enough horror and misery were inflicted in that old house to more than account for all the psychic disturbances and paranormal events that have been observed there for more than 150 years.

Before renovations turned the house into luxury apartments for families of far fewer means, residents said that they had seen Madame Lalaurie herself stomping through the rooms. Some claimed that she'd picked up babies and hurled them down the stairs or beat children until they bled, although child protection authorities rarely accepted these explanations for how younger occupants in the apartments had been abused.

Screams and cries of torment are still often heard emanating from the house. Furniture is sometimes smashed into splinters despite being kept in unoccupied rooms behind locked doors. Occupants occasionally report the sound of chains dragging over floorboards overhead, or the shadowy figures of a small girl pursued by a tall, whip-wielding woman momentarily silhouetted against the windows. Neighbors say that from time to time a young girl is seen leaping from the roof or that tortured faces press against the glass of top-floor windows, wordlessly begging to be set free. Since Madame Lalaurie seems to have gotten away with her crimes and never faced punishment—at least not on this mortal plane—perhaps the souls of her tormented slaves continue to cry out in pain until justice is finally, somehow, achieved.

Haunted House Sold to Hollywood Hunk

Actor Nicolas Cage bought the Lalaurie Mansion in 2007 for $3,450,000. He paid exactly the same amount in 2005 for the former Our Mother of Perpetual Help Chapel on Prytania Street in New Orleans's Garden District, previously owned by vampire writer Anne Rice. Neither place is open to the public, and Cage's plans for these weird properties have not been announced.

Susie Plantation

Ask around Garden City or Centerville in St. Mary Parish for directions to "the haunted house," and you'll likely be directed to Susie Plantation. The old homestead stands by itself roughly halfway between the two communities. Surrounded by cane fields, the house doesn't appear to have changed much since it was built in the early 1800s. It's a squared-off, white clapboarded structure with double porches both front and back.

The house looks welcoming, but the reason locals believe the place is haunted is pretty clear: A single, aboveground tomb stands in the middle of the side yard. Young Addie Harris, who died during childbirth at the age of twenty-two, lived here as a child. Not long before her death, she and fiancé James Stirling Hereford were put in charge of running the facility.

A number of mysteries surround the old house. For one, Mr. Hereford is not buried near Addie, although he likely remarried and chose to spend eternity buried alongside the woman with whom he spent the greater part of his life. Still, it must have been unsettling for Mr. Hereford to look out of the house windows and see Addie's lonely marble sarcophagus out in the rain—or shine—or dimly glowing in the full moon's light, like an accusing presence. There's an eerie epitaph on its weathered slab, which reads, "Weep not: she is not dead, but sleepeth." Although the sentiment seems pure Victorian—an expression of the cult of mourning—there are some who say that it should be taken literally, since the figure of a young, shrouded woman has often been seen in the vicinity of the tomb at night, with a reproachful look of condemnation and regret upon her face.

The story may be more complex than it seems. Photographs taken in the vicinity of the grave sometimes reveal a shadowy figure, not of the young would-be mother but of a man who seems to be attired in the ragged clothing of a field hand. Could there have been a secret tryst? Could she have killed herself out of shame or died while trying to lose her baby? The answers, it seems, went with her to the grave.

Paranormal Playmates at Logan Mansion

Ghosts make lousy tenants. They keep odd hours, disturb the neighbors, create all sorts of ruckus, and all off, they don't pay rent and aren't easily evicted. Worst of all, they seem to like living in a rundown place and don't appreciate anyone else fixing it up. The surest, easiest, and cheapest way to spook the spooks into revealing themselves is to show up with a fresh can of paint and some brushes and act like you're going to do a little sprucing up. They *hate* that.

When Vicki and Billy LeBrun moved into the old Logan Mansion on Austin Place in Shreveport in the mid-1970s, they soon got underway with renovations. One of the features they loved was the house's large unfinished attic, which had served as a rainy-day playroom for the children of former owners and could be refitted as Vicki's baton-twirling school. But the more they tried to fix up the place, the more the house seemed to resist their efforts. Can lids popped off and went missing, paint spilled of its own accord, and newly replaced window glass inexplicably shattered. Exhausted after a typical day peppered with events like this, they'd try to go to sleep, but then lights would turn on and televisions or radios would suddenly blare in unoccupied rooms. The smell of fried chicken often permeated the house, even if salad was the only thing on the dinner menu.

Despite all that, the big Victorian pile was still a little too swanky to call a living hell. But when the overlarge rooms began to feel crowded, the couple realized they weren't alone and decided to do some investigating.

The house had originally belonged to local beer and ice distributor L. R. Logan, who bought a sizeable lot in Shreveport's Ledbetter Heights neighborhood and built the Queen Anne–style house there in 1897. But by the end of World War I, it had become a boarding house, owned by a former Kansas City Southern Railroad conductor named Wade Hampton. Hampton raised fighting cocks in a small pen behind the house and tinkered as a part-time inventor, but no one knows whether either of these activities ever amounted to much. For a while the LeBruns wondered if Hampton himself might be their ghost. After all, an oddball inventor might be the kind of guy who would fry up his fighting roosters if they failed to perform in the ring—that would certainly explain the smell of fried chicken. And if Hampton had been a handyman type, then maybe he was resentful of their amateur restoration efforts. So the "Hampton Is He Who Haunts Us" theory stood for a while.

Little Girls, Lost

But then the LeBruns' historical sleuthing brought a disturbing incident to light. In the late 1970s, a psychic, who was investigating the former Florentine Supper Club across the street, saw a small girl in the upstairs window of the Logan place. She told the couple, and they mentioned the sighting to the employees of radio station KZOZ, which had used the Logan house for its offices and broadcast studios in the years before the LeBruns bought it. Both an engineer and a retired DJ admitted that they'd sometimes seen little girls dashing toward the attic. But every time they followed, there was nothing there, so eventually they learned to ignore it. Then an old document revealed that Hampton had seen her too—so he couldn't be the ghost after all.

The question, then, was who is she? At least two stories emerged as possible answers. One story the LeBruns uncovered concerned a Dr. Randall Hunt who had lived across the street around the turn of the last century. His daughter, Theodora, was considered peculiar and somewhat "unbalanced." She often roamed the neighborhood looking for other children to play with, but whenever she came lurching into sight, the other kids ran away screaming. She

[illegible] to wander into other people's houses—almost no one bothered to lock their doors back then—and if any adults were at home, they'd take her by the hand and lead her back to Dr. Hunt's house. According to one story, in 1904 she entered Logan Mansion at a time when it was unoccupied and made her way to the top floor. Whether Theodora fell or jumped isn't known, but the Logans found her lying on the ground directly below the open dormer window of the attic, her little skull shattered from the fall.

But another story says that a different young girl was one among several children living in the old Logan place after it had become a boarding house. She was the daughter of a teacher living on the third floor, and in 1928 she jumped or accidentally fell out of that same aforementioned window while playing.

We're not so sure there's necessarily a conflict between these two stories, however. What if, just to make a wild speculation, both were true? What if, after twenty-four years of having no [illegible] play with, Theodora Hunt finally saw her chance to recruit a permanent playmate and *pushed* the other girl out the same window? After all, one of the other recurring phenomena at the Logan place has been the sound of voices, plural. From somewhere far upstairs, sounds of a shutting door and at least two faint muffled voices are heard.

Terrifyingly Good Tea at Myrtles

The Myrtles Plantation in St. Francisville is said to be one of the most haunted places in Louisiana. In an old home like that, you kind of expect that a fair number of tragedies have occurred over the years. I've heard many stories, but one particular tale stands out. Most Louisianans will recognize it.

During antebellum times, there was a slave girl who lived with and worked for the family in the main house of Myrtles Plantation. No one knows why, but the girl fell out of favor with the family and she came up with a plan to get back in their good graces. She decided to make tea using highly toxic oleander leaves—we call it "Charleston tea" in the South—which in very small doses can cause one to become quite sick. She gave the tea to members of the family and waited for its effects to kick in, intending to nurse them back to health and redeem herself to the family.

Unfortunately the girl allowed the oleander leaves to steep for too long and when she "administered" the dose she accidentally killed everyone in the family. After realizing what she'd done, she hanged herself. People say the slave girl's ghost haunts Myrtles Plantation, as does the family she poisoned. —*Vincenzo*

Stage Fright at Shreveport's Memorial Auditorium

There's something about an old theater that generates a sense of persistent presences there. Actors are famous for hanging on to more superstitions than ordinary mortals, and it may be in part because, in order to do their jobs well, they have to channel their characters in much the same way spiritual mediums channel the souls of the dead. An empty stage echoes with all the acts and performances that ever made it come alive, and whenever the curtain rises before a new audience, it is to conjure up a moment that transports the crowd into a different state of being for a period of time.

Shreveport's Municipal Memorial Auditorium undoubtedly has more than the average share of theatrical magic and memories embedded in its Art Deco woodwork. Opened just eighteen days after the 1929 stock market crash that initiated the Great Depression, it survived the dark years and went on to launch the careers of now-legendary stars like Elvis Presley, Hank Williams, and Johnny Cash. Two weeks after his first performances in Nashville, Elvis played Shreveport on October 16, 1954, and then signed a contract with the Louisiana Hayride Talent Showcase to perform every Saturday night for $18 a week. A year and a half later, Dutch impresario Col. Tom Parker bought out the deal and then successfully manipulated the twenty-year-old all the way to stardom—and, some say, to death. Presley's bronze statue stands in front of the auditorium now.

Many people who work at the auditorium claim that more than just memories remain in the place. Doors open and shut by themselves in the empty hall several times a day, toilets suddenly flush in empty bathrooms, and old stage controls for lights and scenery seem to have minds of their own. Recordings made by paranormal researchers with special equipment have picked up electronic voice phenomena (EVPs), including audible talking and whispers, as well as clapping and whistling sounds. Other frequently reported phenomena are the sounds of babies crying, racking coughs, uncontrolled laughter, and loud yawns. These sound like horrors, all right, but we can't say if they come from out in the hall where the audience sits or from backstage, behind the curtain. Aren't they, after all, the demons that fill the nightmares of every performer?

Loyd's Hall of Haunts

William Loyd has been his own worst enemy since birth, which by now must be at least a couple of centuries ago. According to legend, as a young man in England he was considered such a scoundrel that his family disowned him. He was forced to drop one of the *L*s in his last name to further disassociate him from the rest of the Lloyds and then was told to leave England entirely.

Being a rogue of low morals and high aspirations, he naturally headed to Louisiana, where he bought a three-thousand-acre parcel of land on Bayou Boeuf near Cheneyville, built a house there sometime between 1816 and 1830, and then set himself up as a planter. The local Indian tribes apparently thought even less of him than his former relatives did, as a couple of flint arrowheads found embedded in the front door of the house seem to attest. As one of his neighbors quipped, "If you'd ordered a wagon train full of rascals but all you got was Bill Loyd, you'd still think you'd got your money's worth."

By 1864, when the Civil War had reached this part of Rapides Parish, wily "Grandpa Loyd" was considered (or else pretended to be) too old and too feeble to fight and chose to sit out the war at home. He invited Union troops to camp on his land and then wined and dined the officers. He may have hoped to curry a few more favors (or at least save his house from being burned down) by offering to tell them where the Rebel forces were hiding.

But if trying to stay on the winning side was his goal, this time it backfired. Following his directions, the Union soldiers walked straight into a Rebel ambush. Unfortunately for Loyd, enough of them managed to escape and straggle back to their campsite at his plantation to point an accusing finger in his direction. Justice was swift. Loyd was dragged out of his house, dipped in boiling tar, and then hanged from one of the oaks in his own front yard. That oak stood until 1957, when Hurricane Audrey finally uprooted it.

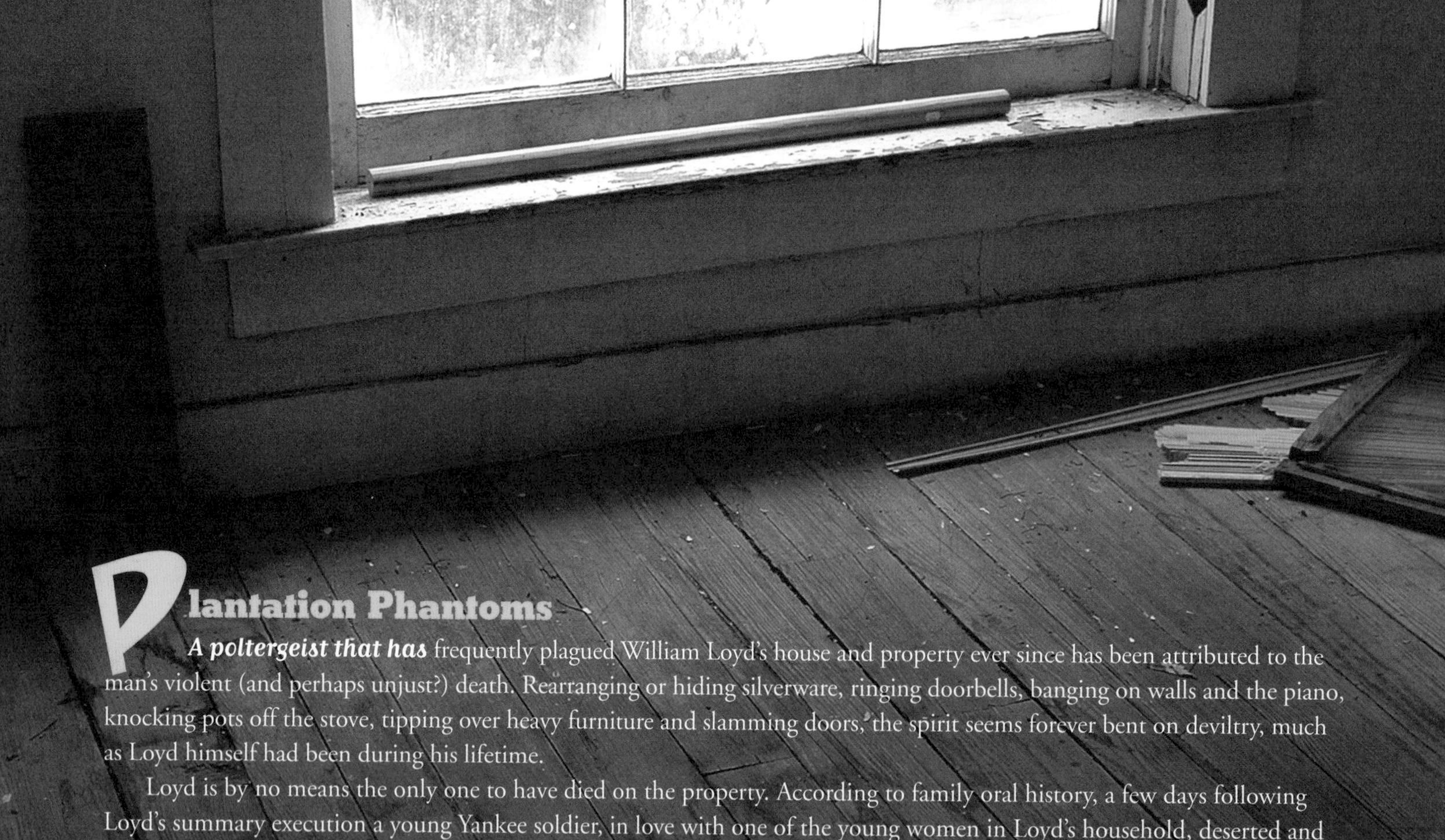

Plantation Phantoms

A poltergeist that has frequently plagued William Loyd's house and property ever since has been attributed to the man's violent (and perhaps unjust?) death. Rearranging or hiding silverware, ringing doorbells, banging on walls and the piano, knocking pots off the stove, tipping over heavy furniture and slamming doors, the spirit seems forever bent on deviltry, much as Loyd himself had been during his lifetime.

Loyd is by no means the only one to have died on the property. According to family oral history, a few days following Loyd's summary execution a young Yankee soldier, in love with one of the young women in Loyd's household, deserted and stayed behind when his fellow troops pulled up their tent stakes to begin the Red River Campaign. He hid in a small storage closet under the roof off the east room on the third floor. When he finally emerged he accidentally surprised (or enraged) Loyd's widow, who stabbed or shot him and then left him to slowly bleed to death on the floor, where bloodstains marking the scene of the incident remain to this day. Unable to lug him downstairs by herself, Loyd's widow tipped his body out a third-floor window and then dragged his corpse into a shallow grave beneath the house.

Another bloodstain marks the spot where William Loyd's niece Inez, jilted at the altar on her wedding day, slashed her wrists and bled to death. Here again, however, the orally transmitted stories vary in the details, since some of the versions insist instead that she jumped to her death through that very same third-floor window, only to be impaled on a big shard of glass when she hit the ground below. Or could this have been the fate of Annie Loyd, yet another niece? Since all the records were destroyed during the Civil War, the various tales and legends about the house and its occupants have become entangled in the turbulent years that followed. Although they do all agree on one thing: Several restless spirits occupy the plantation.

Since the Civil War, more than a dozen families have attempted to live in the slowly crumbling house. But whether driven out by ghosts or daunted by both the ever-advancing decay of the structure and its remote location, none managed to stay for very long. Misfortune and suffering seemed to grip anyone who tried to live there, but each new owner had to discover the curse for himself and then keep it a secret, lest he be unable to resell it to the next unsuspecting buyer.

Harmless Haunts

The old Loyd property changed hands again and again, shrinking from 3,000 to only 640 acres as the forlorn mansion gradually became so overgrown with vegetation that when Virginia Fitzgerald and her husband bought the property in 1948, they had no idea it included the old house. Pulling down the vines that thickly shrouded it, the Fitzgeralds rediscovered the ten-room Georgian manor, cleaning out decades of debris to reveal its "floating" staircase of tiger maple and the beautifully intricate plasterwork of its sixteen-foot ceilings. Confident that they had found a treasure, the Fitzgeralds and their young children moved in as soon as the rooms were cleared and the broken windowpanes replaced. They had not, however, counted on sharing the house with its long-term residents or heard about the ongoing curse, so when tragedy struck, they were unprepared. Within months of moving in, both Mr. Fitzgerald and his daughter were killed in a mysterious accident.

Undaunted by the supernatural, Virginia Fitzgerald chose to remain in the house. Determined to somehow carve out a place for the living among the spirits of the dead, she furnished the place with antiques—including a massive 1878 piano that once belonged to politician William Jennings Bryan and that is still in the house today—and began delving into its past. Some things, like the bullets she found embedded in the stairs, never yielded an explanation, but in time she came to terms with the phantoms. Her surviving son raised a family there and eventually her grandchildren learned to play with one of the ghosts, "Harry Henry," as they called the lovelorn young soldier. Harry entertained them with violin music he played on the broad second-floor veranda and often wandered through the house in his old Union uniform. He and Inez, and another spirit the family called Sally (thought to be a former slave), all seemed to be harmless, even benevolent toward the Fitzgeralds, who had lived in the North before buying the property. But William Loyd apparently never forgave the Union for the tarring and hanging and never ceased his troublemaking until the living Fitzgeralds finally moved out of the mansion into a cozier modern cottage they built nearby.

Loyd's Hall is now being refitted for use as a guesthouse. If you choose to stay there, we recommend you keep quiet about where you're from—if you hail from the South, Harry might not like it, and if you say you're from up North, you might have William to deal with. So mum's the word either way.

Central Hospital Haunts

What is it about mental hospitals that suggests they were intended to make their patients even *more* disturbed than before they got there? Most of them resemble prisons or elementary schools from the 1950s, as if dialing back the clock and making patients feel like they're perpetually stuck in their nightmare childhoods were really the best way to make them feel comfortable. Does anyone *really* have fond memories of fourth grade?

What resident wouldn't be disturbed when the hospital is infested with the real stuff of nightmares: accumulated horrors and unhappy terrors of thousands of patients? It's as if they spent half their lives experiencing night sweats and tremors and then gathered and decided to stay—as certainly seems to be the case at Central Hospital in Pineville, a well-known site for paranormal activity of all sorts.

When Central Hospital opened in the early 1900s it was undoubtedly considered a big improvement over the olden days of psychiatric care. Until the late nineteenth century, mental patients were treated with techniques that would violate the Geneva Conventions' standards today. Patients were locked into metal straitjackets, kept in tiny "restraint cages," or strapped to "tranquilizing chairs" equipped with chamber pots so they could be held sitting upright and immobile for months at a time.

Although those days are happily behind us, there's still more than enough to be afraid of at Central Hospital—but of the paranormal sort. Unit 2 has an elevator that seems to be operated by unseen hands, for instance. In the middle of the night it will begin traveling between floors and opening and shutting its doors with nobody on board. In other units, staff and patients have reported hearing doors slamming loudly and the sounds of heavy rolling objects echoing down the corridors. When the hallways are checked, they're empty and silent, and all the individual doors are firmly secured for the night.

Spooks at Seven

Unit 7 stood unused for many years, but due to overcrowding and renovations going on elsewhere in the hospital, it was reoccupied in 1999. Shortly thereafter staff and visitors began noticing an abundance of unexplained activity—strange glowing lights passing under doors, voices coming from empty rooms, unoccupied chairs suddenly tipping over, objects randomly falling from shelves, clocks keeping wildly inaccurate time, computers and electrical appliances turning on and off at odd times.

Such activity is usually associated with the presence of one or more poltergeists, who are in turn often associated with the presence of certain living people—referred to by paranormal scholars as "poltergeist agents." According to researcher Lauren Forcella, these living agents "are unaware that they are causing the physical disturbances, and . . . usually have no conscious control over how and when the disturbances will occur." Strange physical phenomena are much more likely to happen in the presence of "two or more people who cocreate a psychological dynamic that causes one or more of the people to mentally 'set off' the physical disturbances. Studies and investigations show that agents are typically experiencing repressed or unresolved emotional stress." That sounds like an accurate description of a typical mental hospital.

Even if Central Hospital weren't haunted, it would still be a pretty creepy place. Some of the older buildings are abandoned and are gradually falling into decay. Scattered pieces of broken wheelchairs, old boxes filled with moldy pillows and rotting Bibles, stained mattresses and splintered chairs tell the stories of the broken spirits of the people who lived in some of those buildings. Other parts of the hospital are still in use, but even those feel forlorn and forgotten.

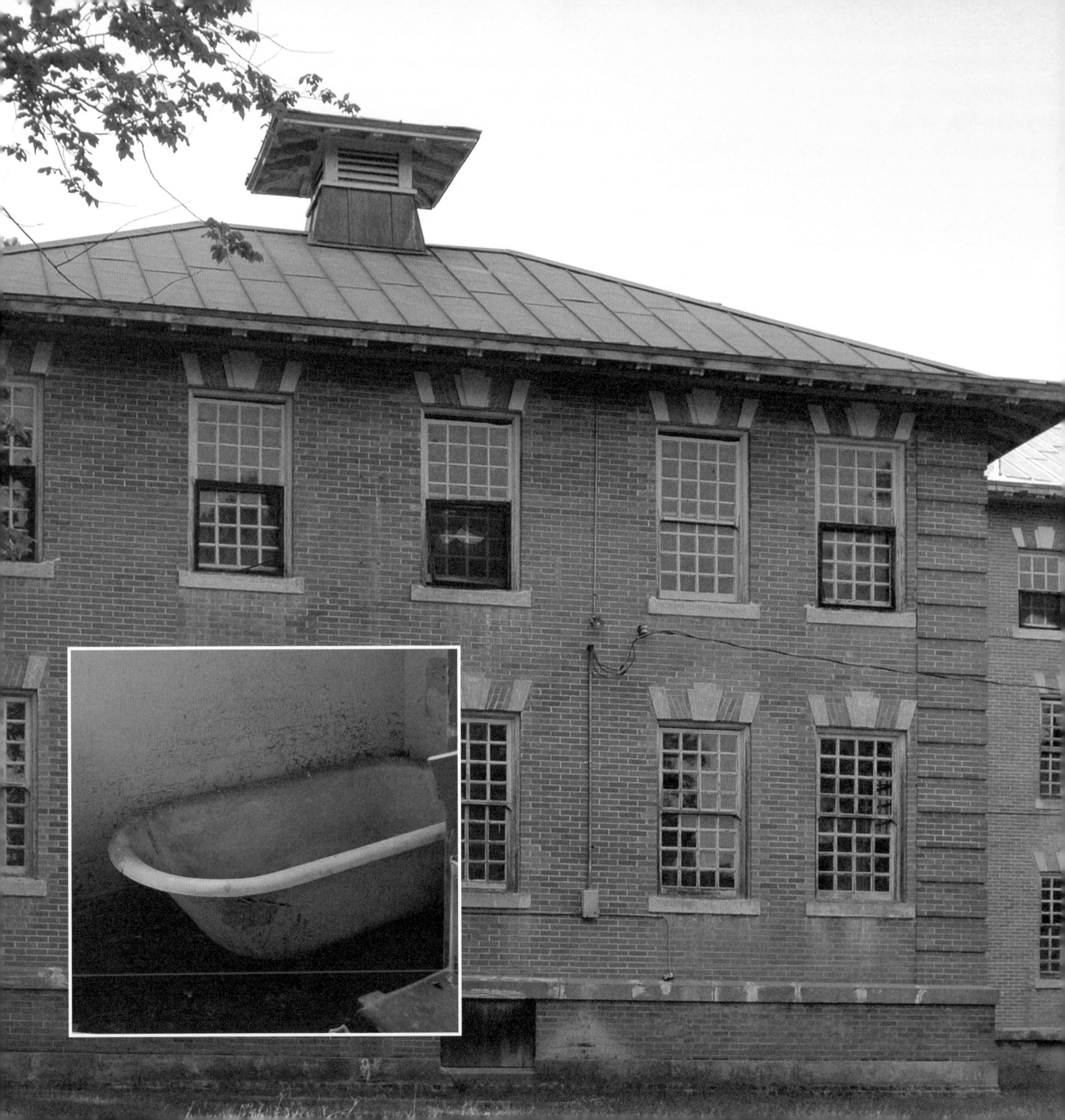

Woman in White

In Ruston, the Center for Biomedical Engineering and Rehabilitation Science on South Vienna Street is a bright, white brick building where researchers and technicians develop equipment to help disabled people lead more normal lives. Everyone there is committed to making specialized devices that fulfill particular medical needs. All highly trained, they're pragmatic and no-nonsense, not the kind of people with uncontrolled imaginations.

And yet much of the staff will tell you about the otherworldly occupants of their building. An apparition haunts three places inside the facility: a consultation room on the fourth floor, an elevator in the hall immediately outside it, and a workshop in the basement. A woman in white is occasionally seen puttering around all three places; and although she's a startling sight to new employees, she is harmless in going about her duties. Doors sometimes open and shut and the elevator may suddenly head from the fourth floor down to the basement and back again; but other than that, she seems to have taken the primary tenet of the Hippocratic Oath to heart: First, do no harm. Her name is Mrs. Evans, and she's there to stay.

open out onto a kind of terrace over the adjacent wing. Those windows hint at the room's original function. Before they had automatic emergency lighting and backup generators, hospitals operated primarily in the daylight. And if the facility were to catch fire, surgical personnel were forbidden to abandon their unconscious patients on the operating table; instead they would have to sew up incisions as fast as possible and drag the patients out onto the terrace to await rescue. When patients died, that elevator took them down to the basement morgue, where autopsies were performed, tumors were sectioned, and amputated limbs were disposed.

Mrs. Evans, it turns out, was the former head OR nurse. She'd spent her whole adult life standing guard at the gateway between suffering and recovery, and between life and the afterlife. She'd seen plenty of patients through storms and fires, accompanied them or their body parts to the dreaded basement, and knew more than most about life's fragility. She was evidently so dedicated and took her duties so seriously that she wasn't about to let her task be interrupted by something as routine as death—especially not her own.

Remains of Ruston Hospital At one time, the Biomedical Engineering building was the old Ruston Hospital. The fourth-floor consultation room, which has wider windows than any other room, was once an operating suite. Now filled with comfortable furniture, the room's windows

Haunted High School

C. E. Byrd High School opened on September 17, 1925, with a speech by aging Caddo Parish school superintendent Clifton Ellis Byrd, who said that dedicating the building was the proudest moment of his life. Dr. Byrd died just five months later and his body was put on display in the foyer of the school; all the students were marched by it to get a good look at his stern-faced corpse. Some people later said that this lying-in-state might have been a bad idea, since many impressionable adolescents began to complain of seeing Dr. Byrd in their dreams, saying he would never let them leave "his" school.

Within a few years of the school's opening, a female student who complained that Dr. Byrd appeared in her dreams was found dead in the shallow end of the school's indoor swimming pool. Concerned parents petitioned to have the tank drained and covered, and soon the pool was converted into a dance studio and gym. Dance students have since described a mysterious cold spot in the room directly above where the girl had drowned. What's more, the girl herself, sporting an old-fashioned black wool bathing suit, has been seen walking around the school, gasping and crying. Sometimes witnesses catch a quick glimpse of her head or a hand that appears out of the floor, as if they are witnessing the girl's drowning.

After the pool was covered in the 1930s, the school community assumed that the worst was over. And so it was, until just before World War II, when tragedy struck again. This time it was a JROTC cadet, found dead of a gunshot wound in a sub-basement area that students called the "catacombs." Because the young man's body had been found behind a locked door, his death was ruled self-inflicted, though no traces of gunpowder were found on his hands and evidence suggested that he wouldn't have been able to aim and fire the gun at himself. Rumors quickly emerged that something else was afoot in the school—something not quite of this world. The rumors seemed confirmed when the apparitions of the drowned girl were joined by sightings of the young man in cadet attire.

There's an old saying that the ideal school boils down to two people sitting on a log: a great teacher and a student. Could it be that C. E. Byrd saw himself as that great teacher but, by dying so soon after his dream school finally opened, he ultimately missed out on getting to sit on the log? Perhaps Dr. Byrd is sitting on a log in the spiritual realm, the drowned girl and the young cadet with him.

Old State Capitol: The Haunted Castle

Some buildings seem to cry out that they're haunted. Outfitted with turrets, towers, creepy corridors, weirdly sweeping staircases, heavily paneled doors that creak on their hinges, stained-glass windows that turn ordinary daylight into crepuscular gloom, they almost seem to scream, "Haunt me, baby! Haunt me bad!" Every town should have at least one such place—some old pile of overblown architecture that makes you want to whistle out of sheer nervousness when you hustle quickly past it at night.

Louisiana's Old State Capitol is just such a place. From a distance it looks like something a kid might build on the beach, but up close it looms threateningly high, with crenellated medieval towers and crossbow slits that bring Robin Hood and the Sheriff of Nottingham to mind. Mark Twain considered it the ugliest building on the Mississippi, referring to it as "a little sham castle" and a "pathetic architectural falsehood" and even suggested that it should have been dynamited to put it out of its misery.

We couldn't disagree more. As aficionados of the weird, we think the Old State Capitol is coolness incarnate.

The Spectral Senator

Not only does the Old State Capitol cry out as a hometown haunt, but it actually delivers the ghoulish goods. What's more, the ghost doing the haunting has been identified as Pierre Couvillon, who served as a state representative and senator from Avoyelles Parish from 1834 until 1851. He would likely have remained in government longer, but he died of an apoplectic fit after uncovering yet another layer of corruption among his fellow lawmakers. Unusual for the Robin Hood–like stance he maintained among his colleagues, Couvillon was apparently outraged by how other wealthy politicians used the privileges of their office to further enrich themselves. During one of his angry outbursts at this perpetual state of affairs, he fell dead.

But maybe Couvillon never left office. Even during the twenty long years between 1862, when Yankee troops set fire to the building and left it a smoking ruin, and 1882, when repairs and restorations finally began, his tall, glaring figure was sometimes spotted wandering among the blackened walls, keeping an eye on things. When the building reopened to government activity in the 1880s, Pierre was among the members of the senate, sometimes casting a vote from beyond the grave (a time-honored Louisiana tradition). Dead or not, he remained a regular attendee until Gov. Huey Long's skyscraping New State Capitol opened in 1932 and the legislature moved to the north end of downtown Baton Rouge, leaving Pierre behind in the little castle.

For a long while it seemed as if Pierre had vanished from the scene for good. The old Gothic building was demoted to a civic activity space and allowed to slump into poorly maintained drabness that barely hinted at its former government grandeur. But finally in the 1980s and early 1990s, a major restoration effort reinvigorated the building's magnificence and, at the same time, possibly reawakened its resident ghost. Pierre was back, and he was excited to be a part of it all again.

Before long, security officers started filing reports of alarms going off and motion sensors registering the presence of moving objects during nights when the building had been securely locked down. Tools and small items left in locked rooms began mysteriously disappearing and then reappearing in other parts of the building. Video cameras revealed nothing, but eventually footprints were discovered when some maintenance work in one chamber (the former state senate) had left a fine powdering of plaster dust on the polished floor. The prints led directly to the former desk (surmounted by his portrait) of Senator Couvillon. That was enough proof to make believers out of the Old State Capitol staff.

Rather than call for an exorcist to rid the building of its spectral senator once and for all, they took the opposite approach and decided to capitalize on it. Nowadays, brochures call attention to the cathedral-like interior dome of the main hall, point out the fossils in the marble flooring, describe the intricate brass hardware on all the doors . . . and encourage visitors to keep a sharp lookout for Pierre, the Capitol ghost.

Cemetery Safari

Long before Dennis Hopper and Peter Fonda took their wild 'n' crazy trip through New Orleans's St. Louis Cemetery No. 1 in *Easy Rider*, the image of labyrinthine, mausoleum-crammed graveyards filled with zombies, nutcases, cracked tombs, and creepy, looming statuary had already become a widely held stereotype of the Pelican State. The trouble with such stereotypes is that there's usually at least a nugget of truth behind them. In the case of Louisiana graveyards, they *are* different from the ones you'll find in the rest of the nation. In this southern state, the dead aren't quickly forgotten or ignored. They're a part of day-to-day life, so much so that in certain parishes the dead have been known to cast votes from time to time. The dearly departed have also been known to emerge from the comforts of their crypts—to praise their family's status, condemn the community for slights or offenses, express regrets . . . or tend to unfinished business.

What we're getting at is that a Louisiana graveyard is often a hotbed of activity. Don't believe us? Here's a collection of tombs, crypts, and mausoleums you won't soon forget.

CORA LEE WILSON
AGED 22 YEARS

NATHAN GOLDKIND
A NATIVE OF
PLOTSK, RUSSIAN POLAND
KILLED IN
SHREVEPORT, LA.
BY GUS LOGAN
JUNE 14, 1885
AGED, 35 YEARS.

The City of the Dead

It's not the oldest, largest, weirdest, or most elaborate of the forty-one cemeteries in New Orleans, but St. Louis Cemetery No. 1 is hands down the city's venerated flagship graveyard. If you hear a native mention "*the* city of the dead," this is the one they mean. Located just outside the French Quarter in what, at one time, used to be the swampy "back end" of town, the cemetery is a maze of old mausoleums full of so many blind alleys and wrong turns that we recommend going when the sun is out, so you can keep your bearings.

St. Louis No. 1 was founded in 1789, after the first great fire to sweep through Nouvelle Orléans destroyed most of its original French structures. Since the city was under Spanish colonial rule during the late eighteenth century, most of the tombs in the "new" cemetery—like most of the houses in the "French" Quarter you see today—utilized a Spanish stucco-over-brick construction after the vast majority of French-built wooden structures went up in smoke.

Although the cemetery itself belongs to the Catholic Archdiocese of New Orleans, the majority of individual tombs are family owned. This accounts not only for the variety that gives the cemetery much of its character but also for the great disparity in condition among the graves. Some are well maintained and glisten with a fresh coat of paint while others are crumbling and falling into ruin—an indicator that a family has died out, moved away, or no longer possesses the financial wherewithal to take care of its mausoleum.

A Tomb Built for Two . . . Thousand

The society tombs in St. Louis No. 1 and other old New Orleans cemeteries that look a lot like large, multidrawer filing cabinets for the dead served a vital function in their day—they made decent burials affordable for the masses. Rob Florence, a committed taphophile and founder of Friends of New Orleans Cemeteries, explains that only the finest nineteenth-century artisans and craftsmen serviced the graveyards and that their prices could be astronomical.

"To cut costs, people would band together in 'Benevolent Associations,' " he says. "These societies would reduce medical bills and help support widows, but their main purpose was to provide a sort of burial insurance, ensuring interment in a consecrated cemetery."

One of the grandest tombs in St. Louis No. 1 is that of the Italian Mutual Benefit Society, which can house the remains of up to 3,600 individuals. Since it was built in 1857 at a cost of $40,000 (the rough equivalent of a million dollars today), it isn't hard to see why dividing up the costs was so crucial.

xxx

The city of the dead is home to handful of well-known graves, the most famous being voodoo queen Marie Laveau, recognizable by the vandalism that scars it and the offerings left in front of "her" mausoleum. Ignorant visitors scrawl three *x*'s (*xxx*) on the structure in hopes that her spirit is still somewhere in the neighborhood and will answer their prayers and wishes. However, as many cemetery historians have pointed out, this graffiti has nothing to do with local voodoo traditions and was probably invented by tour guides. And even if Madame Laveau's spirit is hovering somewhere nearby, it is almost certain that her remains are not in this tomb, which belongs to the Glapion family. If the bones of anyone named Marie Laveau are still in there, they are far more likely to be those of her daughter, Marie Laveau II, who was the common-law wife of Capt. Christopher Glapion. Another tomb, located in the wall against the Iberville Street end of St. Louis Cemetery No. 2, is also locally venerated by those in the know as the "real" tomb of the voodoo queen, but it is probably just as dubious. No one knows for sure where Marie Laveau is buried.

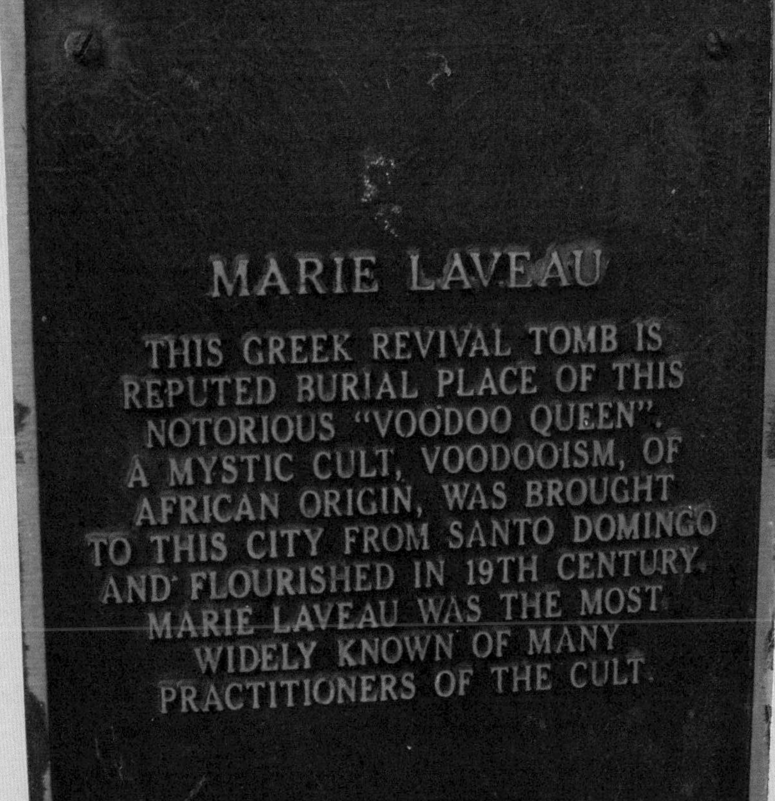

MARIE LAVEAU
THIS GREEK REVIVAL TOMB IS REPUTED BURIAL PLACE OF THIS NOTORIOUS "VOODOO QUEEN". A MYSTIC CULT, VOODOOISM, OF AFRICAN ORIGIN, WAS BROUGHT TO THIS CITY FROM SANTO DOMINGO AND FLOURISHED IN 19TH CENTURY. MARIE LAVEAU WAS THE MOST WIDELY KNOWN OF MANY PRACTITIONERS OF THE CULT.

Holt Cemetery

Located behind the Administration Building of Delgado Community College at 615 City Park Avenue, Holt Cemetery has been the place to bury the poor, abandoned, or otherwise unidentified dead since the late 1800s. In New Orleans, where the water table is just a foot or two below ground level, Holt is the only graveyard where the dead are housed underground.

Those who couldn't afford aboveground burial in a marble mausoleum or brick wall alcove (as is customary in southern Louisiana) could purchase a plot scarcely larger than the hole dug for the coffin. The grave lot would be outlined in wooden boards; but after a decade or two, boards and markers inevitably decay and vanish if they aren't maintained or replaced. Eventually the erosion creates room for another grave in almost the same place. Holt Cemetery has as many as three thousand gravesites marked with homemade monuments of all kinds, but the cemetery might hold the remains of ten or twenty times that many people.

Holt's Heroes

Holt Cemetery is the final resting spot of a number of musical giants, including R&B singer Jessie Hill and "King of Jazz" cornet player Buddy Bolden, whom Jelly Roll Morton called "the blowingest man since Gabriel." One of the key figures in the development of the classic New Orleans jazz style, Bolden was diagnosed with premature dementia before his thirtieth birthday and spent the rest of his life locked up in an insane asylum. The exact location of his remains—buried here in 1931—is unknown, as is the case with so many others interred here.

Dead Can Dance

"That Cora Lee Wilson has jimmy legs," the old man called out. He had seen us taking pictures of her grave, located in one corner of Shreveport's old Oakland Cemetery, and had begun strolling over from the sidewalk to kibitz. "That girl never could stand to be shut in. Her people couldn't keep her at home, not even for one whole weekend. She always loved the dancing." He acted almost as if he'd known her personally, even though it seemed pretty clear that Cora Lee had been in her grave since sometime in the 1870s or 1880s.

Cora's marker said she was dead at twenty-two. Although there is no indication of the year of her birth or death, we figured Cora was born around 1859 and died roughly between 1875 and 1885. In Victorian culture, the calla lily with two leaves decorating the marble plaque at the front of Cora's tomb usually symbolized marriage and the trumpet-like shape of the flower suggested resurrection.

But the grave raised more questions than it answered. Since Cora used her family name, did the calla mean she was engaged? Maybe it was an unhappy arrangement? Or was she not quite ready to settle down?

"Nobody knows," the old man said. "They say she was a socialite, a real party girl. The real story, though, is around the other end." He walked to the back of the low brick tomb and pointed down. "See?" he said. "You can see her coffin. Cast-iron. For some reason, it's not deeper down in there, like it should be. Even in these old box tombs, they were supposed to dig a hole, but for her it looks like they left her on top of the ground."

Then he looked us in the eye. "You may not believe it, but they say she kicks out the bricks from inside and tries to go dancing. Every time they brick it up again, she kicks it out. She's got about the worst case of jimmy legs anybody ever heard of."

Burning Love

Gram Parsons, one of the greatest rock-and-roll artists of all time, is buried in the Garden of Memories Cemetery out on Airline Highway in New Orleans. You'll have to ask around to find the grave. Don't be too surprised if no one knows exactly where it is. Head toward the middle of Section R, look around for a bench, and you'll find the flat bronze slab that marks the legendary rocker's final resting place.

Parsons, who had performed with bands including the Shilos, the Byrds, and the Flying Burrito Brothers, never envisioned being buried in New Orleans. In fact, in July 1973 he made a pact with several friends, including Phil Kaufman and Michael Martin, after attending a friend's funeral. Upon his death, Gram wished to be cremated and have his ashes scattered at Joshua Tree National Monument, in California.

In a strange twist of fate, Gram died of an accidental overdose just a few months after expressing his last wishes. Gram was in the midst of recording his second solo album, *Grievous Angel,* when a visit to a motel in Joshua Tree ended in tragedy. After consuming a fifth of whiskey, several barbiturates, and morphine, he began breathing erratically, and on September 19, 1973, he was pronounced dead at a clinic in nearby Yucca Valley, California. Robert Parsons, Gram's stepfather in New Orleans, made arrangements to have the body shipped to Louisiana for burial. His remains were placed in a coffin and taken to Los Angeles International Airport, where Phil Kaufman and Michael Martin stepped in to carry out Gram's final wishes.

Kaufman and Martin arrived at LAX in a borrowed hearse and somehow convinced the freight handlers at the airport to release Gram's body to them. They then drove to Joshua Tree and attempted a makeshift, homemade cremation. After propping the coffin open near Cap Rock, they doused Gram's body in gasoline and tossed in a lit match before pushing it over the edge. When they saw the lights of a vehicle in the distance, Kaufman and Martin jumped in the hearse and sped away.

On September 21, campers in the area reported the discovery of a "smoldering log" to park rangers, who soon identified it as a partly cremated human body. The amateur attempt had rendered only 40 percent of the corpse to ashes. After the body was identified as the dead rock star, Robert Parsons took the remains back to New Orleans for a private funeral. Kaufman and Martin were each fined $700 for building a fire in a national park outside authorized camping areas, but since there were no laws on the books against stealing corpses, they were never penalized for the theft itself. Several months later, *Grievous Angel* was released. Among the songs on the album were "Love Hurts," "In My Hour of Darkness," and "Hearts on Fire."

Light of the Soul

Harry Offner's tombstone in the Gates of Prayer Cemetery on Canal Street in New Orleans commemorates the years he spent as director of Lighthouse for the Blind, a service organization for the visually impaired. The stone is a scale model of a lighthouse, complete with steps and a tiny doorway for the keeper, windows to illuminate the spiral staircase inside, and glass surrounding the beacon. We don't know if it actually lights up at night, but we wouldn't be at all surprised if it did.

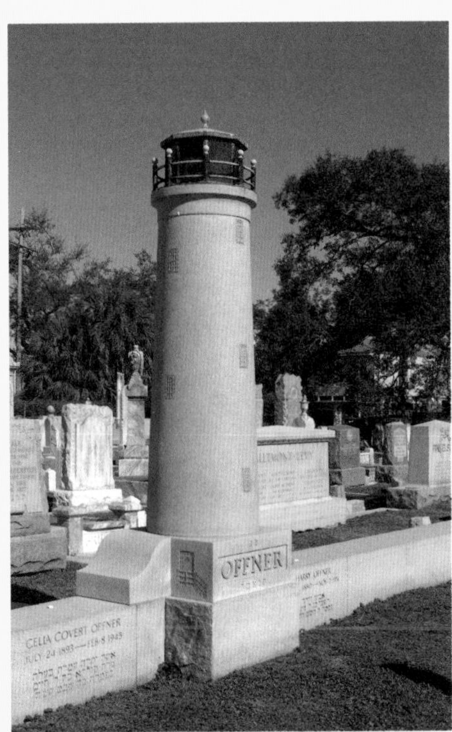

Going Out in Style

One of the grandest monuments in Metairie Cemetery—one of the grandest cemeteries in a community famous for its cities of the dead—is an immense structure. The elaborately carved stone surrounds a solid marble sarcophagus of Eugene Lacosst. Few individuals besides Renaissance popes have had burial sites more ornate or flamboyant. Yet Lacosst was not a great religious leader, revered founder of a nation, or megalomaniacal dictator.

He was, in fact, a hairdresser.

Lacosst saved what he made in his Bourbon Street barbershop and made wise investments. He arranged for his and his mother's remains to be buried at the front of the cemetery in a replica of a cardinal's tomb from the Church of Santa Croce in Florence, Italy. It may have been a case of hair today, gone tomorrow, but what a way to go!

Self-perpetuating Self-portrait

Stone carver Teodoro Francesco Bottinelli, born in Brienno, Italy, created a full-body sculpture for his own tomb in Metairie Cemetery. A similar carving of his wife, Emma Louise Pinardi Bottinelli, stands nearby, looking appropriately approving. With any luck, she'll be doing this for thousands of years to come, since both are hewn of solid granite, the longest-lasting sculptural material of all.

Women and Children First

Atop the Aldigé family mausoleum in Metairie Cemetery is a pair of winged women, desperately clutching each other on the bow of a sinking ship. The figures represent female members of the family who lost their lives onboard the French steamer *La Bourgogne* and whose remains are not contained within the tomb.

On July 4, 1898, the *La Bourgogne* was on its way to La Havre, France, with an estimated 711 people aboard, including a crew of 220. Despite the fog and the rough seas, the captain had ordered the vessel to proceed at full steam. In the dark predawn hours two days out of New York, some passengers thought they heard foghorns nearby and mentioned this to the crew, but they were told not to worry about it and go back to bed. Then, at four forty-five in the morning, *La Bourgogne* suddenly slammed into the British sailing bark *Cromartyshire* some sixty miles from the nearest land. The coal freighter *Cromartyshire* had her bow cut off in the crash and lost two of her masts, but somehow miraculously managed to stay afloat. *La Bourgogne*, however, sank within forty minutes—time that would be remembered by the lone female survivor as a living hell.

Years later Mrs. Victoire Lacasse told how she barely got onto a life raft, and only because her husband had dragged her out of the waters and then forcibly defended her. A mad panic had overtaken the crew and passengers. Wielding knives, revolvers, and oars, men fought with women and children for places on the lifeboats. As Mrs. Lacasse reported, "Suddenly men, women and children, some of them still alive, were spouted out like sticks in a boiling volume. Those poor creatures, those who had the strength, would swim to the rafts and beg to be taken aboard, and, being denied, turn and disappear into the ocean." Only 163 of 711 people survived; 104 of those were crew members. Mrs. Lacasse was the only female survivor of the nearly 300 women who were on the ship, among them the three Aldigés. Another ship, the *Grecian*, towed the survivors to Halifax, Nova Scotia.

After news of the behavior of *La Bourgogne*'s crew spread, an international court battle ensued. Although the French company that owned the ship was eventually found not legally liable for the loss of life, steamship lines everywhere amended the Law of the Sea to state in no longer uncertain terms that in the event of future mishaps, women and children should be saved first.

It wasn't long before the revised law was put to its first major test, with eerie parallels to the *La Bourgogne* tragedy. Another ship, steaming recklessly fast through northern waters and also a bit off course due to faulty navigation, had a collision at sea. And once again there was a tremendous loss of life, but when the *Titanic* struck an iceberg and went down in 1912, more than 74 percent of the women and 52 percent of the children lived to tell the tale.

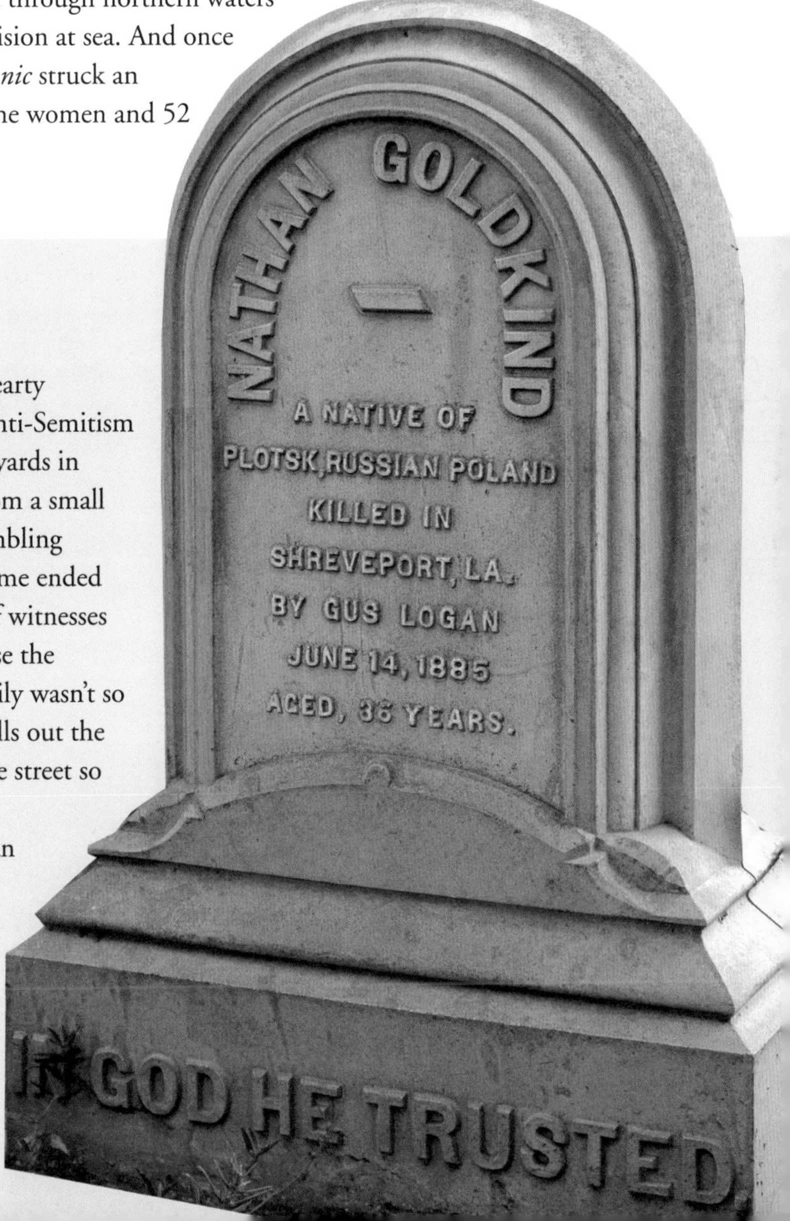

Grave Reproach

Even in its earliest days, Shreveport extended a hearty welcome to Jewish immigrants who had struggled against harsh anti-Semitism in Europe and western Asia, and some of the earliest Jewish graveyards in the state were established there. Nathan Goldkind, who hailed from a small village in Poland, ran with Shreveport's rough-hewn riverboat gambling crowd. Inevitably this led to his undoing, when in 1885 a card game ended in a shooting that left him dead at thirty-six. There were plenty of witnesses to the crime, but after the trial the murderer was pardoned because the consensus was that Goldkind had earned his fate. Goldkind's family wasn't so willing to forgive and forget, however. Goldkind's monument spells out the name of his killer—Gus Logan—in Oakland Cemetery, facing the street so that everyone who strolls by can read the indictment.

The monument is made of a cast metal promoted by Victorian funeral homes as "white bronze" but was really zinc. Still, over more than a century, it has held up a lot better under Louisiana's weather than most monuments made of far more expensive materials, such as marble or granite.

Brothel's Beacon

Of all the tombs in New Orleans's most magnificent necropolis, the one that attracts the most attention never actually bore the name of the person who made it famous. On the outer loop of Metairie Cemetery's Avenue F, keep an eye out for a life-sized bronze statue of a woman who looks as if she's eager to get back inside the crypt—this is the mausoleum of Josie Arlington, infamous madam of the city's historic red light district. A well-known local legend maintains that once in a while, when it's dark enough, the statue limbers up, turns around, and strolls through the graveyard. Perhaps, they say, she's in search of her earthly remains, which were removed from the crypt ten years after interment.

Mamie Dübler, born in New Orleans near the end of the Civil War, grew up during a turbulent period in the city's history. Amid the ethnic unrest, uncontrolled urban growth, and frequent outbreaks of disease, a lively culture of art and entertainment emerged. The birth of jazz, and burgeoning Mardi Gras celebrations—and of course, the proliferation of saloons, brothels, and bordellos—put New Orleans on the map as the Babylon of the South. By age seventeen, when Mamie started seeing a small-time thug named Phil Lobrano, she had already become a fixture in the city's budding prostitution industry. As her fame and reputation grew, she began using various aliases—Little Mary, Josie Alton, Josie Lobrano, Josie Lobrano d'Arlington, and Josie Arlington—and by 1886 she was running her own brothel in the French Quarter on what is now Iberville Street. In an effort to create the finest establishment in town, Josie began referring to her business as Le Chateau, claiming that her girls were imported examples of European aristocracy.

Vixen of Vice

Aware that they couldn't eradicate prostitution, city officials attempted to regulate it. On January 29, 1897, prostitution was outlawed throughout New Orleans, save for the thirty-eight blocks between St. Louis Cemetery No. 1 and No. 2. Named for Sidney Story, the alderman who proposed the law, "Storyville" became the nation's first legally designated prostitution district. Saloons, brothels, and cribs proliferated, so much so that by 1917, when prostitution was once again outlawed, nearly every building in the district had been converted to either a bar or a bordello.

Josie Arlington was determined to make the most of Storyville's bordello boom. She became the district's vixen of vice, opening a new over-the-top house of ill repute: The Arlington. Crystal chandeliers, paintings, and sculptures by well-known artists; plush velvet-upholstered furniture; and a piano bar were just the beginning. Food, liquor, and illicit entertainments were always available and always top-notch.

The Arlington continued to service well-to-do gents until a 1905 fire gutted much of the building. Although Madam Josie escaped uninjured and was soon back in business, her brush with disaster left her shaken and painfully aware of her own mortality. While The Arlington was being restored and refitted, she spent a small fortune on a grave plot and personal mausoleum in Metairie Cemetery, the city's most fashionable graveyard. The crypt is a testament to opulence in the afterlife: made of red marble from Maine with carved bronze doors, twin urns symbolizing sacrifice and eternity, and a statue by an artist from Düsseldorf.

The bronze statue of the woman at the tomb's door has provided locals with a topic of conversation ever since it was installed there in 1911. Some say it represents Josie seeking admission—whether to home, heaven, or high society depends on whom you ask. Others believe the statue symbolizes the young women she welcomed in and taught her trade of harlotry.

Flaming Tomb

Shortly after Josie's death in 1914, people within earshot of the tomb claimed they heard something pounding on those big bronze doors from time to time. But whenever they'd approach to investigate, the noise suddenly ceased and all they'd find was the statue with its hand frozen just inches from the door. Others have witnessed flickering lights dancing over the mausoleum while the stone altars seemed ablaze. Over the years there have been many attempts to explain the phenomenon of the flaming tomb. Practical-minded folks suggested that dancing lights had something to do with a flashing red light that marked a toll road near the cemetery; once the red light was taken down in the mid-1920s, the flames no longer appeared.

In 1924, Josie's heirs put her cemetery plot and mausoleum up for sale. During the ten years after her death, they had somehow squandered her hard-earned fortune, and, after selling the mansion on Esplanade Street, the only thing left to liquidate was the mausoleum. Josie's remains were removed from the crypt and transferred to an undisclosed location. The new owners soon moved their own dead into the crypt and carved their family name above the door. Almost to the day, the mysterious flames ceased to appear.

Pyramid Power

French-American pharmaceutical magnate Lucien Napoleon Brunswig had a pyramid-shaped family mausoleum built in 1900 for his first wife and ten-year-old son, who had both died within a month of each other in 1892. Brunswig joined them and several other family members in 1943.

Located in Metairie Cemetery, the pyramid is likely based on the design of the tomb of ancient Egyptian artist Sennedjem. It features an Egyptian temple-style entryway and a mournful female figure gesturing toward its bronze doors, which are guarded on the other side by a sphinx. What this arrangement means remains a mystery. The standing woman wearing Egyptian jewelry has an eye on her forehead and may represent the Egyptian goddess Hathor, known as the "mistress of heaven" and the goddess of mothers, children, and love. Hathor was also called the "eye of Ra" in her other role as goddess of the dead. But she's wearing a Greek himation (woman's toga), so she might represent Persephone, the Greek goddess of the Underworld, too.

As Seen on TV

Eliza Jane Wilder Thayer Gordon was the sister-in-law of Laura Ingalls Wilder, author of *Little House on the Prairie* and other books about life in the wide-open Great Plains. Known in real life as a bossy, hardheaded woman, Eliza Jane appears in the books as the domineering older sister in *Farmer Boy* and the mean schoolteacher in *Little Town on the Prairie*, but why she would want to have this memorialized on her tombstone is anybody's guess. Although she and her relatives spent much of their childhoods in places like Minnesota, Wisconsin, Kansas, and the Dakota Territory, many of them wound up in Louisiana—living in Crowley, Kinder, and Lafayette (where Eliza Jane is buried in the Protestant Cemetery)—as unsuccessful rice farmers. But somehow, *Little House on the Rice Plantation* never quite made it to syndicated television.

Drive-By Condolences

In Louisiana, your idea of a pleasant drive would involve getting the AC set right where you want it and the radio tuned to your favorite station. The last thing you'd want to do is get out of your car for anything short of a life-or-death situation. And at Verrette's Point Coupee Funeral Home in New Roads, even death isn't a good enough reason. It's one of the few mortuaries in the nation to offer a drive-by viewing option for special friends and family who don't feel like dressing up from the waist down or prefer their own musical ambience to mourn by. After the coffin cruise, the next stop is the nearest drive-in for some fries and a shake. After all, life is for the living.

Cemetery Symbolics

Half the fun of visiting old cemeteries is learning how to "decode" the hidden messages on the graves: Upside-down torches symbolize the extinguishing of life, anchors mean hope, pyramids symbolize eternity, flying hourglasses are intended to warn us that time flies, lambs represent innocence, ivy means life everlasting. To modern eyes, the motif from a grave in St. Louis Cemetery No. 2 in New Orleans may just look like a bouquet of pretty flowers. But the average Victorian would have had no trouble interpreting it because each flower had a particular meaning. The pansy, daisy, lily of the valley, and rose gathered here suggest that the tomb holds an unmarried teenage girl (indicated by a broken rosebud that had barely begun to bloom), who was considered gentle and innocent (as symbolized by the daisy). She will always be remembered (the pansy signifies remembrance), though now she's in a happier place awaiting resurrection (according to the lily of the valley). Hundreds of such combinations make it possible to say all kinds of things about the deceased—without using a single word.

PerPETual Care

Why are pet cemeteries so disturbing? Maybe it's the overdone sentimentality or the jarring association of overly cute names like Mopsie or Miss Pinklepaws alongside monikers like Killer or T-Rex. Or it could be that the miniature headstones contradict the real losses they memorialize, juxtaposing play and sorrow in a way that can hardly avoid looking ironic. When they're overgrown and abandoned, like St. Bernard Pet Cemetery in the Toca community of St. Bernard Parish, pet cemeteries are still more unsettling. Promises to never forget our beloved companions seem as broken as the stones on which they're engraved. Such places can't help but be haunted by unsettled spirits of forgotten, unhappy souls.

Founded in the 1950s or early 1960s by Grace Thompson and her husband, the defunct St. Bernard Pet Cemetery is hidden in the thick overgrowth close to the end of Bayou Road. In its early days, the quiet business was well suited to the Thompson family; Grace filled in the income gaps between funeral services by teaching piano lessons and daughter Dorothy Lou had a relatively normal childhood, all things considered. And then one day, Mr. Thompson went missing. Surprisingly Grace didn't seem much affected by his disappearance—she continued to give music lessons and put pets away until her own death some years later. By then, Dorothy Lou had grown up and married. She and her husband took on the task of maintaining St. Bernard Pet Cemetery, keeping the graves clean and the weeds at bay.

A few years later, the rows of miniature memorials had grown so long that a caretaker was hired to help with the upkeep of the graveyard. Not long after that, Dorothy's husband vanished. This time the disappearance was considered a little *too* convenient, and local authorities sent out a search party. It wasn't long before her husband's body was discovered, holding a pistol as if he'd shot himself, but also wearing a glove—a detail that struck many folks as strange. Why would he put on a single glove if he were going to kill himself? Dorothy Lou was taken into custody for questioning but, because there wasn't enough evidence to book her, she was released that same afternoon. And then a few weeks later Dorothy Lou went missing, only to be discovered by fishermen in a nearby bayou who reeled in her half-rotted corpse wrapped in chains. By then, the caretaker had disappeared as well. As far as any of the neighbors know, he never returned. The case remains unsolved.

Doggie Depression

One of the most popular monuments in Metairie's vast necropolis memorializes an outstanding representative of humankind's best friend. When Austro-Croatian immigrant Francis Masich died in 1893, his faithful dog refused to leave his side, accompanying his body to the wake and funeral. Even after the memorial services were long over, the dog would run away from home to return and keep forlorn vigil by its dead master's mausoleum. Refusing to eat or be consoled in his bottomless grief, the poor pet eventually perished. The tearful stone that the family erected to memorialize the pup's undying faithfulness is often redecorated by anonymous visitors, especially on August 16 (Feast Day of Saint Roch, the patron saint of dogs), August 26 (National Dog Day), November 1 (All Saints Day), and Christmas. Perhaps it's no accident that those first dates are also among the classic hot and humid "dog days of summer." Don't let that discourage you from paying your respects; the determined dog deserves it. He's on Avenue H in Metairie Cemetery.

Matrimonial Madness in Monroe

Every town has its rascals, and in the 1870s, Monroe had Sidney Saunders. He showed up one day claiming to be a Confederate veteran from Mississippi and soon opened a small grocery. But the shop was probably just a front for Saunders's unlicensed but very profitable gambling tavern.

In 1875, Saunders returned from a business trip in the company of a young mixed-race woman named Annie and her infant son. Annie was introduced as Saunders's wife, and the boy was named Willie St. John Saunders. Rumors spread that their living arrangement was one of convenience; according to official 1880 census records, Sidney was still single and Annie had kept her maiden name.

Betting and barkeeping were lucrative for a while, but in 1886 Saunders's luck began to turn. Little Willie, now twelve, suddenly died of unexplained causes. Then, two years later, a mysterious fire broke out in one of the buildings Saunders owned and quickly consumed a number of adjacent structures, gutting much of downtown Monroe. Angry merchants claimed that Saunders had committed arson as part of an insurance fraud scheme, although a lawsuit and series of lengthy investigations into the causes of the fire remained inconclusive. On January 22, 1889, after receiving numerous threats and spending years living under constant fear of a lynch mob, Sidney Saunders bought a cemetery plot.

Just ten days later, neighbors answering Annie's screams for help ran into the Saunders home and found Sidney bleeding to death of a gunshot wound. Doctors who arrived at the scene could do nothing to save him, and the cause of death was listed on the death certificate as suicide. The only problem with this determination was that Saunders had been shot in the back of the head.

Historian Lora Peppers has described the rumors that swept through the city: "Was it murder? Suicide? Was Sidney planning his suicide or planning for any eventuality when he bought the cemetery plot? Did someone who lost a business in the big fire decide to get even? Did Annie finally have enough of Sidney and decide once and for all to be free? Can a person bent on suicide shoot himself in the back of the head?" None of these questions has ever been cleared up. The biggest question of all, however, remained whether Annie and Sidney had ever really married.

Once it was revealed that Saunders had amassed the then-enormous personal fortune of $83,000, his siblings disputed Annie's legal right to the estate, asserting that she'd only been his ward, or worse, his maid. Annie insisted that she and Sidney had legally wed in St. Louis, and a copy of the marriage license was sent for. When it arrived, proving her claim that she and Sidney had made their union legal on March 25, 1875, she won the suit. But it was a Pyrrhic victory, for her portion of the estate had been whittled down to only $7,250 and a small piece of property in Texarkana, Arkansas.

Elks Mound

***In 1912,* German immigrant Albert Weiblen built a club tomb for members of the Benevolent and Protective Order of Elks to fraternize forever in New Orleans's Greenwood Cemetery. Naturally enough, a larger-than-life elk stands proudly on top of the tumulus-style burial mound, which features eighteen internal chambers and a bronze door surmounted by a clock permanently pointing toward the eleventh hour. Just don't forget the old saying: "Those who expect to be saved at eleven sometimes die at ten thirty." So don't wait.**

Annie used the bulk of the remaining money to erect a monument to Sidney in Old City Cemetery. The stern-looking statue of a mustachioed Sidney holds a scrolled parchment document in his left hand—an engraving of the marriage certificate that proved Annie's case.

She insisted that the statue be placed as high as possible atop a small tumulus and that it be turned so it could look down upon the part of the cemetery where the Monroe society folks who had despised them for so long had their own family plots.

A Crypt Built for Three

Annie's fury turned to obsession, some say to near madness. She kept a key to the crypt and often spent days in the tomb with the remains of her late husband and son. After a while, she moved a desk and chair into the tomb, then a sewing machine, her son's bicycle, and even curtains. For the next several years she spent the bulk of every day hunkering down inside the tomb, reading and sewing and keeping her loved ones company.

Despite Annie's dedication to her deceased family, she eventually met someone else and remarried. In 1891 she moved to Texarkana, where she lived for a number of years as the mayor's wife. When her new husband died in 1925, she discovered that he had secretly divorced her fourteen years earlier, a turn of events that embroiled her in yet another estate inheritance suit. She once again fought it and won, but sadly died two weeks later in a fiery accident after a gas stove set her clothes alight. Annie's remains were brought back to Monroe to join Sidney and Willie in the family crypt, although no inscription was added to mention her return.

Despite the marble marriage license, the legitimacy of Sidney and Annie's union is still questioned today. According to Lora Peppers, "In 2001, researchers with the Ouachita Parish Public Library found a copy of Sidney and Annie's marriage register in the records of the city of St. Louis, Missouri. The record is word for word what is engraved on the scroll on Sidney's monument. The register was not filed and recorded until April 24, 1889, fourteen years after the marriage and almost three months after Sidney's suicide, right in the middle of Annie's fight with Sidney's siblings. Coincidence?"

A poem is engraved on the side of the statue's pedestal:

Sidney I could have well forgiven
That last seeming cruel act of thine
(for you wanted me with you in heaven)
Had you, with your life, taken mine.

Angèle's Obelisk

Although it's not one of the more ornate markers among the elaborate tombs lining the streets of Metairie Cemetery, the imposing obelisk that commemorates young Angèle Marie Langlés is certainly one of the most peculiar, for it was erected against the wishes of the deceased's family. Madame and Mademoiselle Langlés were among more than five hundred passengers lost at sea after the steamship *La Bourgogne* sank on July 4, 1898, just two days after setting off for France. Shortly after the accident it was discovered that their wills diverged on a number of key points, including the designated beneficiaries and instructions for how the estate was to be handled.

It was thus left up to the courts to decide which of the two wills to honor by determining which woman had survived the other. The case was ultimately argued before the Louisiana Supreme Court, and after much debate the judges came to a decision: Because she was younger, Angèle had probably taken longer to drown than her mother, and so the court would honor Mademoiselle Langlés's will. The younger woman's will requested that a large tomb be erected for her in the event of her death, and the court therefore ordered her heirs to spend $3,000 from the estate (roughly equivalent to $355,000 today) to erect a memorial. Lest anyone doubt the legal basis for this extravagant decision, the executor of the will made sure that the reference number to the case—105 LA. 39—was carved into the granite pedestal just below Angèle's name.

Barelli's Tomb

The Barelli mausoleum in New Orleans's St. Louis Cemetery No. 2 depicts a disaster along with its imagined outcome. On November 15, 1849, the steamboat *Louisiana* exploded seconds after it pulled away from the New Orleans docks to head upriver, destroying two adjacent steamers and a small supply boat, and killing more than 150 people.

The scene carved into the front of the Barelli tomb shows the moment of horror, with the bow of the steamer in the lower right-hand corner, the supply boat being crushed and overturned while people on the docks are struck by shrapnel from the exploding boilers. Joseph Barelli's young son (for whom the tomb was built) was among the victims. Above the mayhem the boy's veiled body is welcomed into heaven by an angel, and at the top of the scene a triangle with an eye represents the all-seeing God as Trinity. The tomb holds the boy's earthly remains—some say all that was recovered from the site of the accident were young Barelli's watch and a fragment of his coat sleeve.

The Crenshaw Children

One of the saddest-looking bunch of kids you'll ever see are the Crenshaw children, whose collective grave is marked by a group of life-sized marble statues in the middle of Magnolia Cemetery, at North Nineteenth and Main Streets in Baton Rouge. However sad they might have been, their parents, William and Mary Crenshaw, were surely even more distraught. They buried three children in the same year. Their oldest daughter, Fannie, died in 1858, followed three days later by their six-year-old son (and father's namesake) Willie. Then four months later, one-year-old Mattie passed, too. The tomb also holds the remains of a baby whose life was even shorter, memorialized only as the Nameless One.

Tomb's Tomb

***Mr. Tomb's tomb* is in Pineville's Mt. Olivet Cemetery.**

A Grave ID

There's this story about a little boy out in Springfield who fell off his bike and was run over by a truck. There were only a few witnesses, but nobody recognized the truck or could give a description of the two men in it.

The morning after the funeral, the boy's parents returned to the grave site. On the back of the tombstone they found engraved stick figures and houses in little squares and triangles, as if drawn by a child. The scene showed what happened at the site of the accident. Each stick figure had a name underneath it: the little boy, the three witnesses, and the two men in the truck. The mother recognized the handwriting under each stick figure: It was that of her dead son.

The engraving is still there to this day. I have personally been to this graveyard before and have seen the tombstone. You get the weird feeling that a little kid is looking up at you or standing right there with you. —*Blake Taylor*

Grace Episcopal Graves

The churchyard of Grace Episcopal Church in St. Francisville—one of Louisiana's oldest Protestant churches—is home to several outstanding monuments.

First Lt. Daniel Bowman of West Feliciana Parish was thirty-seven when he died in the Philippine Islands during the Moro Insurrection following the Spanish American War. Unfortunately he never got to shoot. A Moro warrior crept into his tent one evening and stabbed him in the heart as he slept. Bowman's marker includes his hat, rifle, belt, sword, canteen, bullet pouch, backpack, and commendation from the War Department. The military accoutrements are accompanied by a tree stump, symbolizing a life cut short, the Rock of Ages for faith, and clambering ivy, to signify fidelity and immortality.

Edward Newsham's monument, erected by his wife, includes an image of their young son. The fern sprouting from the rock stands for sincerity and sorrow, while the palm fronds mean spiritual victory and eternal peace. At the bottom of the monument are the words "Faithful Ever to My Trust."

Dr. Ira Smith moved to Louisiana from upstate New York to build a plantation he called Troy, after his hometown. He died on Christmas Day, 1850, leaving instructions that his mausoleum should be "built of lasting materials and present a pleasing appearance." The family hired cemetery architect J. C. Wells of New York City, who assured them that a granite tomb in the Egyptian style would answer that request very well.

Do Not Disturb

The instructions—"Do Not Open"—carved into Mrs. J. T. Jones Jr.'s grave in New Orleans's Valence Street Cemetery might seem completely unnecessary. But believe it or not, the vast majority of people who were laid to rest in a New Orleans graveyard fully expected their graves to be opened—and not just once. The tradition in the city's aboveground family mausoleums is to slide the coffin into its tomb, seal it up, and then let nature take its course for a year or two. Those hot, buggy summers work their magic, reducing the remains to next to nothing in a jiffy. The next time a family member passes away, the vault is reopened, the scant contents of the previous coffin are tipped out and bagged up, and the remainder either put inside the new coffin (if it's the spouse) or shoved toward the back to fall into a common holding pit called a *caveau*, where the remnants of all the previously deceased family members are already waiting. As long as a year and a day have gone by since the last coffin was inserted, state law allows the old to make room for the new.

This approach saves money and space. Some family graves may hold the mingled remains of as many as sixty to eighty individuals from several generations, despite having only a few currently occupied "decomposition units" (i.e., coffins). It's one way to make sure that the "family that lays together, stays together." Although many tour guides will insist that aboveground burials are a New Orleans innovation made necessary by the shallowness of the water table, it's really a centuries-old European tradition to treat the dead as moveable objects. French, German, and Italian churches used to hold the stacked-up bones of former parishioners in their charnel houses, while the catacombs below cities like Paris or Rome were crammed with the calcareous remains of millions who used to be buried elsewhere.

Apparently Mrs. J. T. Jones Jr. wanted nothing to do with these old ways, no matter how sensible they might be. Her wishes were carved in stone, expressing her very British desire to stay put and let the sleeping dead lie.

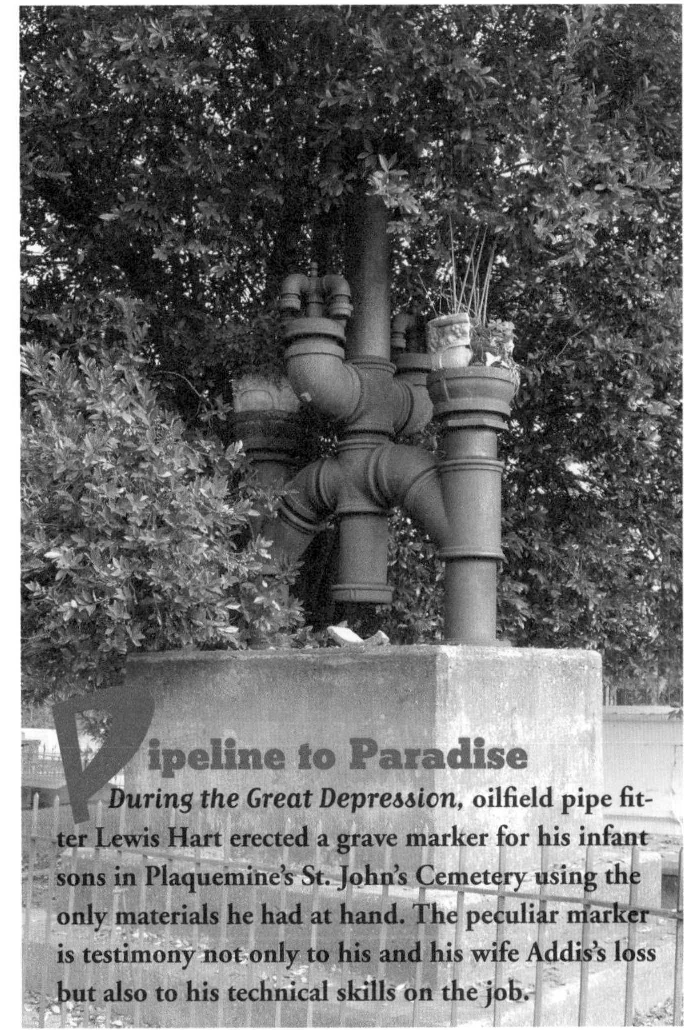

Pipeline to Paradise

***During the Great Depression,* oilfield pipe fitter Lewis Hart erected a grave marker for his infant sons in Plaquemine's St. John's Cemetery using the only materials he had at hand. The peculiar marker is testimony not only to his and his wife Addis's loss but also to his technical skills on the job.**

Abandoned in the Bayou State

There's a big difference between places that were let go because they outlived their necessity and those that were damaged and uninhabitable. Even before Hurricanes Katrina and Rita forced residents to flee New Orleans in 2005, Louisiana had more than its share of uninhabited homes and buildings.

Take, for example, the eighteenth- and nineteenth-century mansions of wealthy Creoles who mimicked the architecture and decor of ancient Greece and Rome. Sometimes they even built artificial ruins in their gardens because the effect looked "picturesque." Unfortunately, after the devastation of the Civil War there was no need to fake Louisiana's ruins.

So many Louisiana industries have gone the same way, as sawmills and sugar mills replaced cottage businesses and then were replaced themselves by refineries and other forms of "progress," only to be left to rot in the heat and humidity. In abandoned mills, one can still almost hear the clank and whir of machines and the shouts of workers. In abandoned jails, the arguments of prisoners echo off the graffiti-scratched walls. And lonesome schools still resound with the shrieks of children, abandoned asylums with the screams of the infirm. . . .

Well, just take a look through these pages, and maybe you'll see what we mean.

The Pea Farm

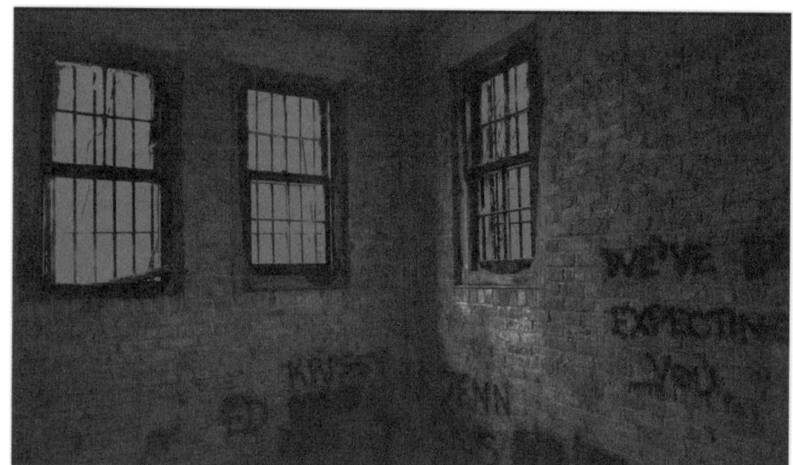

In the woods west of Shreveport, a couple miles out Seventieth Street beyond the West Shreveport Industrial Park, a collection of ruins known locally as the Pea Farm is a frightening relic from a ruthless era. From the end of the Civil War to the 1940s, black convicts—the unemployed, hitchhikers, and "troublemakers" incarcerated on trumped-up vagrancy or disturbing-the-peace charges—died on prison chain gangs and were buried in unmarked graves. The *pea* in the name refers not to crops the convicts raised to feed themselves but to *P* as in "prison," "punishment," and "penal servitude."

Tucked out of sight from the rest of the world, conditions at the farm went unnoticed by the rest of society. Though most of the thick iron bars that once divided the cells were sawed out and sold for scrap long ago, other horrors of the old place are still plain to see: windowless punishment cells in the damp basement; bolts on walls where unruly prisoners were shackled and beaten with leather straps; abandoned living quarters near the lake where guards passed their spare time drinking, playing cards, or brandishing guns on horseback; and tent villages exposed to sweltering heat and bugs in summer and pneumonia-inducing chills in winter.

Many of the Pea Farm's prisoners never left the place alive. A potter's field, surrounded by a rusting wrought-iron fence, contains the remains of post–Civil War casualties. But as the decades wore on—the prison closed in the early 1960s—subsistence crops were sewn in fields fertilized by corpses that had been unceremoniously dumped in shallow graves.

The Pea Farm is currently owned by a major corporation. We were told the owner is having trouble selling the place because groundwater percolation and soil consistency samples keep turning up something funky. We also heard that the site is haunted—that at night the screams and moans of all those who disappeared and died here echo through the halls of the old main building. Sometimes, we were told, people hear the harsh slap of leather straps and rubber hoses. Then come the screams and whimpers of prisoners whose daytime reality was far worse than any nightmare. It wouldn't surprise us if the place is haunted: It takes a very long time for the aftereffects of cruelty and suffering to diminish and then, finally . . . to fade away.

Pea Farm Hanging

After about one and a half minutes of gently swaying from the rope, the killer-rapist was pronounced dead and ordered to be cut down. Upon hitting the ground, the man opened his eyes. Still alive! The mother pulled a .32 pistol from her handbag and shot him in the chest until her gun went *click, click, click*. And still she kept pulling the trigger. . . .The mother was arrested but never charged. Technically the man had already been pronounced dead before she started shooting. *—Lee Erwin*

The Priory of Storms

Up Highway 1081, several miles north of Covington, is a forbidding and peculiar complex that until twenty years ago housed several hundred nuns belonging to the Order of Saint Benedict. Benedictine nuns had come to New Orleans from Kentucky in 1870 but soon left the sinful city and settled north of Lake Pontchartrain, where they founded the St. Scholastica Priory and opened some of the first schools among the Indians. The old priory was abandoned in 1988 and left to the destructive whims of nature. A cemetery near the slowly rusting hulk is still used for the occasional funeral service, but the hundreds of cells that once rang with chants and prayers now echo only with the sounds of whistling wind and the flutters of trapped birds.

Saint Scholastica, who died in 543 A.D., was the twin sister of Saint Benedict. One night during a visit, Benedict stood up to leave before Scholastica was done talking. She brought her hands together in prayer, the story goes, prompting a fierce storm and preventing Benedict's departure. Since then Scholastica has been the patron saint of bad weather and convulsive children, because of their "stormy" seizures.

Our friend Karen Ciccone tells us that during the last years all those women were confined to their duties, the place may not have been all goodness and piety. Although the details have been clouded and the names have been lost in the decades of retellings, one rumor tells of a conflict between a young novice, who had barely begun her life of chaste and sanctified service, and an older nun, who took a liking to her that was not quite sisterly. The nun began concocting reasons to wander by the novice's cell, interrupting her whenever she was not praying and demanding comforts not normally provided to those who have taken holy vows.

When a priest came to hear their separate confessions, he was shocked but sworn to confidentiality, so he did nothing to interfere. The novice found herself trapped as well, and, after months of running from the nun, killed herself. As a suicide, she could not be buried in the priory cemetery; instead she was interred in a nearby paupers' graveyard.

The nun outlived the novice by only a few months, supposedly dying of loneliness and guilty remorse. They say it was sometime after the nun's funeral that the priest confided the truth to his superiors. Curiously, the priory closed shortly thereafter.

According to the tale, two shadows appear in the priory on stormy nights—the nervously swift novice floats by silently followed by the slower-moving, darker shadow of the nun, accompanied by the sound of jingling keys. But was the nun's mission to demand unreciprocated love, or to ask for forgiveness? No one knows.

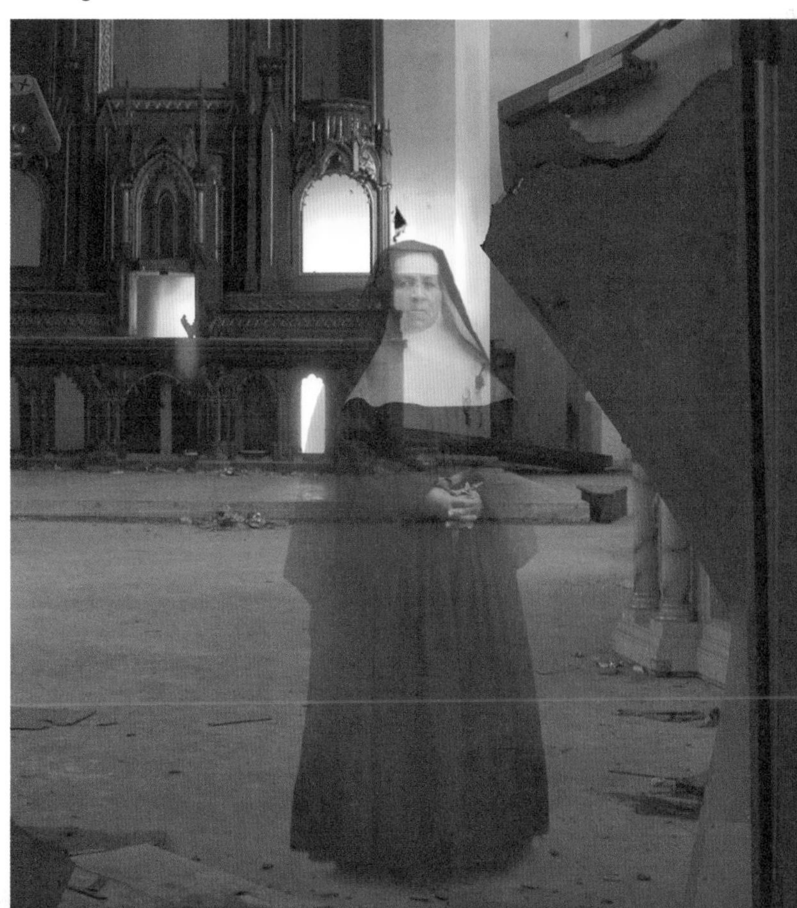

Keachi College

Fieldwork in search of the weird can sometimes be confusing. Depending on which map you consult, a town in western DeSoto Parish can be spelled Keatchie, Keatchi, Keitche, or Keachi, and pronounced either KEE-chee or key-CHAI. In any case, the town itself, while only a ghostly shadow of its former self, is a charming collection of old buildings, many of which are now listed on the National Register of Historic Places.

There's also a one-story school on the site of the former Baptist Union Female College (also called the Keatchie Female College, Keachie Women's Academy, or Keachi College), organized in 1856 or 1857 to offer the maid of arts and mistress of English degrees to women seeking higher education. The college had barely begun awarding diplomas to its first graduates when the Civil War began.

During and after the Battle of Mansfield and Pleasant Hill (sometimes known as the Battle of Sabine Crossroads or the Battle of Pleasant Grove) the college was requisitioned as a Confederate hospital. From April 7–12, 1864, army surgeons performed unmedicated amputations, resulting in wagonloads of arms and legs to be hauled off and buried. A large hole in the side yard for burying buckets of soldiers' blood, and a morgue set up on the school's second floor.

According to eyewitnesses, the smell of "seared flesh, clotted blood, splintered limbs, and dismembered corpses" filled the air. The wounded were "sickening sights. Some shot in the face, both eyes out, head bent, arms, legs, everywhere." Describing a similar scene in Pleasant Hill, historian Vicki Betts remarked on "how numbed the children came to be at the sight of the dead soldiers, so much so that some were caught jumping from body to body and crowing like roosters."

For local people such as Lafayette Price, the horror had only begun when the fighting ended, for the dead were buried in mass graves. According to Price, "They just dig a big hole and put 'em in and threw dirt on 'em. I went back after two or three days, and the bodies done swell and crack the ground. The dead of both armies were laid head to foot and the whole hillside was wrapped up with soldiers and the unburied dead. When the earth began to warm later in the season, huge cracks appeared in the ground. It swelled up in ridges, like a big mole run, and the entire hillside turned green with flies."

The largest Civil War battle west of the Mississippi also turned out to be the last major Rebel victory; both students and townsfolk were left psychologically and physically scarred for years. Alums of Keachi would recall for decades afterward the screams of the wounded soldiers as young women frantically shredded and scraped towels and linens

to make "lint" for stanching blood or making disposable bedding, while inscriptions gouged into walls by the wounded and dying remained visible as long as the building stood. Despite years of scrubbing and repainting, students continued to complain they heard screams, saw pooled blood dripping down the stairs, and smelled cauterized blood vessels and the stench of gangrenous flesh.

In 1879 the school began admitting male students, but they too were troubled by the horrible groans and strangled cries of wounded and dying soldiers. Not long after Louisiana College opened in Pineville in 1906, Keachi College closed, then burned to the ground. When a new school opened on the same site, pupils dreamed of men in bloodstained uniforms.

Now the place is abandoned, except for the occasional black snake slithering through heaps of fallen lumber or gaping holes in the floor, and the birds that have built nests under the eaves. During the day, that is. At night, it's a whole different story.

Lonesome Tower

A lone tower looms over the weeds and old railroad tracks between Half Moon Lake and the Flat River near Taylortown, Bossier Parish. The tower is a rough, three-story affair with Gothic arches and crumbling buttresses, covered in Spanish moss and mired in local legend.

One story has it that a plantation owner lost his wife in childbirth. Years later a horse-riding accident left him dependent on his teenage daughter. When she died on her wedding day, her father, now an old man and alone for the first time in his heartbroken life, set fire to the plantation's chapel. When the smoke finally cleared, only the Lonely Tower remained; and on certain nights, when there's no moon and the sky is overcast, people say they hear the bell ringing a mournful toll and see a glowing figure in a wedding gown waiting for her groom.

Another tale of more recent vintage claims the groom was killed in a car accident on his way to the wedding. According to this version of the facts, the distraught bride then did one of three things: clambered up the tower and immediately flung herself from it, hanged herself from the bell rope, or set fire to the church in her anguished madness and then ran into the flames.

Ellerbe School

"Location, location, location," Realtors are so fond of saying, but it's precisely the location of a 1950s school southeast of Shreveport that has captured the imagination of explorers of the weird. Leaving the city behind, Ellerbe Road (Highway 523) continues, seemingly interminably. Just before its junction with Highway 1 in Caspiana, there sits a former school that has unsettled many.

Some claim the old Ellerbe School had been a Baptist seminary whose preacher-professors performed sadistic biblical punishments on their pupils to teach them firsthand how Jesus suffered at the hands of the Romans. Others insist it was a black elementary school that sheet-wearing bigots made sure would never be integrated. Still others maintain that its students were hobbling paraplegics struck by a terrible polio epidemic. But some blame its emptiness on something else entirely: a homicidal maniac.

The school closed, many say, after the last principal was exposed as a child molester, a pedophile who silenced his victims forever to prevent parents from learning the vile truth. According to this old rumor, the screams of his young prey are still heard echoing down the long corridors.

Another version claims that the school janitor was the child killer, not the principal. He stared at the kids with snakelike eyes, they say, and swallowed his chewing tobacco juice instead of spitting it out. High on concentrated nicotine, he'd lure children into his broom closet and snuff out their young lives. Found out, the janitor chained the doors closed, set fire to the building during a PTA meeting, then hanged himself from the school's water tower as the fire consumed them all. After that, the few families remaining in the community fled. The school never reopened.

For visitors to the old Ellerbe School, it is *they* who inevitably end up feeling like ghosts, wandering invisibly through corridors, reviewing scenes of their own dimly remembered pasts.

Ellerbe's Vanishing Janitor

The oldest stories told about the Old Ellerbe Road School have to do with why it was abandoned in the first place.

Apparently one day a janitor in the school vanished into thin air. There was no trace of him at all. His car was still in the parking lot but he was nowhere to be found. Rumors started swirling and the schoolkids started getting really worked up about it. One night a few of them decided they would find the janitor and rescue him. They had a sleepover, snuck out, and went to the school. They were never seen again. Hysteria overtook the town and the school closed, never to reopen.

Nowadays if you go in the school at night you can hear the sounds of children playing in the distance. No matter where you go, it sounds far away. If you run to the sound, it seems to move to a different spot. There's also the sound of a school bell. People have also told me they've seen strange lights coming from the school's windows at night.

Be careful if you decide to visit the Old Ellerbe Road School. Not only is it frightening, it is truly dangerous.

—Tex LaRone

The Devil's Mill

If what we heard across Louisiana is true, many an abandoned building has morphed into a church for satanists. In the southern outskirts of New Iberia, colorful stories and "folk art" suggest that a cluster of forbidding overgrown ruins has provided just such a meeting place. Built in 1920 to make cardboard from rice straw, a by-product of the town's three rice mills, the Charles Boldt Paper Mills—with it's cracked smokestack, windowless rooms, rusting sheds, and acre of blasted concrete—is now home to snakes, nesting birds, and Satan worshippers.

We heard tales of caverns beneath the mill where "evil-doers" regularly gather to do stuff like sacrifice small animals, chant church hymns in reverse, engage in self-mutilation, and perform odd rituals with sea salt, gunpowder, and sulfur. These activities are of real concern to a group of investors who hope soon to transform the site into an RV park and a chain restaurant.

It's a creepy place, all right. We got there late in the day, and only by bushwhacking the waist-high weeds with a stick were we able to eventually find our way to the main building, decorated in satanic-looking graffiti. Pentagrams were etched into the soil, and swastikas and scary spray-painted faces adorned the walls.

We made our way further into the old mill, but a loud rumble of thunder made heading back to the car seem like an awfully good idea. We barely made it to shelter before a late-summer deluge that colorful-talking folks call "frog stranglers" struck with terrifying force. Strange, we thought, since just before we'd headed toward the old mill, the sky had seemed still and almost cloudless. How could it have come up so quickly? By the time it was over, the path we'd taken to reach the mill was under water. Without rubber boots there was no going back. The possibility of those caverns would have to remain tantalizingly unconfirmed.

Maybe you should go and take a look yourself, before it is turned into yet another franchise eatery. But if you decide to check it out, please do be careful. It might be a good idea to keep a crucifix and a few holy cards handy just in case you run into some other folks whose purposes aren't as chaste and pure as your own. That is, unless you happen to be one of those people who believe that if you can't beat 'em, join 'em. In that case, you're on your own.

—Allen and Lauren

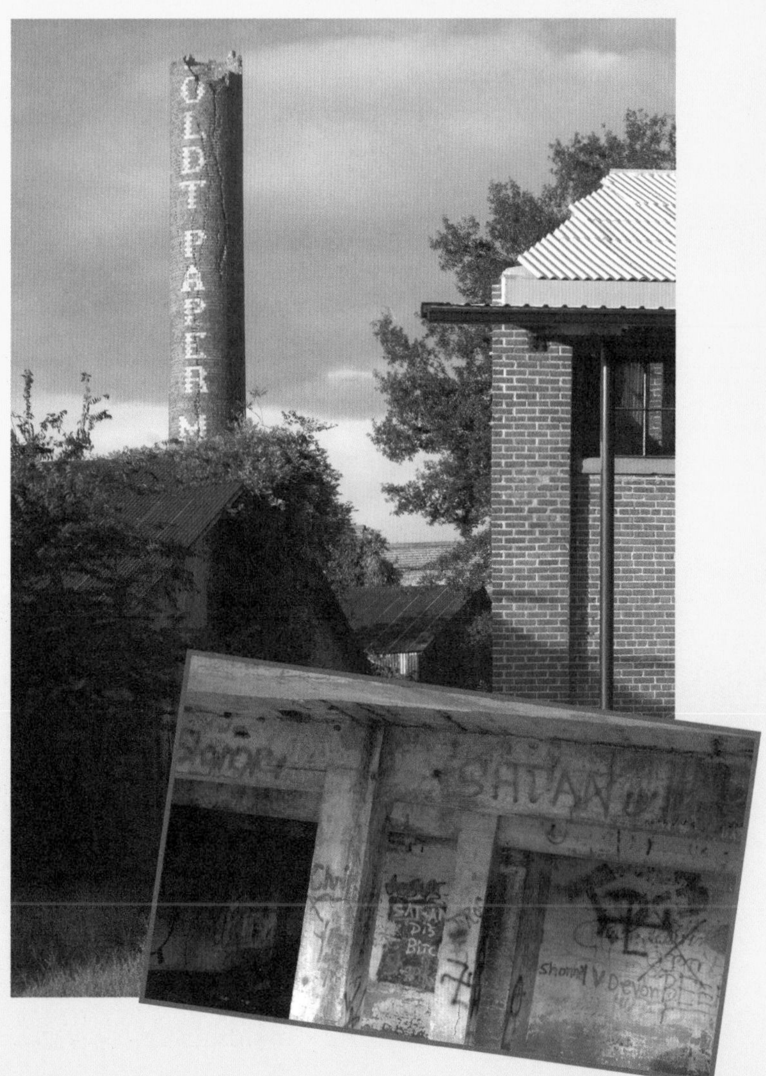

Up in Smoke—Plaquemines Parish Courthouse

Plaquemines Parish Courthouse lies along the Mississippi left bank near the hamlet of Pointe a la Hache. The epitome of abandonment, the building has vines climbing through broken doors and windows; a thicket of gnarled, Spanish moss-covered live oaks on its grounds; a grim jail tucked behind it that would have made the Devil's Island penal colony look good; and a sinister tower housing a clock without hands. Every hour or so, a handful of vehicles arrives on a small ferry from places such as Nairn, Happy Jack, and Port Sulphur. Otherwise, the courthouse seems like a relic from a ghost town.

It is certainly a relic from a bygone age, and one that not everyone recalls with relish. Its most famous denizen was thuggishly brutal archconservative Judge Leander Perez, who ran Plaquemines and St. Bernard Parishes as a petty segregationist dictatorship for the first half of the twentieth century. Perez was so brazen at rigging elections that candidates he supported (and thereafter manipulated) sometimes won with majorities that were greater than the entire amount of eligible voters. The living, the dead, and the famous could cast votes on Plaquemines ballots. People like Charlie Chaplin, Babe Ruth, and Herbert Hoover were among those who unknowingly helped elect Perez henchmen without ever having heard of the candidates. A rabid leader of both the White Citizens' Council and the Louisiana States' Rights Party, Perez had a special prison built near the mouth of the Mississippi to hold civil rights demonstrators. His racist and anti-Semitic attacks reached their peak when he engineered the burning of a newly integrated Catholic school in St. Bernard Parish in 1962. For this he was excommunicated from the Catholic Church, though he was reinstated shortly before his death in 1969 so he could receive a Christian burial.

We'd only stepped out of the car and taken a couple of snapshots of the old courthouse when a pickup appeared out of the heat mirage in the distance and slowed to a stop. An old man leaned out only long enough to say, "You know, Katrina didn't do that. That was a matter of pure arson, sir" and then drove off. He was referring, we knew, to the evening of Saturday, January 12, 2002. Fifty-nine-year-old James Chancey, owner-operator of Vernon's Cycle Shop in Gretna, set fire to the parish courthouse to destroy evidence in several criminal cases pending against him and some of his associates. By then, Chancey was an experienced arsonist, having conspired with at least two of his friends in insurance fraud schemes by setting fire to a truck and a house they owned so they could file claims for the damages. Chancey had also

conspired with the former owner of his retail store to bilk the sheriff's office for the cost of undelivered motorcycle parts. The sheriff's office records were among the documents slated for torching that evening in 2002.

The entire 1890 structure was quickly sheathed in flames, and although a hastily assembled human chain of volunteers from the community tried to remove as many files as possible, most of the civil and criminal records were quickly destroyed. The loss of the building, including the offices of the district attorney, parish assessor, and parish council, was a major setback for local government. Judge Anthony Ragusa attempted to offer encouragement, saying, "We can survive this. We've survived hurricanes and other emergencies in Plaquemines Parish." But this was three years before Katrina, and now the courthouse and most of the surrounding community are gone. Parish court is now held in a temporary location nearly thirty miles away in Belle Chasse, and Chancey is serving a term in prison for the $2.5 million dollars in damage he caused.

Judges' Drive

Pointe a la Hache (French for "tip of the ax") is located on Highway 39, about an hour southeast of New Orleans. As you leave the Crescent City, the first part of that road is still called Judge Perez Drive, originally named for Leander Perez. But now that some of his mineral rights schemes have come to light—by which he'd bilked the government and his fellow citizens out of more than $80 million—his local reputation has been tarnished. However, rather than go to the trouble and expense of replacing all that roadway signage, officials in St. Bernard Parish came up with a genuine Louisiana-style political solution: Now Judge Perez Drive is named after the late Melvyn Perez, a more favorable judge from St. Bernard Parish.

Pontchartrain Beach

If you take Elysian Fields Avenue in New Orleans all the way north from the Marigny up to the south shore of Lake Pontchartrain, you end up at an unexpected site: an abandoned mid-nineteenth century lighthouse that seems too far inland to be doing anyone in a boat any good at all. Beyond it is a wide expanse of grass, and then a seawall with a forbiddingly high gate. If someone can give you a boost to take a peek over the seawall, you'll see another expanse of grass, a few palm trees, and then finally, the lake itself. It's hard to believe it now, but not so long ago this emptiness contained the "Coney Island of Louisiana," Pontchartrain Beach Amusement Park.

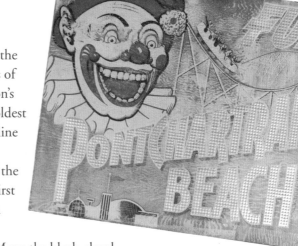

Pontchartrain Beach opened in 1928 at Zephyr Park, next to the Old Spanish Fort amusement area on the west side of Bayou St. John, but moved to the end of Elysian Fields Avenue in the early 1930s. Before that, the abandoned lighthouse had marked the entrance to a small harbor in a fishing community called Milneburg, which had been built out into the lake on stilts. Milneburg had the distinction of being the terminus of the nation's second-oldest railroad line and the home of the world's first real train station.

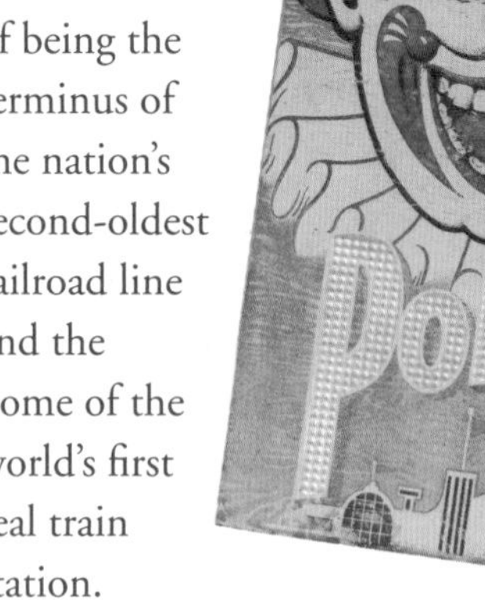

Smoky Mary, the black-cloud-belching locomotive that first serviced it, was so weak that the departure schedules were determined by the wind direction and sails were often raised to help move it along. Even so, the trains ran along Elysian Fields until 1935.

By then, the Huey Long administration had ordered the Milneburg harbor filled in and the stilt houses removed—hence that wide expanse of grass. In the era of segregation, Pontchartrain Beach was for "Whites Only," while a few miles along the lake to the east, Lincoln Beach was built some years later for "Colored" residents of the city. When both amusement parks were integrated in the early 1960s, Lincoln Beach closed. Pontchartrain Beach closed in 1983, when the amusement-seeking public was drawn toward the newer, flashier attractions being built for the New Orleans World's Fair of 1984.

For more than half a century Pontchartrain Beach had been one of the most popular sources of entertainment in the state. Its signature ride, the Zephyr, was among the largest wooden roller coasters in the South, while other rides included the Zephyr Junior, Smoky Mary, the Bug, the Ragin' Cajun, the Calypso, a haunted house, Ghost Train, Laff in the Dark, and The Monster. Bumper cars, Ferris wheels, concession stands—it's hard to look at the emptiness of the site now and visualize all it once was. "The Beach" held live concerts with national acts like Elvis Presley and Jerry Lee Lewis, as well as special areas for dolphin, magic, and high-diving shows and a petting zoo.

If the site where all this took place seems too empty and depressing, you can see a few bits and pieces of the rides at, strangely enough, the Veterans Memorial Park in Kenner, next to Louis Armstrong Airport on Williams Boulevard between Seventeenth and Eighteenth Streets. Here you can find the top of the wooden-trussed "lift hill" from the Zephyr (the first big climb that really gets a roller coaster rolling), a handful of tiki gods rescued from the former Bali Hai restaurant (one of the famous eateries at the old amusement park), part of the petting zoo, and some of the abandoned signs—they've all been saved and re-erected as a homage to a time before video and air-conditioning made popular entertainment a solitary, indoor endeavor.

Pontchartrain Beach Memories

Pontchartrain Beach always had a slightly frightening air about it that made it exciting. The Rotor was a centrifuge ride in which people would stick to the walls when the floor dropped out. There were scary clown faces everywhere and creepy-looking "painted children" you had to stand next to, to see if you were tall enough to ride. And there were talking garbage cans with lion and clown faces that would suck trash into their dark round mouths with amazing vacuum force while demanding, *"Feed me trash!"*

But the most exciting and terrifying part of Pontchartrain Beach was the Zephyr, a wooden roller coaster that got noticeably ricketier with each passing year. An archway over the top of the tallest hill had a blinking red light and a sign that said, DANGER: 20,000 VOLTS. This left a big impression on us as we clanked up the hill to that first big drop. Despite that and other warnings, legend had it that someone riding in a front car had once stood up and grabbed the arch, then tried to drop back down into one of the rear cars but fell to his doom. Past the peak, as gravity took hold of the cars, the ride was incredibly rough and noisy and dark. Totally out of control. The park eventually added tunnels that seemed about to decapitate you as you whipped into them. It was the best roller coaster ever.

One day in the late 1980s, after the park was torn down, I was riding through Kenner with a friend when I noticed something interesting a short distance from the road. We stopped to investigate and discovered a park filled with pieces from the demolished Pontchartrain Beach park. There was one of the hideous YOU MUST BE THIS TALL TO RIDE children, a car from the Zephyr, and, most wondrously, the top of the tallest peak of the Zephyr! There it was on the ground within touching distance—the wooden trusses, the word *Zephyr*, the arch with the red light, and the DANGER sign—all things that still live in my mind as danger in the dark and the sky. *—Karen*

DeRidder Jail's Rooms with a View

Next to the parish courthouse in the heart of DeRidder is a strange old structure that everyone still calls the Hanging Jail. Swelteringly hot in the summer and freezing cold in winter, it was deemed a health hazard in 1984 and shut down by court order.

When it first opened in 1914, the courthouse was considered an architectural wonder for its day. The design was based on "collegiate Gothic," an architectural style popular with colleges and universities at the time, featuring pointed Tudor arches, balconies, and tile roofs, along with dormers and bay windows. The facade resembled a posh frat house from the good old days of raccoon coats and pennant-shaped team flags. A 1922 article in *Mechanix Illustrated* even compared it to a "grand mansion or private clubhouse."

Inside, however, it was a different story. Iron cages within each room kept most prisoners out of reach of windows. Walls were nearly two feet thick and up to fifty prisoners shared hard steel bunks designed to accommodate about a dozen inmates. A long dark tunnel connected the jail with the courthouse next door, so that prisoners didn't interact with the public. All the cells opened onto a large central stairwell that spiraled up through the middle of the building, allowing the six jailers to monitor what was happening in each cell. Capital punishments were carried out on a gallows in the stairwell in full view of the inmates, the idea being that the display might serve as a learning experience for the prisoners.

Hanging-Jail Haunts

On March 9, 1928, when Molton "Mosey" Brasseaux and Joe Genna were both executed for the murder of forty-five-year-old local taxicab driver Joseph Brevelle, the "hanging jail" earned its name. Just after lunchtime they walked up the spiral staircase. One at a time they plunged three levels down before their necks broke. Joe Genna, twenty-five, was pronounced dead at 1:06 P.M., and Brasseaux, twenty-six, died twenty-three minutes later.

There are still a few old-timers in DeRidder who remember that day in vivid detail: how their teachers kept looking at the classroom clocks, how the whole elementary school was deadly quiet all morning long, and how they all rushed outside at recess to press their noses against the school fence just in time to see two plain coffins emerge from the front of the jail and carried down the street.

There are others, however, who claim the two killers never really left the old jail, at least in spirit. Reports of strange evanescent figures seen by numerous witnesses (jailers and prisoners) suggest the old structure may be haunted by the restless spirits of the two men lurking around the moldering cells where they were kept in adjacent solitary confinement cells awaiting their deaths.

Whether or not that's true, the old Hanging Jail in DeRidder would probably exude unrest and dread in any case. Maybe it's the calendars scratched into its walls, marking off the slowly passing days of many a lengthy jail term. Or maybe it's the graffiti that speaks of unfulfilled longing for sex or salvation, or the old rusty doors that squeal and groan like sound effects from a horror movie. But most of all it's that staircase and the memories of those who observed so closely what happened there.

Prison of Pain

A sharp bend in the Mississippi River west of Carville, Iberville Parish, loops around a 320-acre compound surrounded by high fences and patrolled by military police. Behind the barbed wire and guard posts stand aging buildings that once belonged to one of the most peculiar institutions in American history. For more than a century, individual Americans—including children—were captured in surprise raids by police or bounty hunters, restrained in handcuffs or leather straps, and brought here in the dark of night to be held captive for the rest of their lives. Nineteen-year-old debutantes were arrested on their way home from cotillions. Boy Scouts still in their uniforms were grabbed leaving their meetings and dragged into waiting station wagons. Children were seized from classrooms and never seen again. Most families could do nothing, as the prisoners' names were changed to keep their whereabouts and even their existence a secret.

From then on, they were forbidden to vote, be alone with the opposite sex, send sealed letters, have visitors, or ever leave the premises. On the handful of occasions when a woman conceived a child, the newborns were immediately snatched away and given up for adoption. And anyone with an outside source of income—including military veterans on small government pensions—was forced to pay for their own food and rent.

As the years passed and friends and relatives on the outside forgot about them, only the radio and the occasional arrival of a new prisoner connected them to the rest of society. Their world gradually shrank to include only this cluster of buildings and walkways, ending at the fence surrounding them.

The strange thing is, none of the people who wound up here had committed any crimes or conspired to harm anyone. They weren't terrorists and this wasn't the precursor to Guantánamo Bay, although some of the similarities are striking. These Americans had disappeared into the compound near Carville because they'd been diagnosed with a frightening disease. The place where they found themselves imprisoned was officially (in the 1980s) called the Gillis W. Long Hansen's Disease Center, named after a Louisiana congressman who was a member of the Long political family, but until then it was known locally as the Leper Colony.

Leprosy in Louisiana

In the early days, leprosy—now called Hansen's disease—horribly disfigured its victims without actually killing them and had long been one of the most feared diseases. In biblical times, lepers' homes were burned and the sufferers were sent into exile as outcasts. During the Middle Ages, they were forced to attend their own mock funerals and treated thereafter as if they were already dead.

Leprosy came to Louisiana with the first European settlers, and by 1785 a New Orleans "pest house" was constructed beyond the city limits to contain its victims.

But frequent attempts to burn down the shelter by citizens who were afraid of the disease eventually brought about its relocation to a more remote part of the state. In 1894, numerous leprosy victims were forced onto a barge for a nighttime voyage upriver, to a defunct plantation called Indian Camp owned by the state.

Its real mission was kept a secret. Locals were told the high fences were for an ostrich farm and were ordered to keep away from it to avoid having their eyes pecked out by the giant birds. For nearly thirty years the colony was run by the state as a permanent quarantine for diseased Louisianans, but in 1921 the federal government took it over and sent people there from all over the country.

Once in a while patients managed to escape, although their experiences in the outside world often drove them back. One escapee in the 1920s made it as far as Washington D.C., where he was able to walk directly into a congressional committee meeting and lay out his grievances against the conditions at Carville. Federal guards were too afraid to lay a hand on him. After news got out that he'd bought something at the train station with a $2 bill, no one within fifty miles would accept bills in that denomination for several days, for fear of winding up with the one he'd touched.

By the 1950s, Hansen's disease was far less terrifying than in the early days when it rendered victims legless, lipless, and blinded, with hideous crablike claws for hands and patches of missing hair. Although the disease was still incurable, advances in medicine made it possible to control the disease and prevent it from spreading without incarcerating the patients. By then, however, it was too late for most of Carville's inmates to return to the outside world. Their outside friends and family ties were long gone, few had learned a modern trade, and many still bore the horrible scars of their disease.

As they slowly died off, most of them were buried in the compound's military-style cemetery near the old incinerator. The earlier practice of burying people with only their serial numbers on their stones gradually gave way to the use of full names, although many of those were the "new" names they'd received when they were first brought to Carville. The center slowly shrank, eventually occupying only a handful of the original buildings, turning into a ghost town as one building after another was abandoned. In 1999, the Hansen's Disease Center closed for good.

However, the compound didn't stay closed for long. Like a mummy rising up from an ancient tomb, a new horror brought it back to life: mass death. Within weeks of Hurricane Katrina, the old Gillis Long Center reopened under a new incarnation as the Disaster Mortuary Operational Response Team (DMORT) headquarters. Re-outfitted as a giant morgue, the DMORT facility processed the many hundreds—some insist thousands—of bodies that were either claimed by Katrina or disinterred when her floodwaters caused their long-buried coffins to resurface.

The new center (recently taken back by the state) is now a high-tech death facility and includes a fully air-conditioned supermorgue with "anti-skid, easy-to-clean floors" and "modern casketing operations," per DMORT's newsletter, plus business offices and conference rooms, a lounge, a recreation room with televisions and separate sitting areas "for socializing," a fitness center with weights, treadmills, stationary bikes, elliptical trainers, pool table, air hockey table, and "a great dining hall, with an impressive commercial quality kitchen." Although the facility saw use for only six months after Katrina struck, it now stands guarded around the clock and remains ready for the next time a lot of people die.

The Stowaway

Discovering the secret shadows of a place you thought you knew is frightening. It's like finding out that the friendly guy at the bakery moonlights as a serial killer or that your kindly old aunt is involved in a drug ring.

Stow's Bar in Ruston is a bit like that. The ground floor of the old place is one of those beer dives with graffiti and pool tables that some folks call colorful or seedy, but not scary. The upper floors of the same building are less predictable, cold and foreboding even on a sultry day. Behind a locked door and a steep flight of worn wooden steps is a former boardinghouse, hotel, home for the elderly, and clinic. Before that, according to what we heard, it was a Confederate hospital. Plenty of evidence to support all these uses is scattered throughout those floors, including sagging beds, piles of old magazines, boxes of cotton batting that rats have taken up residence in, and, in one room, an abandoned operating table.

We met a guy who said he'd tried to spend a night upstairs and then changed his mind. "I realized I wasn't alone," he said, ". . . my girlfriend and I heard something scraping, and then some footsteps just like somebody was walking toward us down the hall. But I flashed my light down that way and didn't see nothing! I told Carla we should get out of there, and I acted like I was doing it for her sake, but the truth was I was probably more afraid than she was. I thought all those stories about the upstairs at Stow's was just a joke, but after that, I didn't think so anymore. There's *something* up there. Not just birds, but something big and heavy enough to make the boards creak.

From Sweets to Suds

Stark and impressive ruins a few miles south of Lecompte in Rapides Parish are all that is left of the Meeker Sugar Refinery. But what, exactly, became of the northernmost sugar mill in Louisiana?

The Meeker refinery was built in 1912. This rural industrial complex was created to centralize regional sugar production, since the quality of sugarcane products was extremely inconsistent. In its heyday, the Meeker warehouse held up to twenty thousand barrels of sugar. Meeker was abandoned in 1981. Nowadays, a company that makes detergent ingredients occupies part of the site. Next to that, the hollow brick shell of the old sugar refinery stands like a ruined cathedral, the holes in the walls that once held ventilation fans looking like openings for stained-glass windows.

Lafitte Drive-In

Local jokesters in **Erath and Abbeville, and such as our friend Richard Gibson, like to quip that nowadays the old Lafitte Drive-In Theater shows only continuous reruns of the same feature film: *Gone with the Wind.***

INDEX

Page numbers in bold refer to photos and illustrations.

WEIRD LOUISIANA

ACKNOWLEDGMENTS

For her endless hospitality I can't thank Deborah Luster enough; hers was a home base away from home for nearly all my explorations. I'm also deeply grateful to Kristie Cornell, Kathy Vellard, and the inimitable John Preble for the warm welcomes and snug harbors they offered in their own respective corners of the state. Tom Aicklen, David Brown, Francis Broussard, Alicia Devora, Richard Gibson, Rob Florence, Erin Pyles Habich, Dana Holyfield, Mike Jenkins, Antoinette K-Doe, Carolyn Long, Lauren Mendes, Steve Smith, and Katie McDonald Windham all went well out of their way to guide me toward many of the most interesting sites described in this book. Karen Ciccone, Ted Degener, Anton Haardt, Larry Harris, Sam Hodges, Guy Mendes, Allen Tumey, John Turner, Michel Varisco, Karen Wood, and Ed Meyer (of Ripley's Believe It or Not!) helped me track down still other stories that appear here. Dan Weiner, Margo Moss, David Bertrand, Skip Stander, Blainey Kern, and the rest of the Kern family threw open the magic doors to unforgettable experiences of Mardi Gras—unfortunately, with all the other weirdness in Louisiana to cover, there was not enough space left over in these pages to include everything they gave me such rare opportunities to see.

Diane D'Amico and Sarah Atwood of the Alexandria Country Inn & Suites, Tricia Crowder of the Bossier City Microtel, Glenn DeVillier of The Myrtles Plantation, Renée Kientz of the St. Tammany Parish Tourist Commission, Erin Pyles (now Habich) of the Shreveport Bossier CVB, and Sherry Smith of the Alexandria

Pineville CVB provided places to rest and time to pursue clues to the weirdness to be found in each of their communities. I am also indebted to Bob Norman, Lee Erwin, Terry and Kim Isbell, Pat Jolly, Victor Klein, "Blake Pontchartrain," Katherine Ramsland, Troy Taylor, and the myriad other researchers, journalists, librarians, law officers, paranormal investigators, and local historians scattered across the state who generously shared their knowledge in order to make this book possible. Finally I need to thank my editors, Mark Moran and Mark Sceurman, whose patience and trust seem to know few bounds, and my wife, Teddy, without whom I could no longer imagine enjoying life enough to accomplish much of anything.

One of the best things about getting to do a project like this is making new friends (in addition to many of the folks mentioned above, I must also include Steve Allen and Claire Hedlund) as well as the chance to further old friendships. At the end of many a long, hot day, Chris Sullivan was always great to share a laugh and beer with. *Bon temps*, indeed!

PICTURE CREDITS

All photos and illustrations by the author or public domain except as noted below:

Page 18 Lafayette Public Library; **26** courtesy of Billie E. Robertson; **33, 52** East Baton Rouge Parish Library; **38** Beauregard Parish Library; **39** Acadian Museum, Erath; **41** Grant Parish Library; **72–73** St. James Parish Library, Vacherie; **111–112** Ryan Doan (ryandoan.com); **116** Ryan Doan; **117–118** courtesy of Dana Holyfield; **119** © Rich Phalin; **126** courtesy of Anton Haardt; **133–134** East Baton Rouge Parish Library; **135** courtesy of Anton Haardt; **136** © Shani Miller; **137** © Andrzej Tokarski; **139** Ouachita Parish Public Library; **145** left courtesy Antoinette K-Doe; **147** courtesy Jefferson Parish Sheriff's Office; **247, 248** inset © Mike Rosebery (www.flickr.com/people/mikerosebery); **251** Shreve Memorial Library; **256** right courtesy of Karen Ciccone.

SHOW US YOUR WEIRD!

Do you know of a weird site found somewhere in the United States, or can you tell us about a strange experience you've had? If so, we'd like to hear about it! We believe that every town has at least one great tale to tell, and we're listening. It could be a cursed road, haunted abandoned site, odd local character, or bizarre historic event. In most cases these tales are told only in the towns in which they originated. But why keep them to yourself when you could share them with all of America? So come on and fill us in on all the weirdness that's lurking in your backyard!

You can e-mail us at: Editor@WeirdUS.com,
or write to us at:
Weird U.S., P.O. Box 1346, Bloomfield, NJ 07003.

www.weirdus.com